AF608336

NICHOLAS NIXON

NICHOLAS NIXON

CLOSING THE DISTANCE

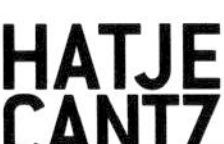

THE WAY OF ALL FLESH

Gilles Mora

Many people know about Nicholas Nixon primarily through a single series: his emblematic images of the Brown Sisters. Begun in 1975, and still ongoing, it consists of Nixon's photographs of his wife Bebe in the company of her three sisters, taken each year according to an immutable ritual, all four posing facing the photographer in a rigorously identical arrangement. In this way, the viewer becomes a witness of the temporal dimension of humans and their aging, as subtle as it is ineluctable. It is an eminently Proustian theme, one dear to the artist who is openly influenced by the French writer of time and memory, in whom few American photographers have shown an interest, leaving the task of assuming this mantle to their European colleagues. The rest of Nicholas Nixon's work is less well known, apart from among a few enlightened amateurs and specialists eager to take an interest in his full corpus.

In the eclectic and prolific American photography scene, which underwent a huge revival, and reached its apogee between 1960 and 1985,[1] Nicholas Nixon has always played an ambiguous and uncertain role in the eyes of photography historians. Many of the books published in the 1980s to accompany exhibitions by American photographers then in vogue ignored him. It fell to Peter Galassi —who would succeed John Szarkowski as photography curator of MoMA in New York in 1991—to showcase Nixon's photographs. In 1988, he organized the solo exhibition, *Nicholas Nixon: Pictures of People*, at the prestigious institution—which had actually shown his work since 1976—accompanied by a catalogue.

The reasons for this hesitation are to be found in the spirit of an oeuvre that does little to conform to the expectations created by the generation of photographers that, during Nixon's early career in the mid-1970s, had come to dominate the American scene. His work was neither triumphant street photography—Garry Winogrand, Diane Arbus, Lee Friedlander, and Danny Lyon—nor aesthetically ambitious fine-art photography— which Nixon always shied away from, seeing himself above all as a photographer, not an artist[2]—whose proponents included Paul Caponigro, Walter Chappell, Ralph Gibson, and Robert Mapplethorpe. All of whom

1 See Gilles Mora, *La Photographie américaine, 1958-1981. The Last Photographic Heroes* (Paris: Seuil, 2007).

2 See Carlos Gollonet, "Conversation with N. Nixon", in *Nicholas Nixon*, exhibition catalogue, Madrid: Fundación Mapfre, 2017, p. 27.

were subject to the aesthetic of small-format and instant photography, or that of the "colorists" such as William Eggleston, Joel Meyerowitz, or Stephen Shore.

With Nicholas Nixon, we are dealing with a complex photographer who might be said to have eluded the habitual codes of American photography at that time. If we must find bonds of affinity (and often friendship), it is no doubt with names such as Emmet Gowin, Robert Adams, Harry Callahan, or perhaps, in a different style, William Gedney. These photographers share with Nixon a similar kind of sensual or even intimate dimension. All of them create demanding photography whose driver initially seems documentary, but which relies on *empathy* with the subject, the opposite of distance, irony or over-formalization, and whether the result of random capture, based upon "aesthetics of sudden apparitions" (Garry Winogrand) or scrupulous composition (Ralph Gibson). They were also photographers, who followed Walker Evans and fell within a more literary than artistic frame of reference. Nicholas Nixon initially studied literature (graduating from the University of Michigan), and constantly refers to it, particularly, as noted earlier, the work of Marcel Proust. In an interview with Carlos Gollonet, Nixon kept returning to his literary influences, which are broader than one might think (from William Faulkner to Flannery O'Connor, Charles Dickens to Robert Frost), stating that they have been more important to him than those of painting or even photography.[3] As for the latter, it is Henri Cartier-Bresson to whom Nixon refers as the inspiration for his own interest in the medium. And it is from the French photographer's formal mastery that he borrows his own aesthetic credo: only form can guarantee content. Nevertheless, it would be impossible to distil Nixon's style. His choice of a large-format camera—rare during an era dominated by the 35mm aesthetic and which he has used exclusively since 1972—corresponds to a *scrutinizing* vision of the world. It escapes the approximations of instant photography and guarantees each print's tactile quality, which he has preferred throughout his career. Robert Adams also worked like this, even if he was more engaged in a quest for beauty than Nixon, or Emmet Gowin. They were to contribute to the revival of large-format cameras, with Nixon's avowed intention being to use it like the more flexible, less rigid small or medium formats, which permitted greater proximity with the subject.

3 Gollonet, *Nicholas Nixon*, p. 24.

This notion of *closeness* is at the heart of Nicholas Nixon's photography. His rather unexpected ties to the legendary New Topographics group might lead us to imagine that Nixon was wholly in line with that movement launched in 1975, which intended to revolutionize the vision of the American landscape observed through an impersonal, coldly clinical distancing, by "cleansing" it of lyricism and visible subjectivity.[4] Nixon did not let himself be trapped

4 Under the title *New Topographics: Photographs of a Man-Altered Landscape*, the exhibition was presented in 1975 at George Eastman House in Rochester, NY.

in this inevitably reductive vision, emerging as an outsider from the beginning: he was the only one among the 11 group members to confront the urban landscape, with his views of Boston, often taken from low angles and reminiscent of images of New York taken by Charles Sheeler in the 1930s. With one phrase in the introduction of the exhibition catalogue in 1975, he set out his position and, at the same time, hinted at his reticence regarding this draining aesthetic: "The world is infinitely more interesting than any of my opinions about it." Far from a systematized, neutral distancing, Nixon's photography would bring him ever closer to his subjects and involve fewer landscapes than human beings. This could be seen from 1977 onwards, when he undertook his series of figures seated on their porches in front of their homes in Boston and in the southeast United States, which recalled William Gedney's photographs of the same subject taken in the late 1950s in Kentucky. Besides the stylistic interest of these images—in which Nixon attempted to use a large-format camera as though it were a Leica, combining the spontaneity and flexibility of the 35mm with the marked descriptive aspects of large negatives—they perfected his strategy of "coming closer" to his subjects, which transformed the photographic act into a human experience of photography. Few American photographers were concerned with these ideas at the time (excepting Ralph Eugene Meatyard or Diane Arbus), being more attentive to techniques and visual strategy than to the existential effects set in motion by their work.

When discussing his engagement with his subject, Nixon evokes the interactions between the operator, his camera, and the human subject. It is a kind of implicit contract, which implies, of course, relations of an emotional nature and, often, sensuality. From 1987, he began his celebrated series of AIDS patients, whom he photographed from the onset of their illness to the terminal phase. The series raised many ambiguities about the motivations that allowed it, and was criticized for a "voyeuristic" approach to death and disease. The problem Nixon raises can be formulated as: can we make art with human distress, or simply document it? He resolves this dilemma with a simple response in which he considers himself as a photographer first and foremost, and no longer as an artist. This shift from documentation towards aesthetics, since Walker Evans, had fuelled American photography. When Nixon affirms his position as a photographer, he removes with one gesture his images' ambiguous status, while bearing in mind the contexts of their reception: documentary in a book, much more aesthetic on the walls of a museum or gallery. This explains how in his work, he chooses the book form as the culmination of series around a theme or subject, and prints for contexts when artistic or tactile qualities come into play that can only be communicated by them. The series on AIDS patients and that of elderly people in their final days spurred many photographers of his generation who were lacking inspiration to imitate him. The early 1990s saw a proliferation of such subjects, the majority of which failed to convey Nixon's extreme sensitivity, his reserve when approaching a theme while nevertheless asking a lot.

His photographs of couples might best illustrate his concept of closeness with his subjects, involving what can be described as "photographic closeness". The images, which he began taking in the late 1970s and continued into the 2000s, appear unique within the panorama of American photography. They bring to life the carnal presence, a concern from which Nixon has never departed, including in work such as still lifes or landscapes. Several of these couple images also transgress the sexual doxa of traditional America, such as those that took interracial relationships as their subject. Although Nixon has always rejected the idea of any kind of intimacy in photography, the artform can at least, in his view, provide a powerful evocation of it.[5] It is through the close-up that Nixon achieves this effect. A rare shooting technique when used with a large-format camera, the close-up for the photographer creates a complicity with the model, given how essential it is to be accepted in this game where an implicit contract between photographer and subject is established.

While this aesthetic can be applied unproblematically to family intimacy (as we see with the images that Nixon takes of his children or his wife), the close-up requires more complex strategies in the case of couples outside of the photographer's domestic sphere. By earning the trust of his protagonists, this is Nixon's tour de force in his *Couples* series. Only Diane Arbus before him was able to bring such gravitas to the photographic act, the weight that would lead to her suicide.

Flesh and skin—both their aging and sensual apogee—are at the heart of Nixon's photographs. As it was, though in a more controlled register, in those of Edward Weston or in the nudes of Harry Callahan, when he photographed his wife Eleanor; even, to go further back, in Charles Sheeler's nudes, which many of Nixon's images undeniably recall. In Nixon's work, however, the interlocking of bodies, folds of skin, through the ages of life, have a sensual attraction often lacking overall in contemporaneous American photography, but without the exhausting, exhibitionist provocation of a Robert Mapplethorpe. Nixon affirmed this tactile sensuality of bodies and objects photographically, within a fundamentally puritanical cultural context that rendered such a striking display of uninhibited desire and its omnipresence misunderstood. If Nixon's images—including his still lifes, with or without plants—reveal one thing, it is the relationship that photography maintains with matter, first and foremost, human matter: far from driving it off towards the abstract shores of type or essence, Nixon celebrates its personal singularity. So, as a loyal Proustian, he also reveals the evolutive marks of human matter's temporality, heavily accelerated in the processes of disease and corporeal decline. The way of all flesh.

[5] Gollonet, *Nicholas Nixon*, p. 17.

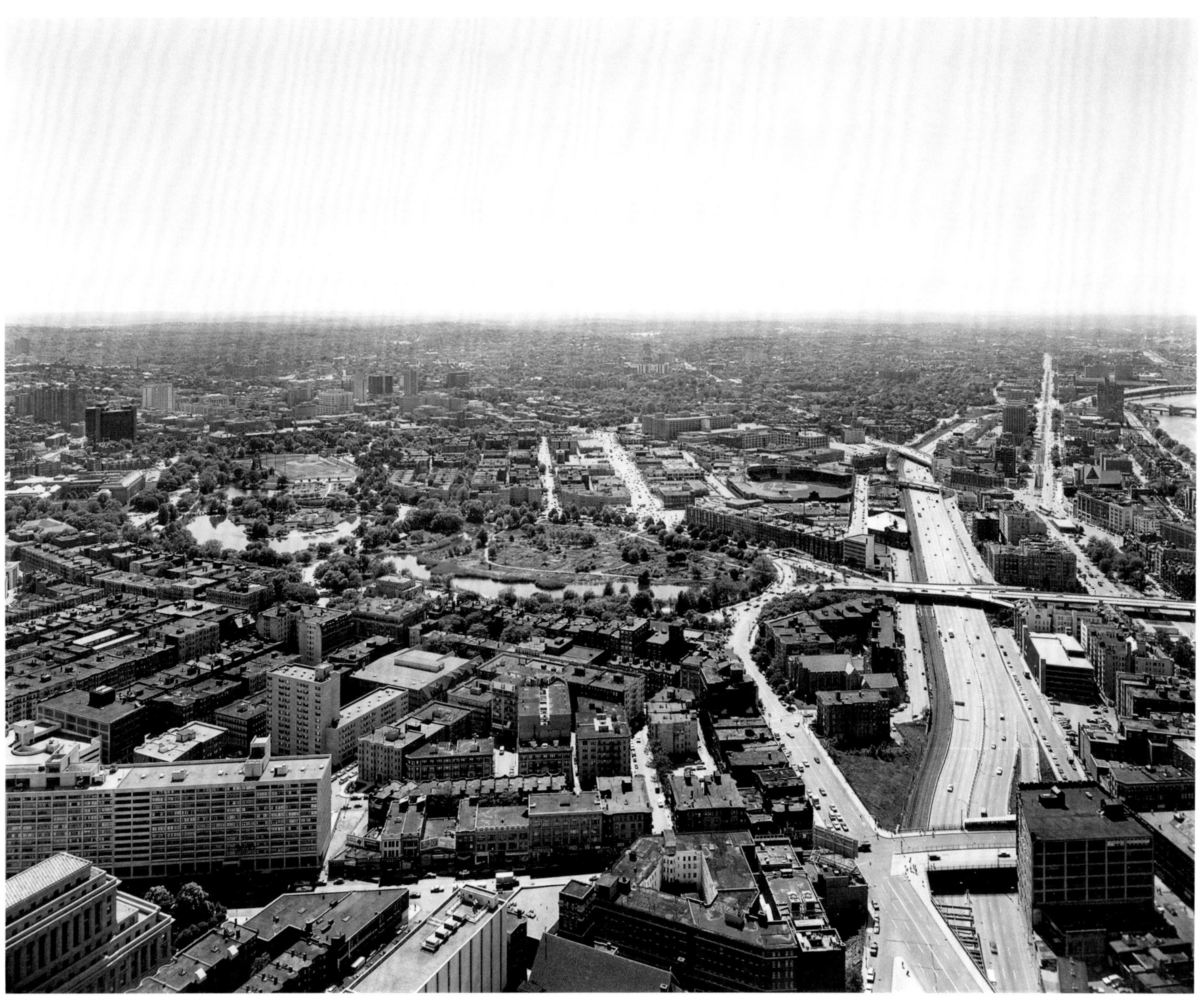

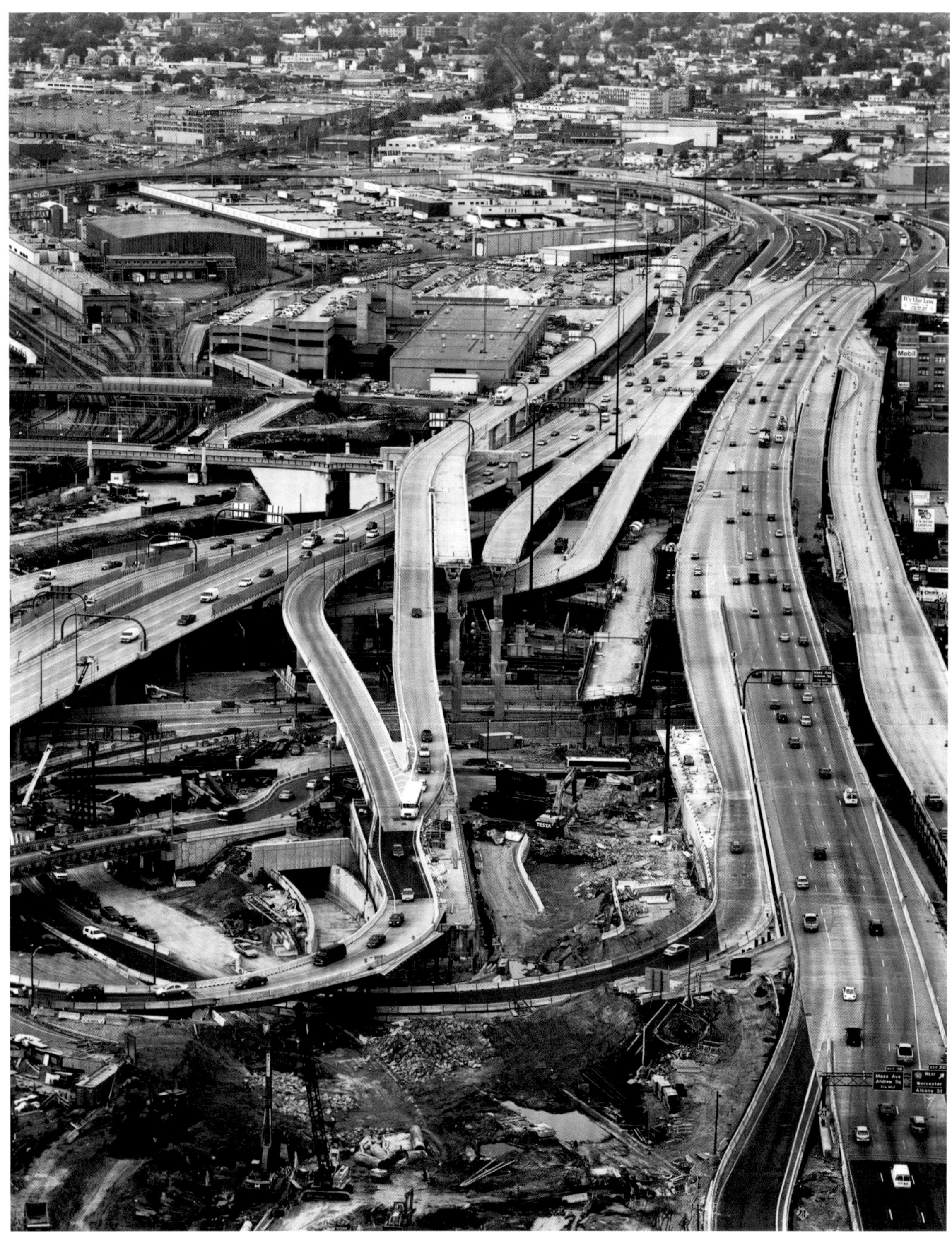
Mass Ave
Andrew Sq
Worcester
Albany St
Mobil

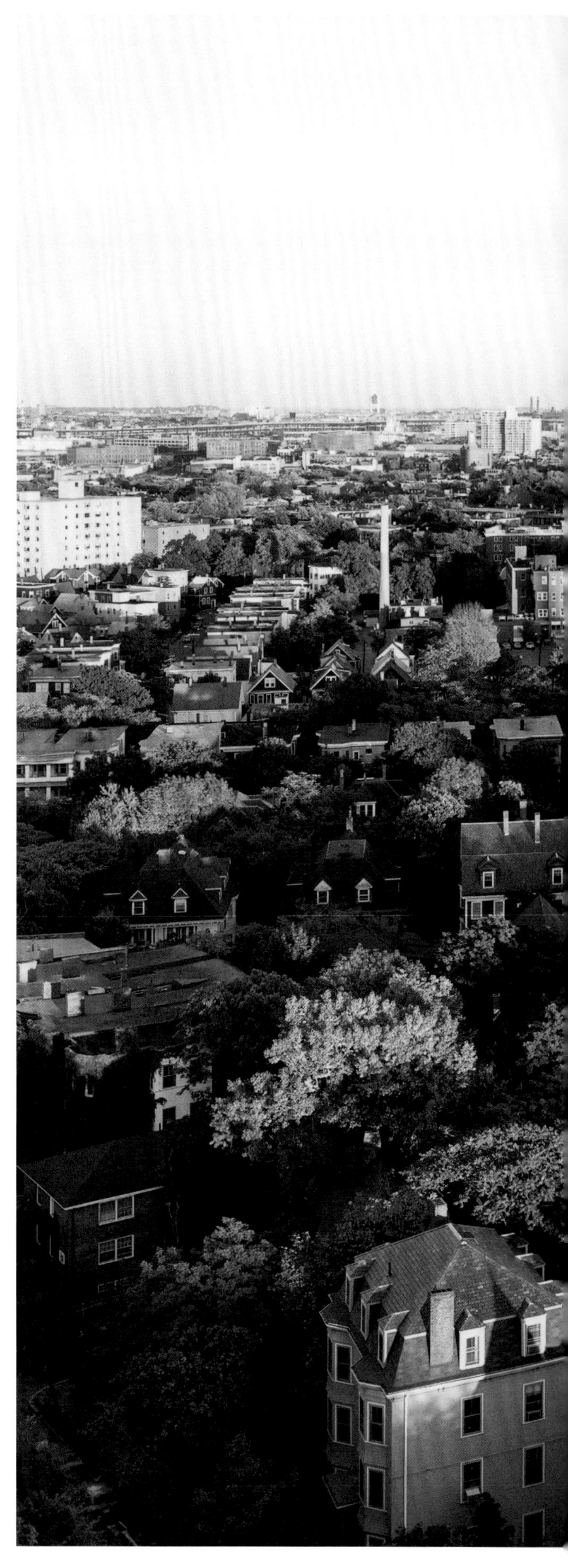

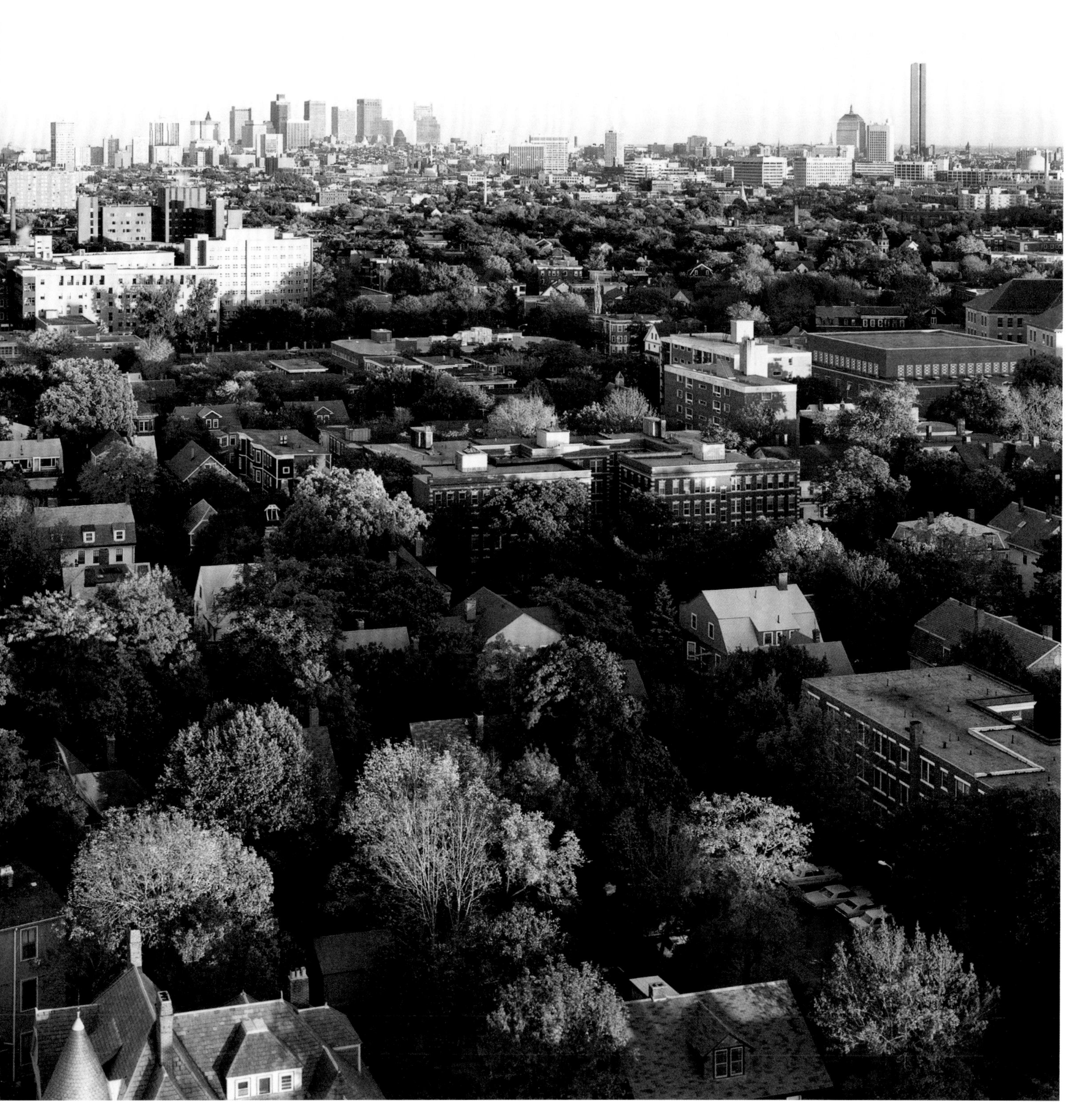

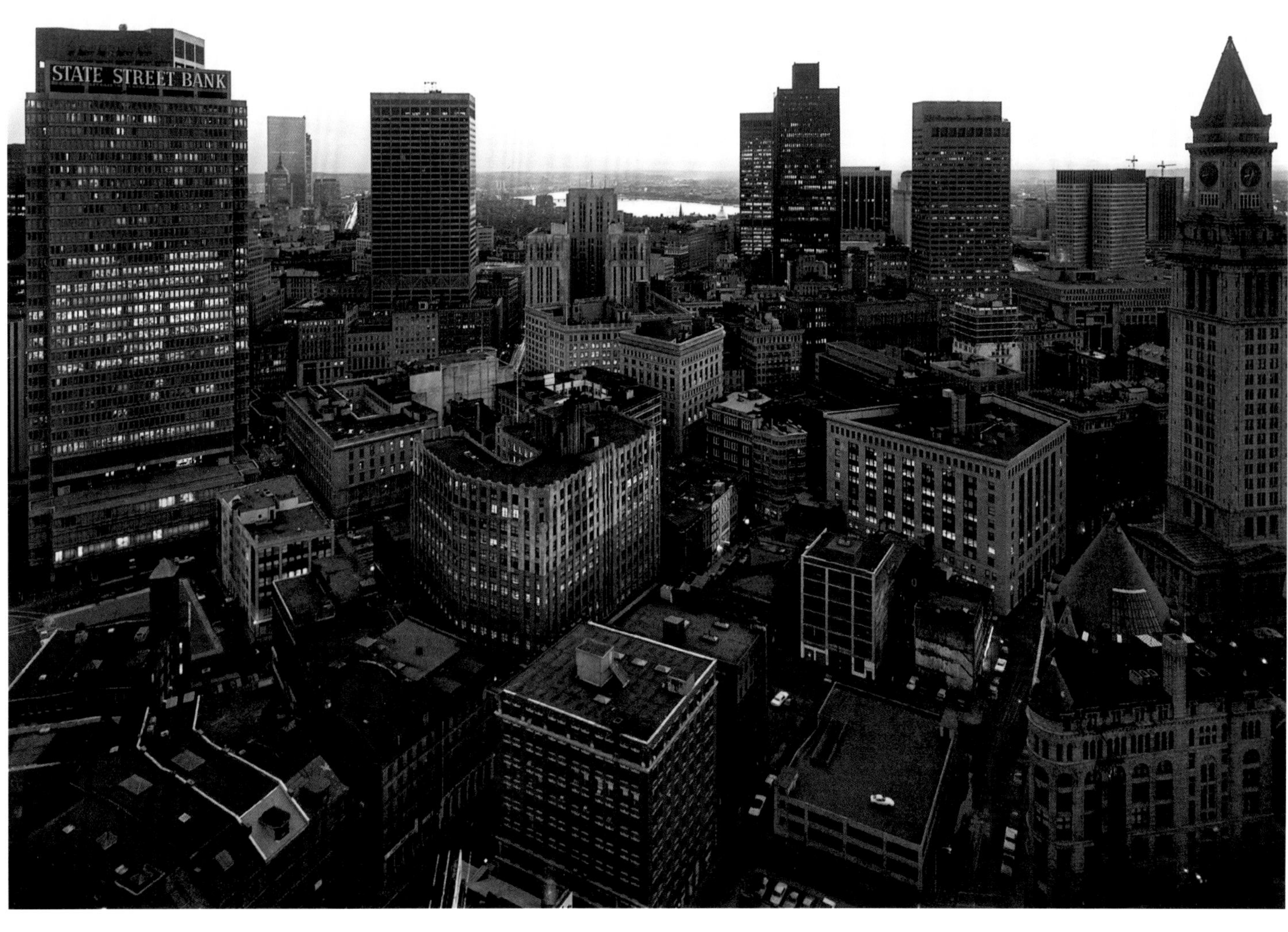
STATE STREET BANK

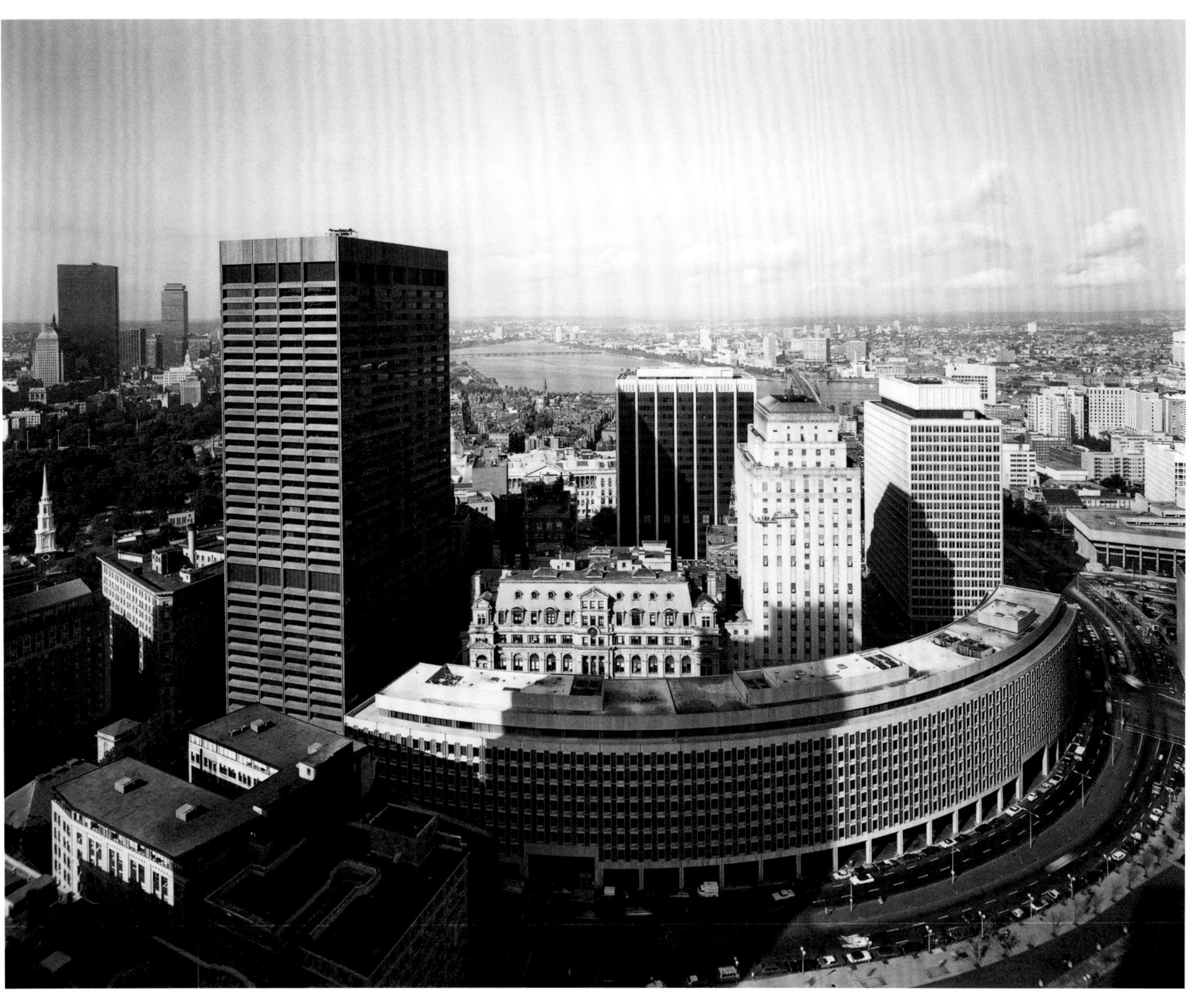

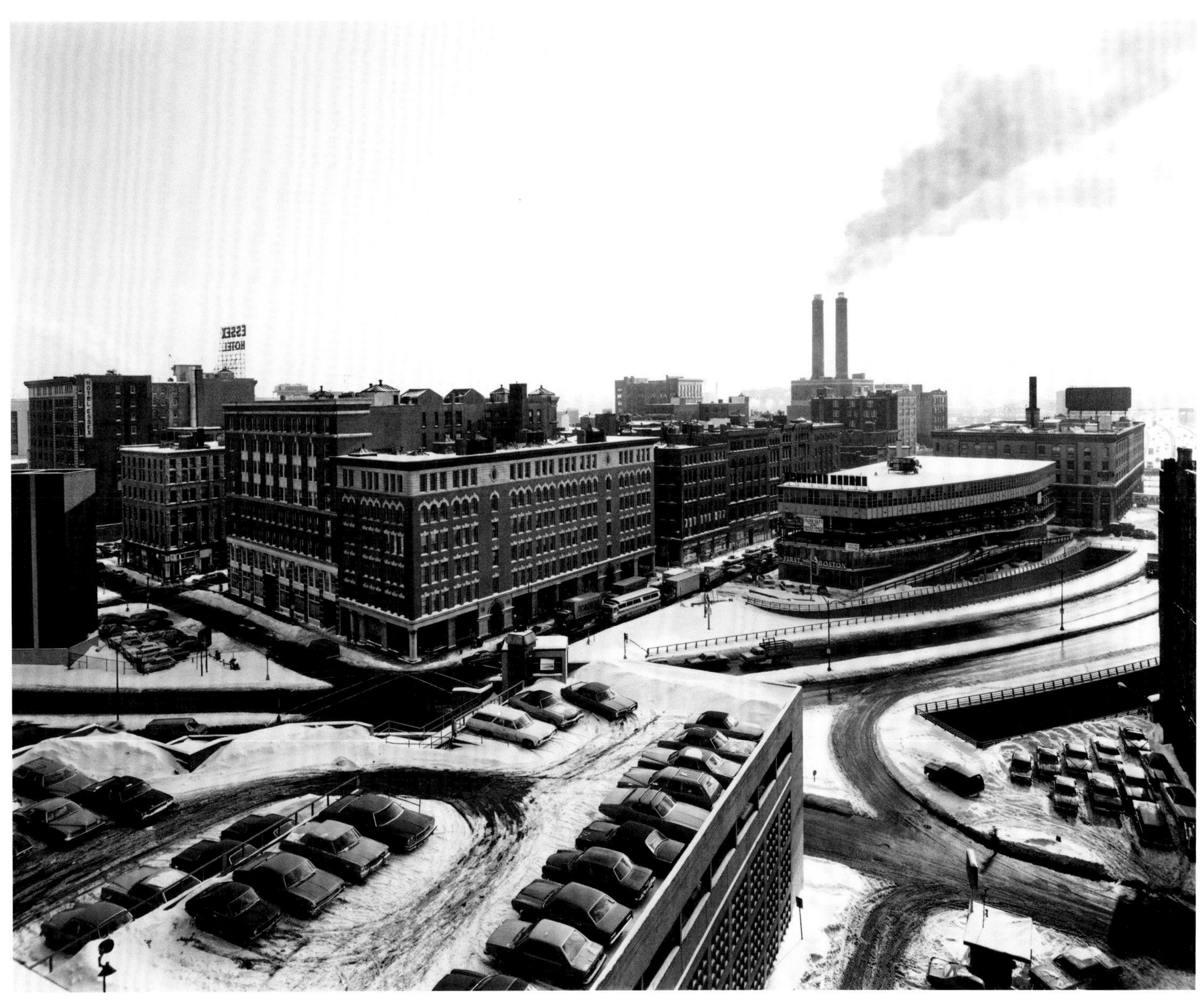
ESSEX
HOTEL
FIRST
BOSTON

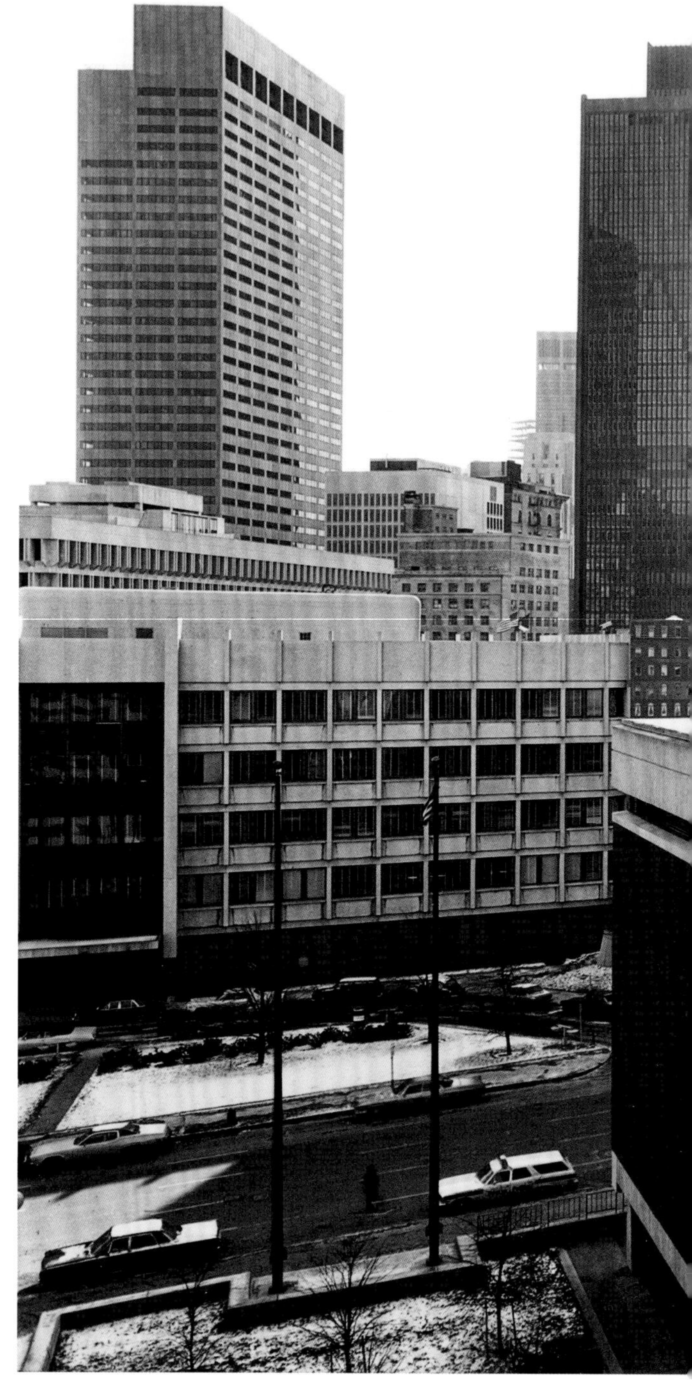

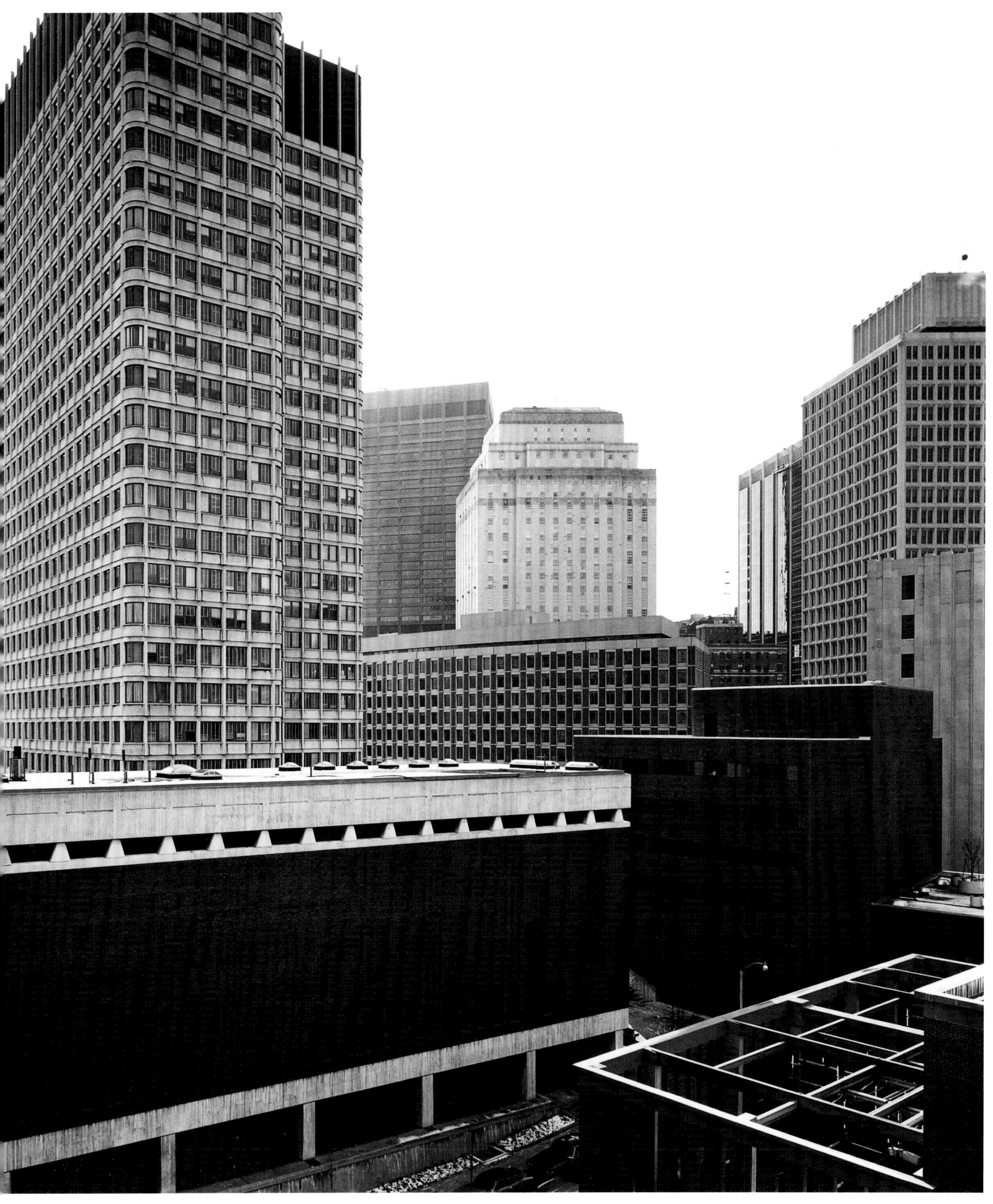

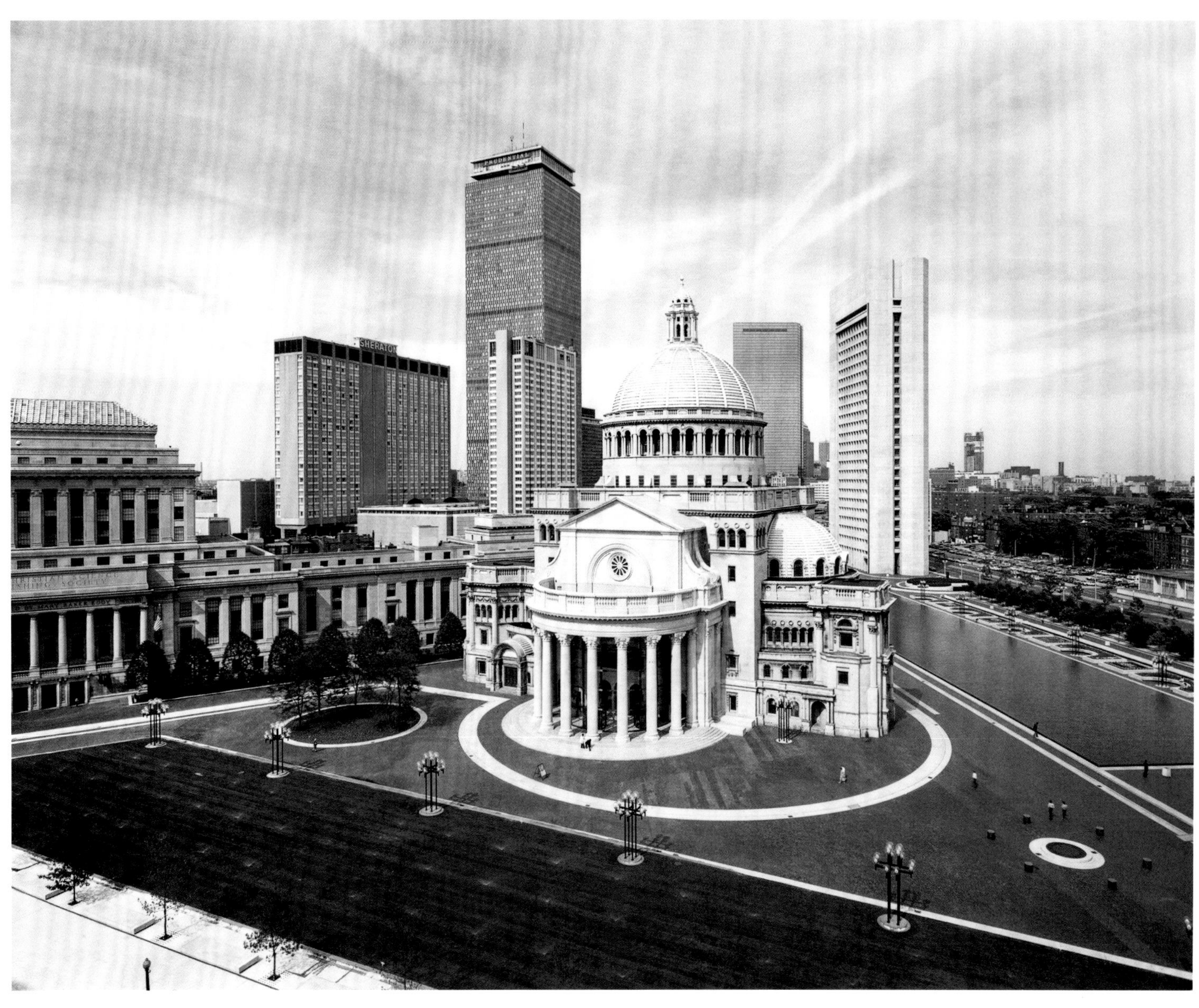
PRUDENTIAL

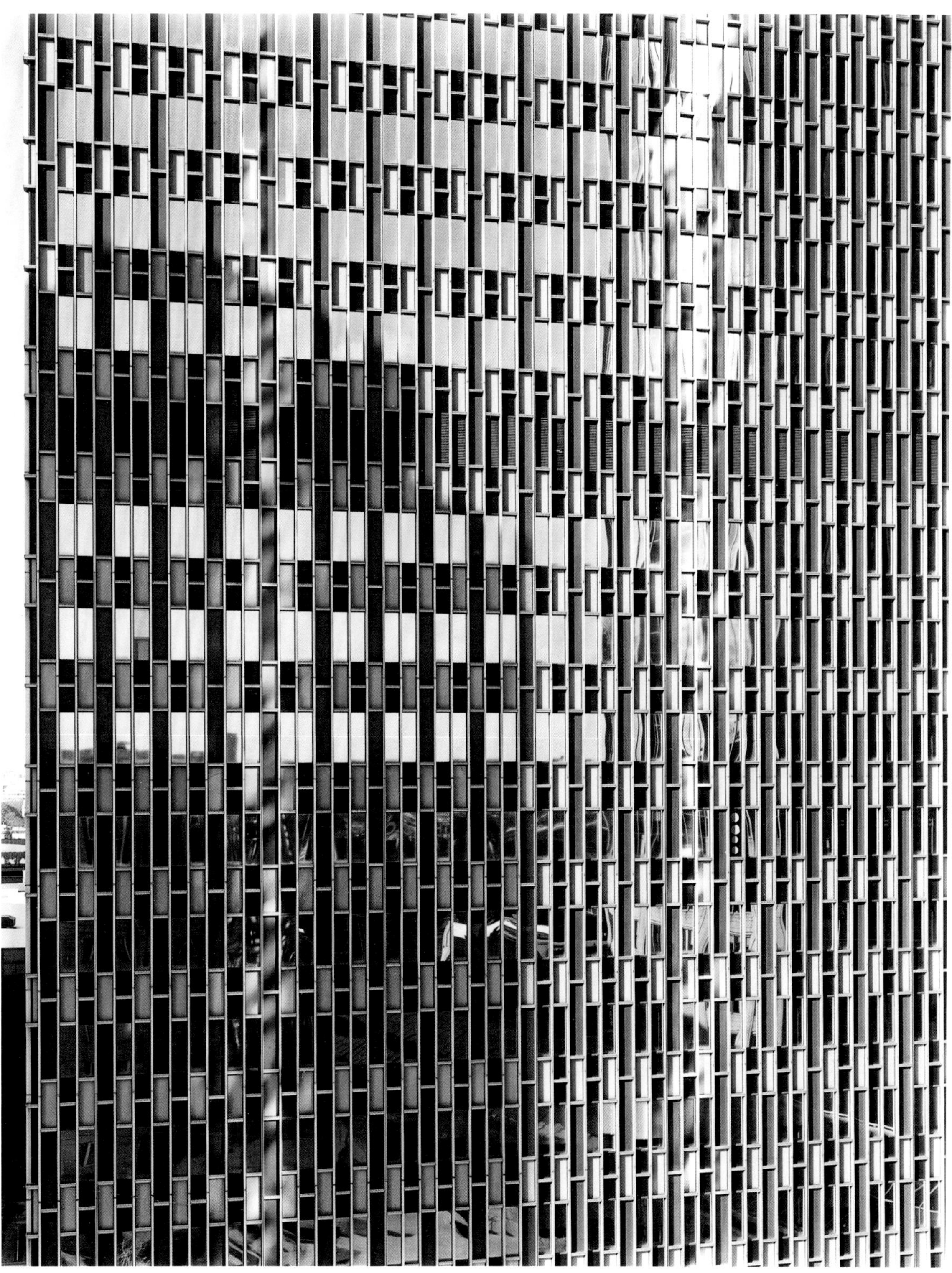

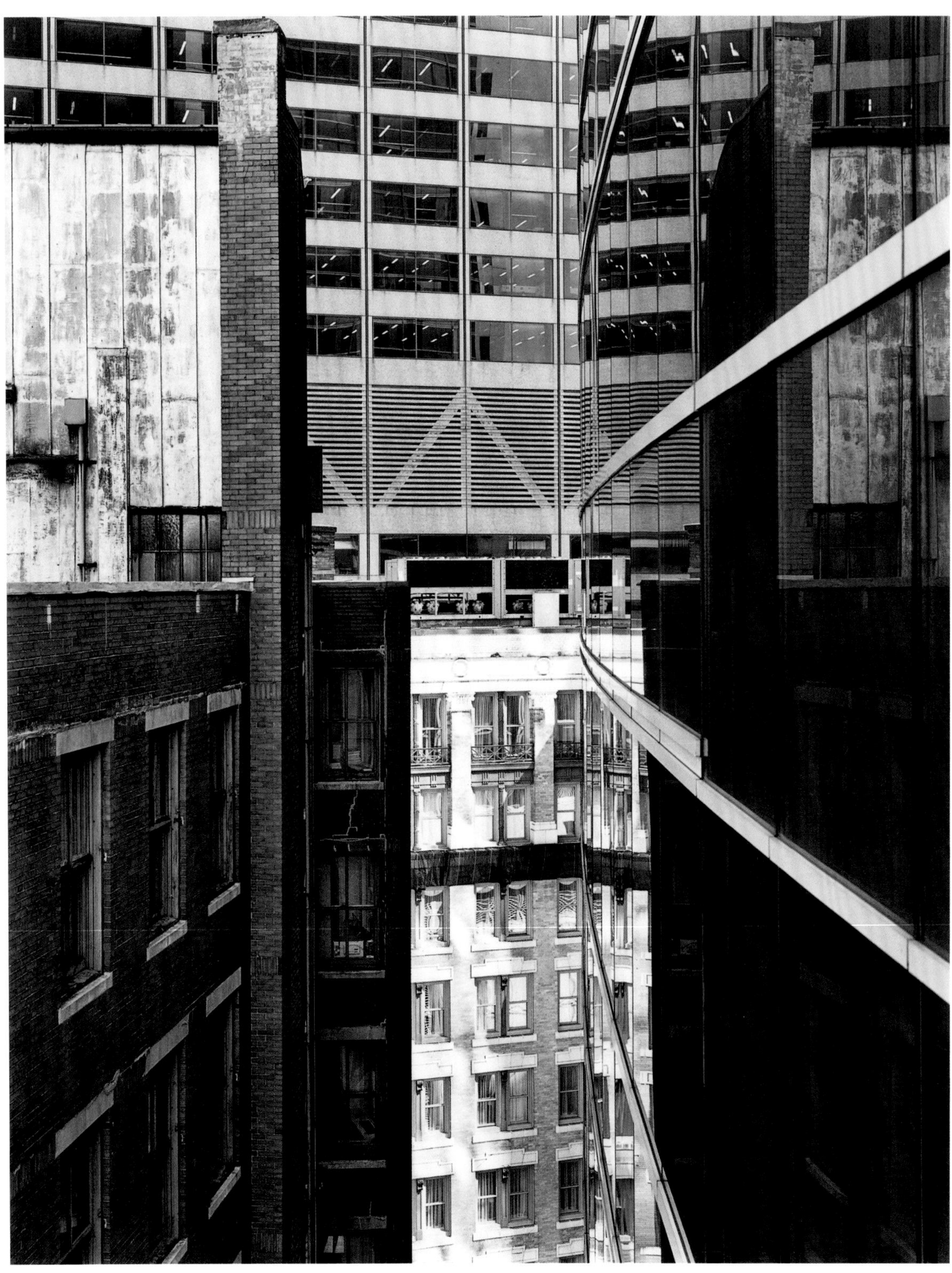

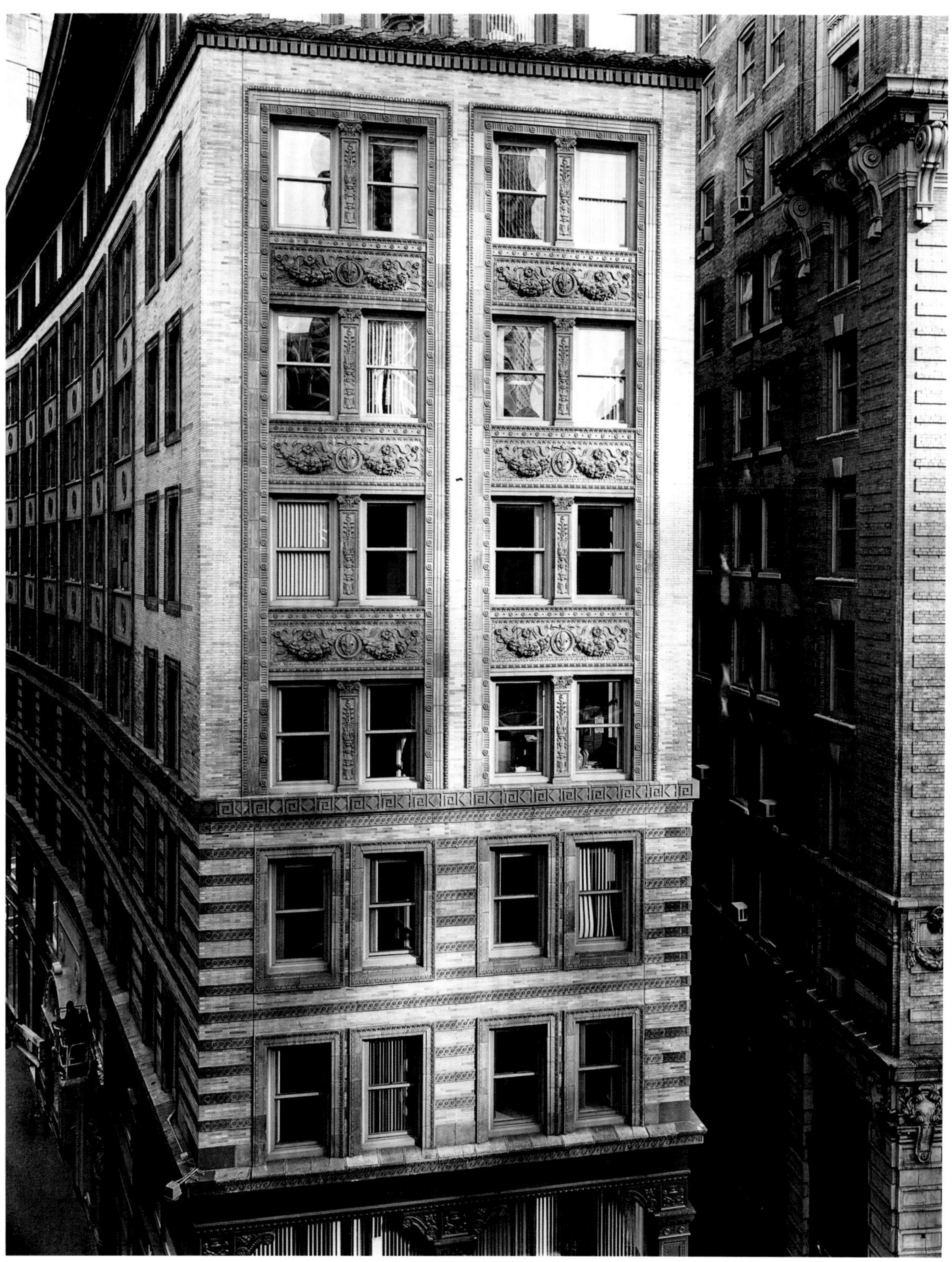

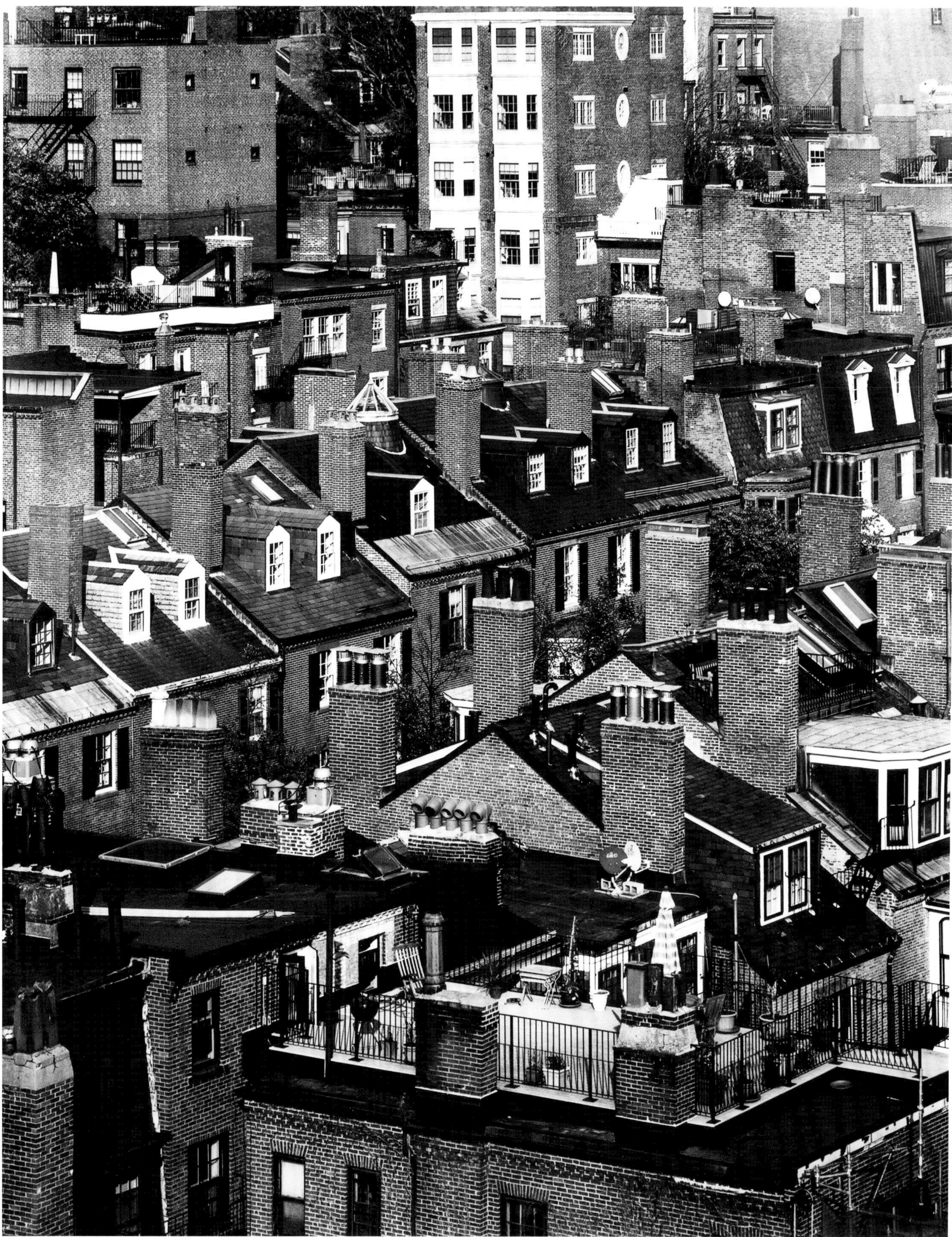

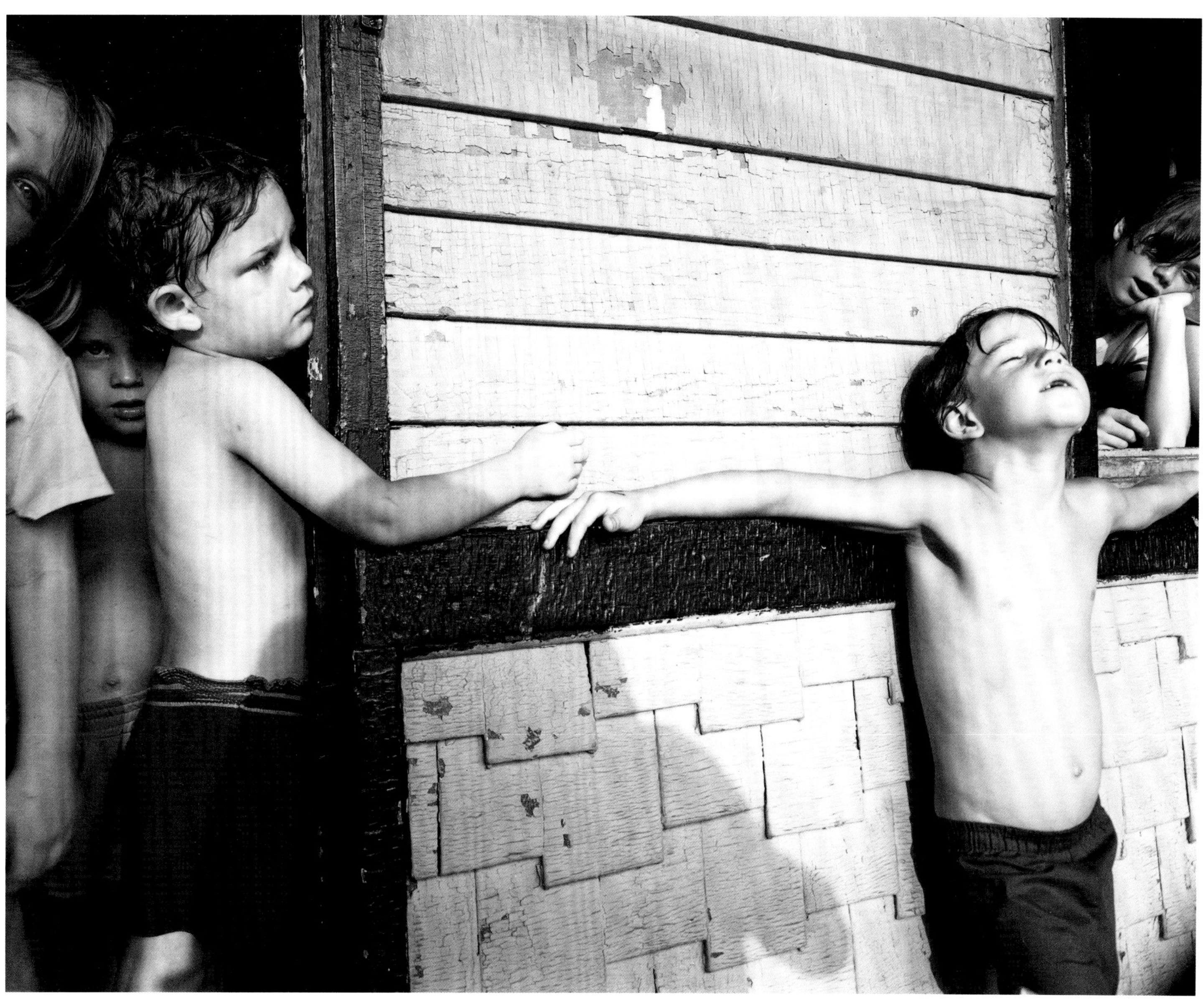

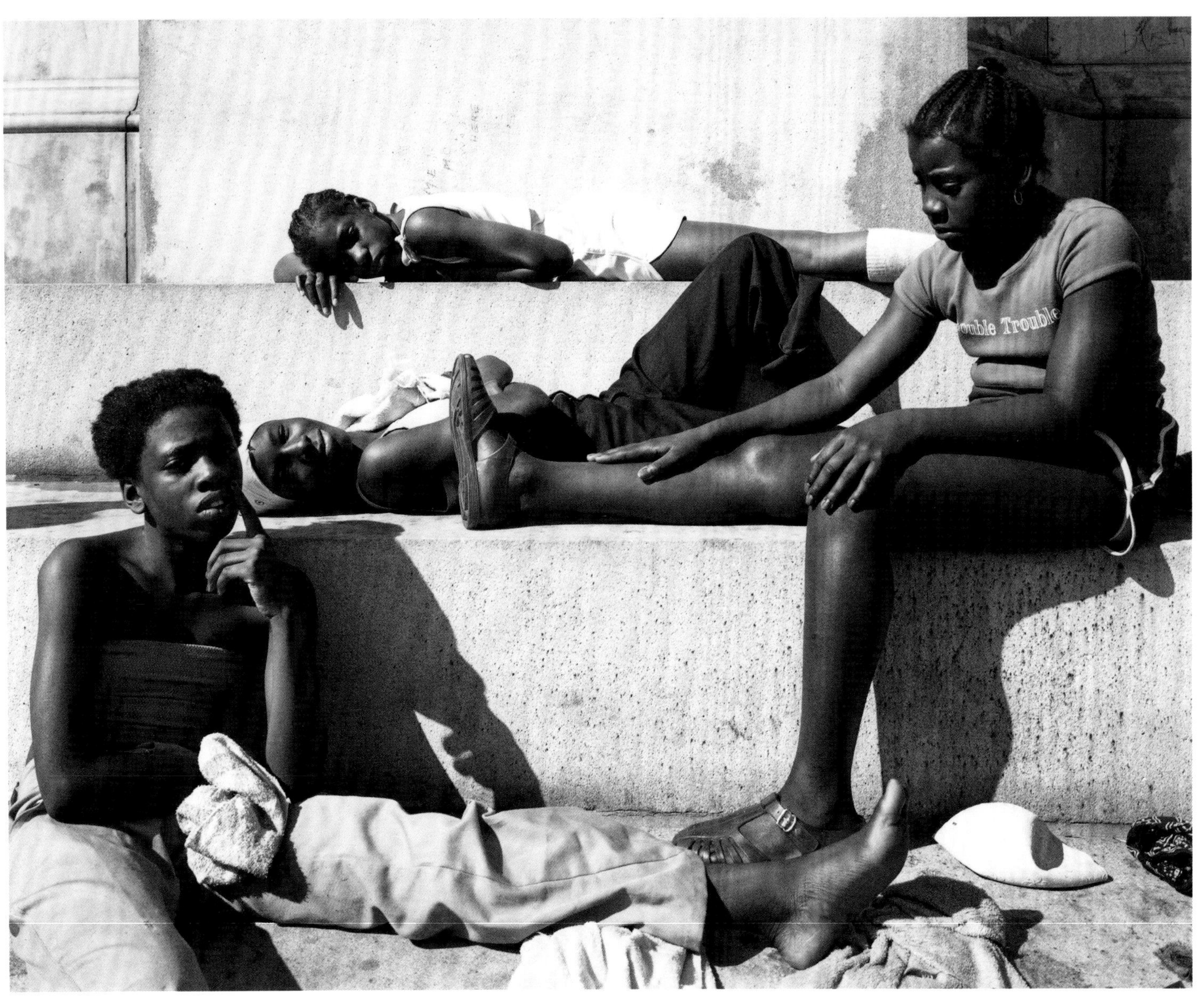
ouble Trouble

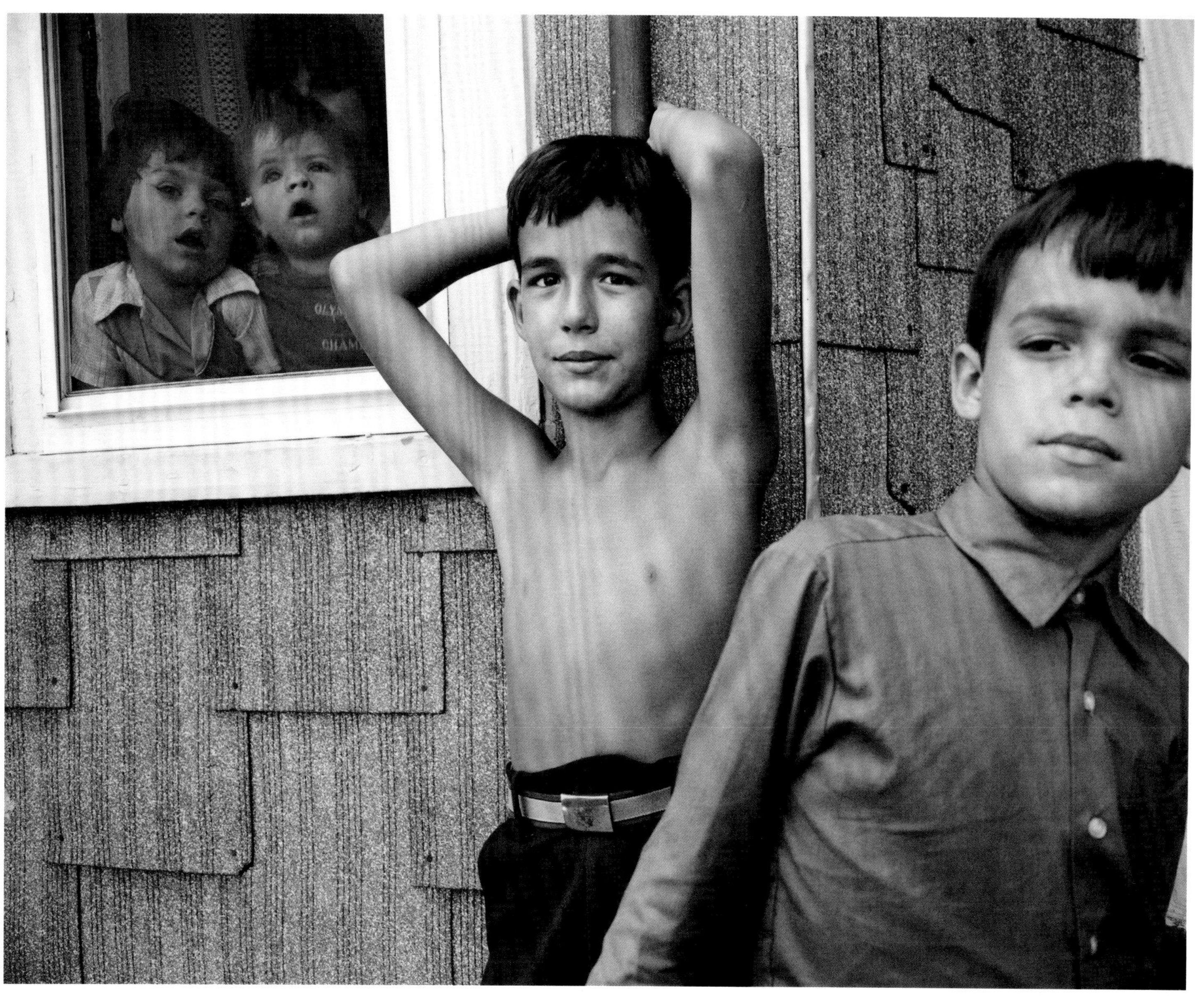

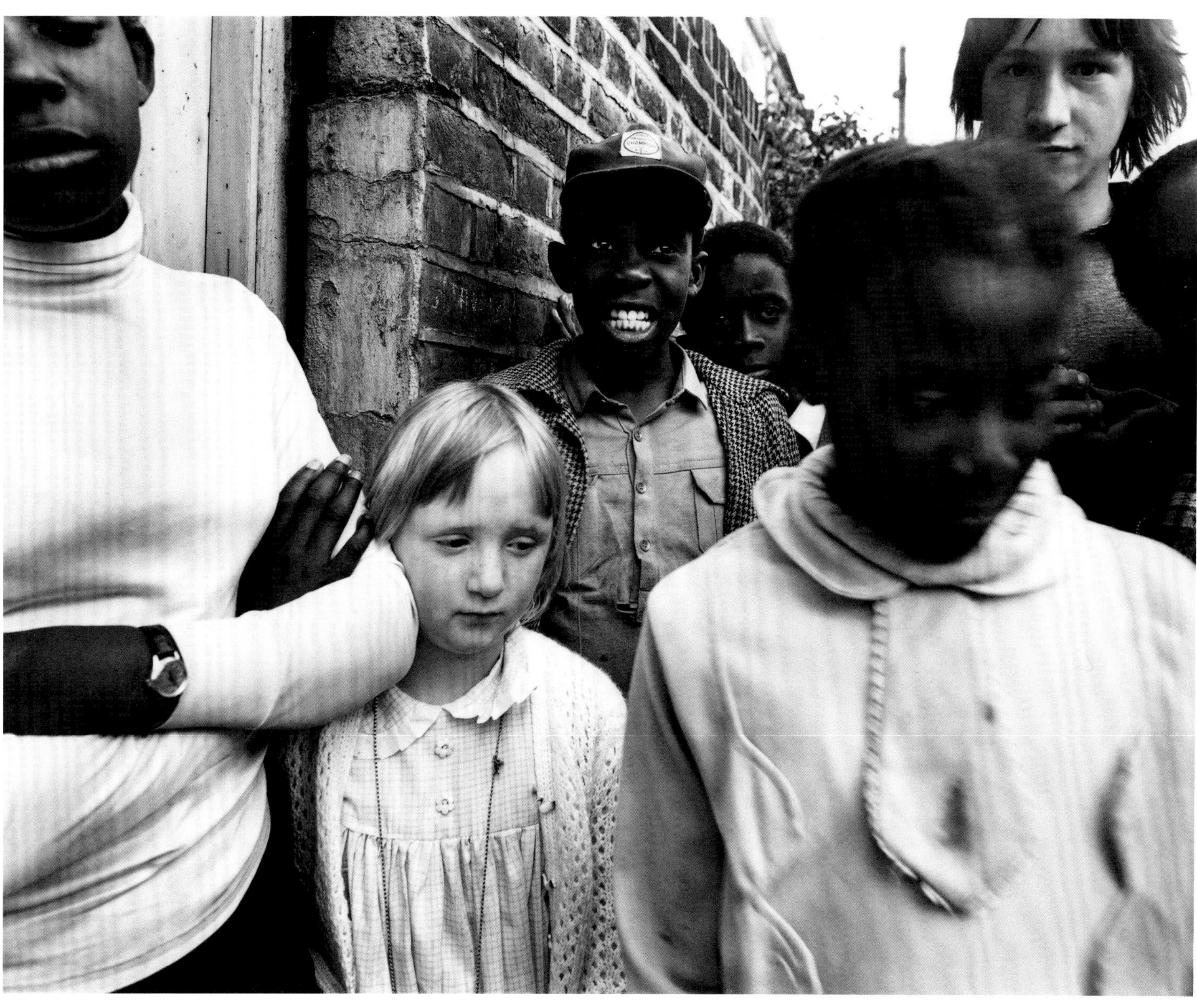

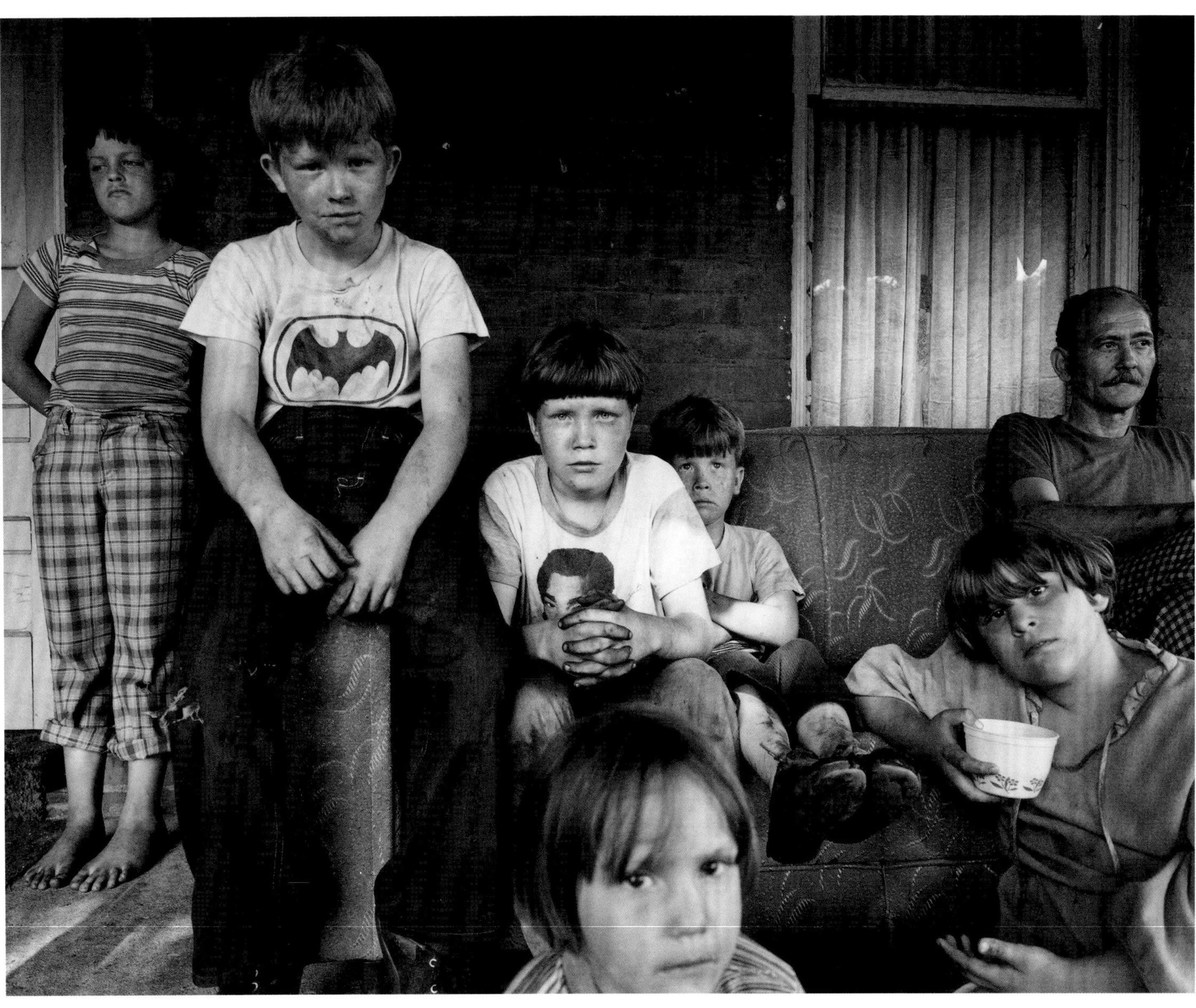

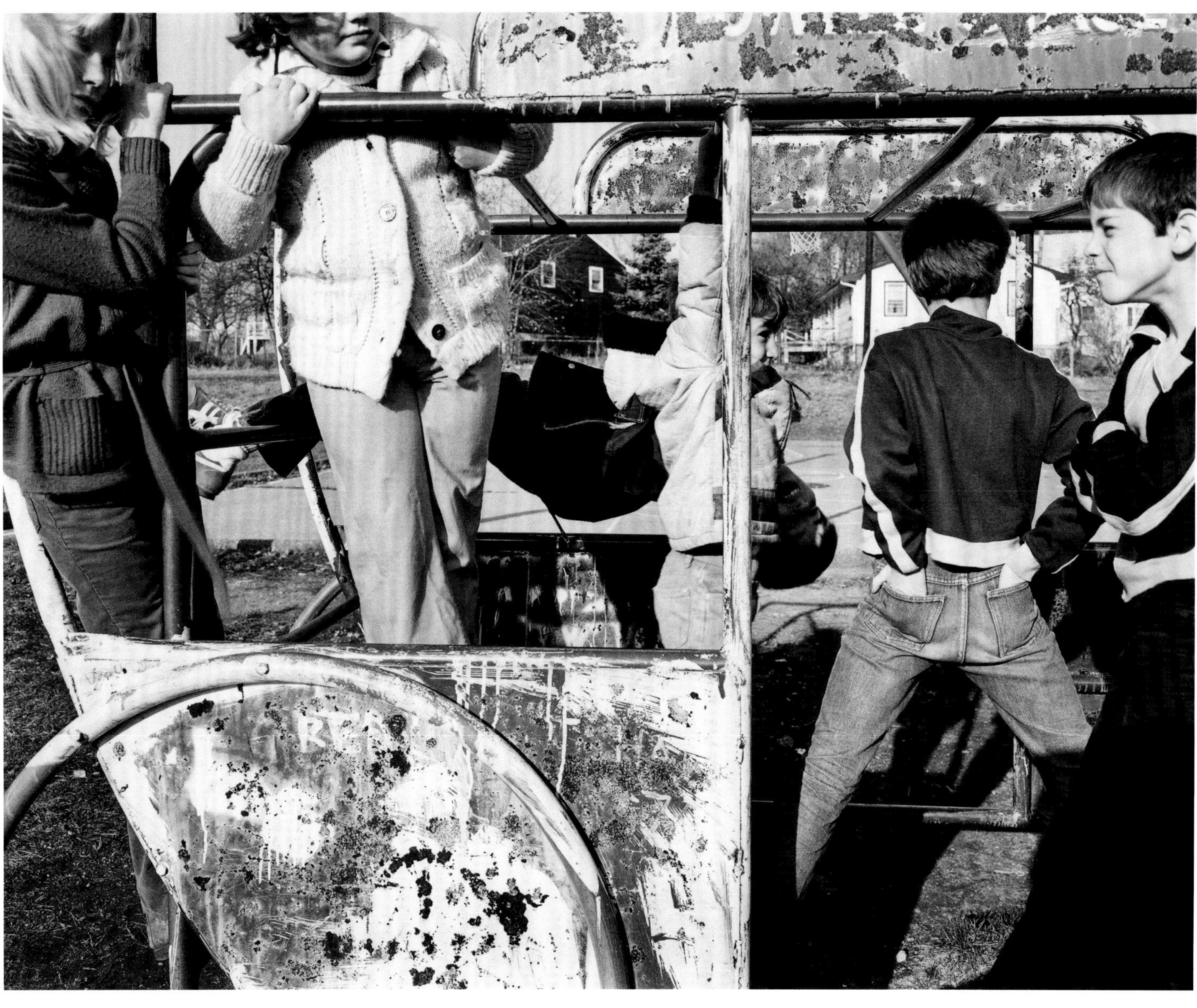

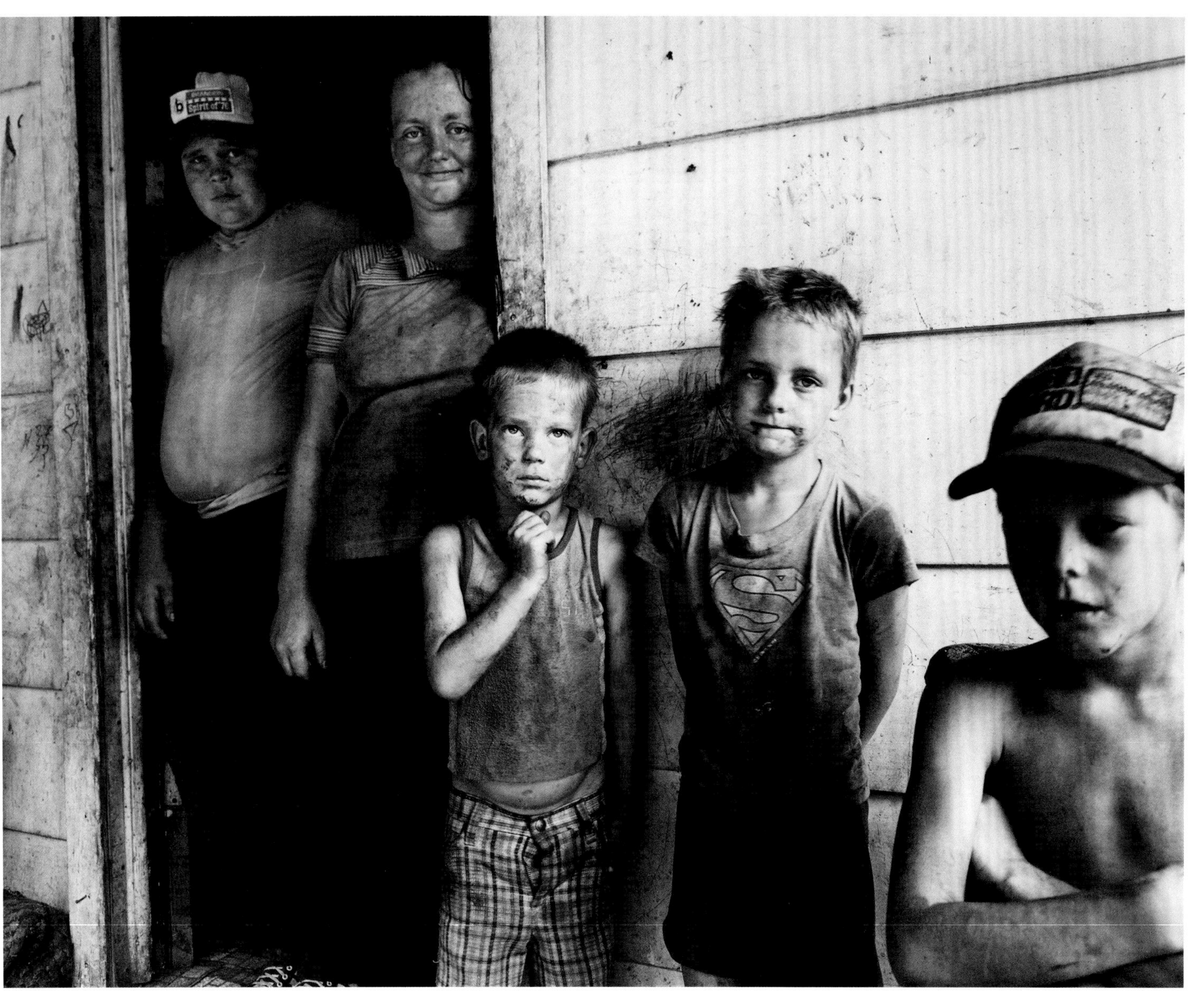

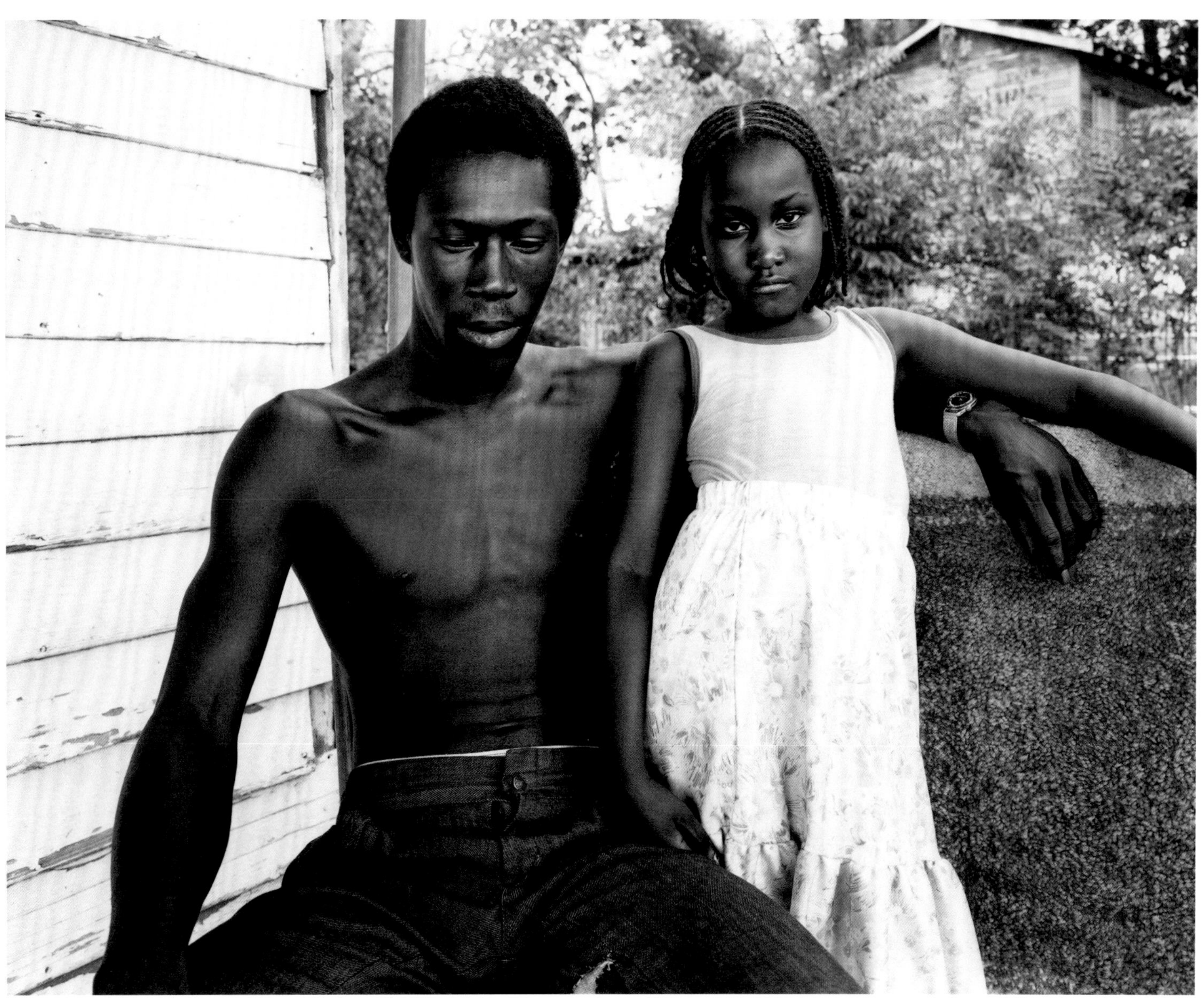

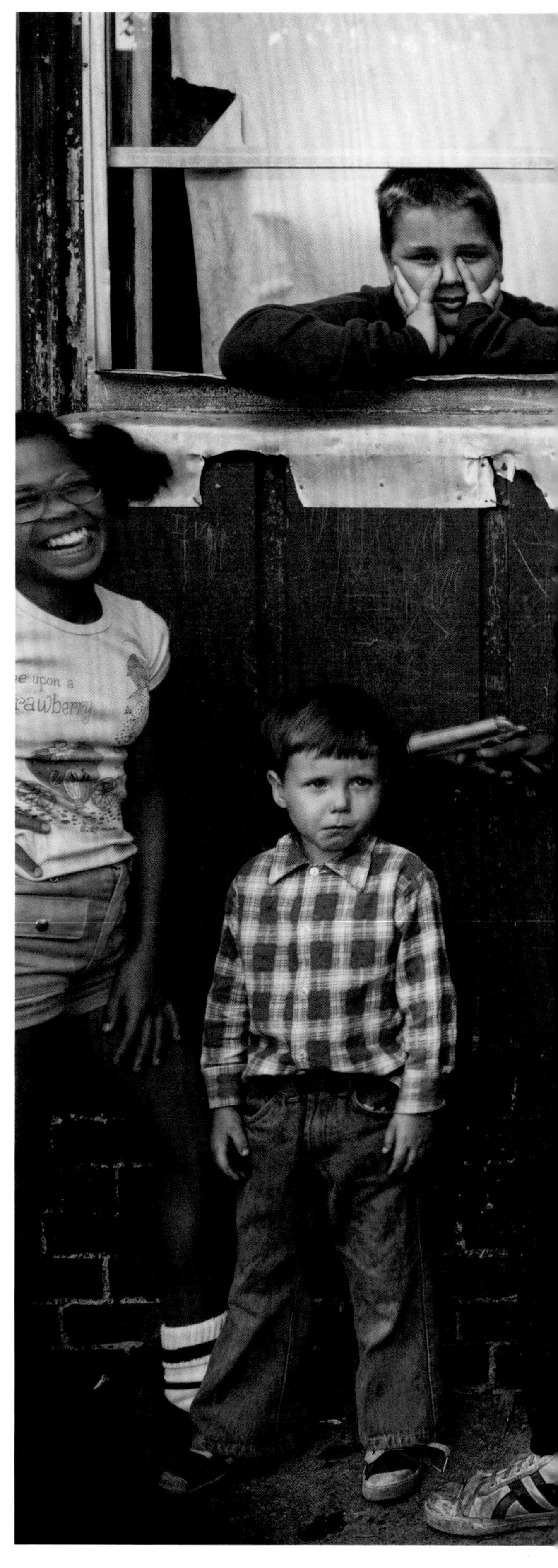

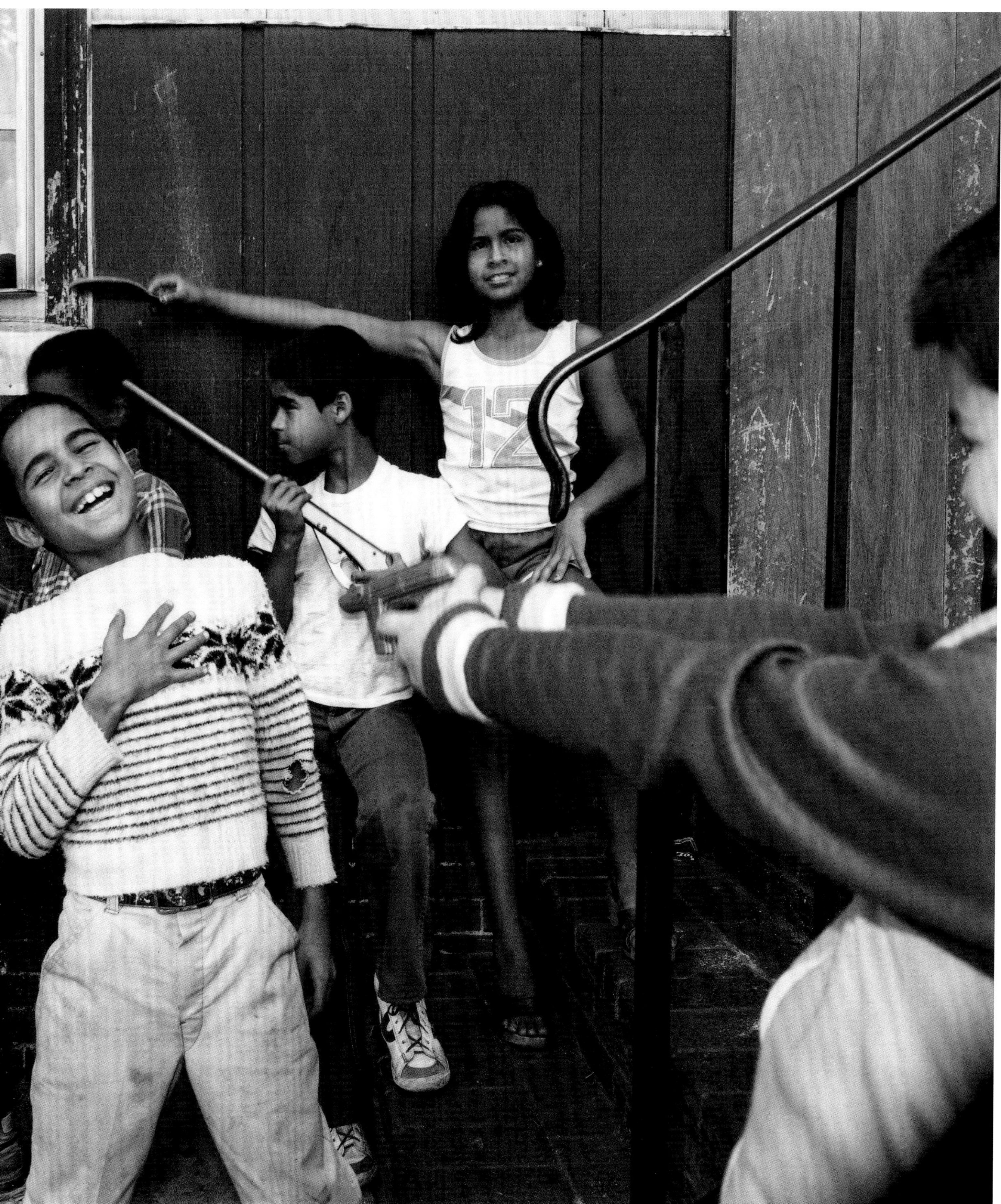
12

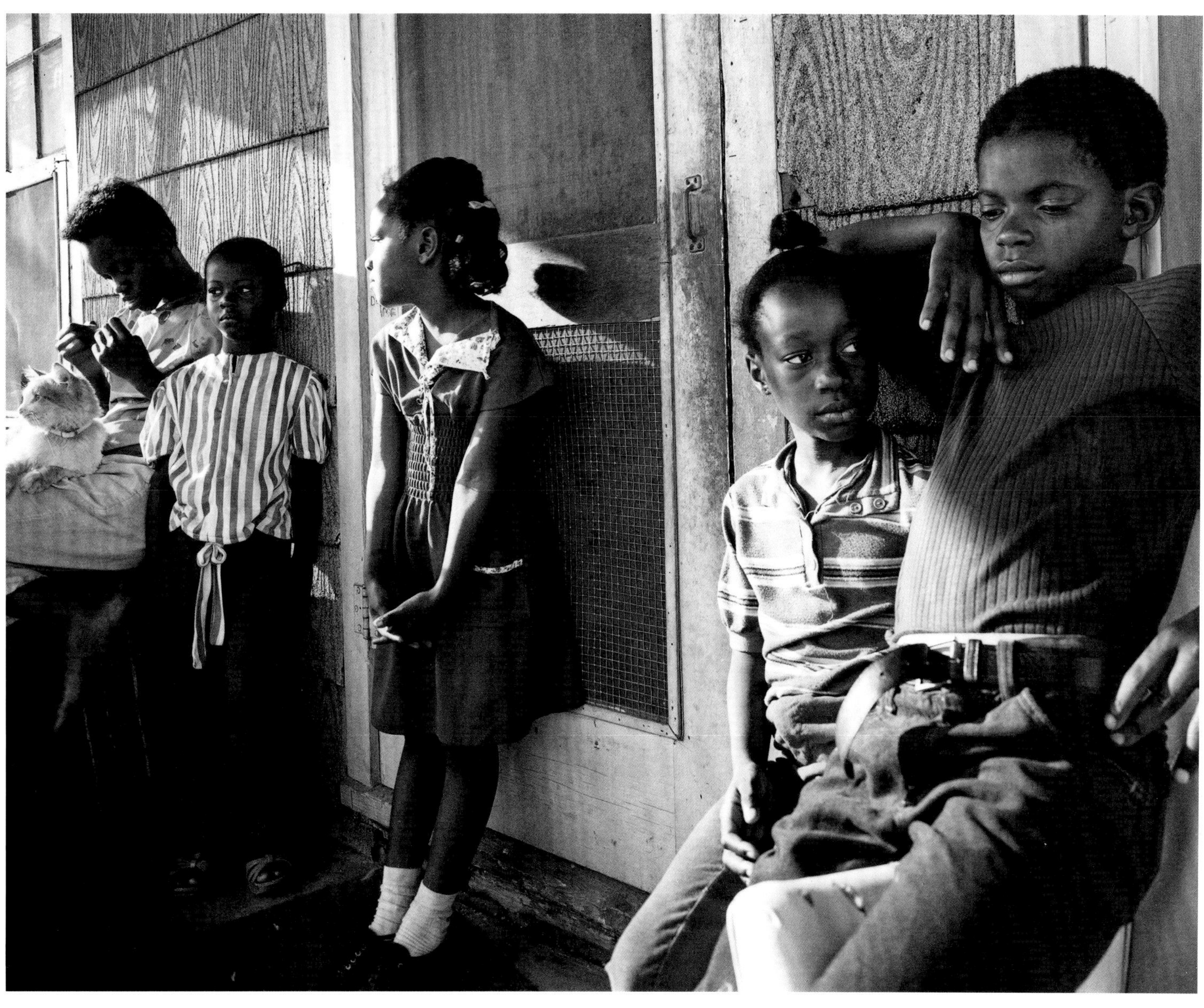

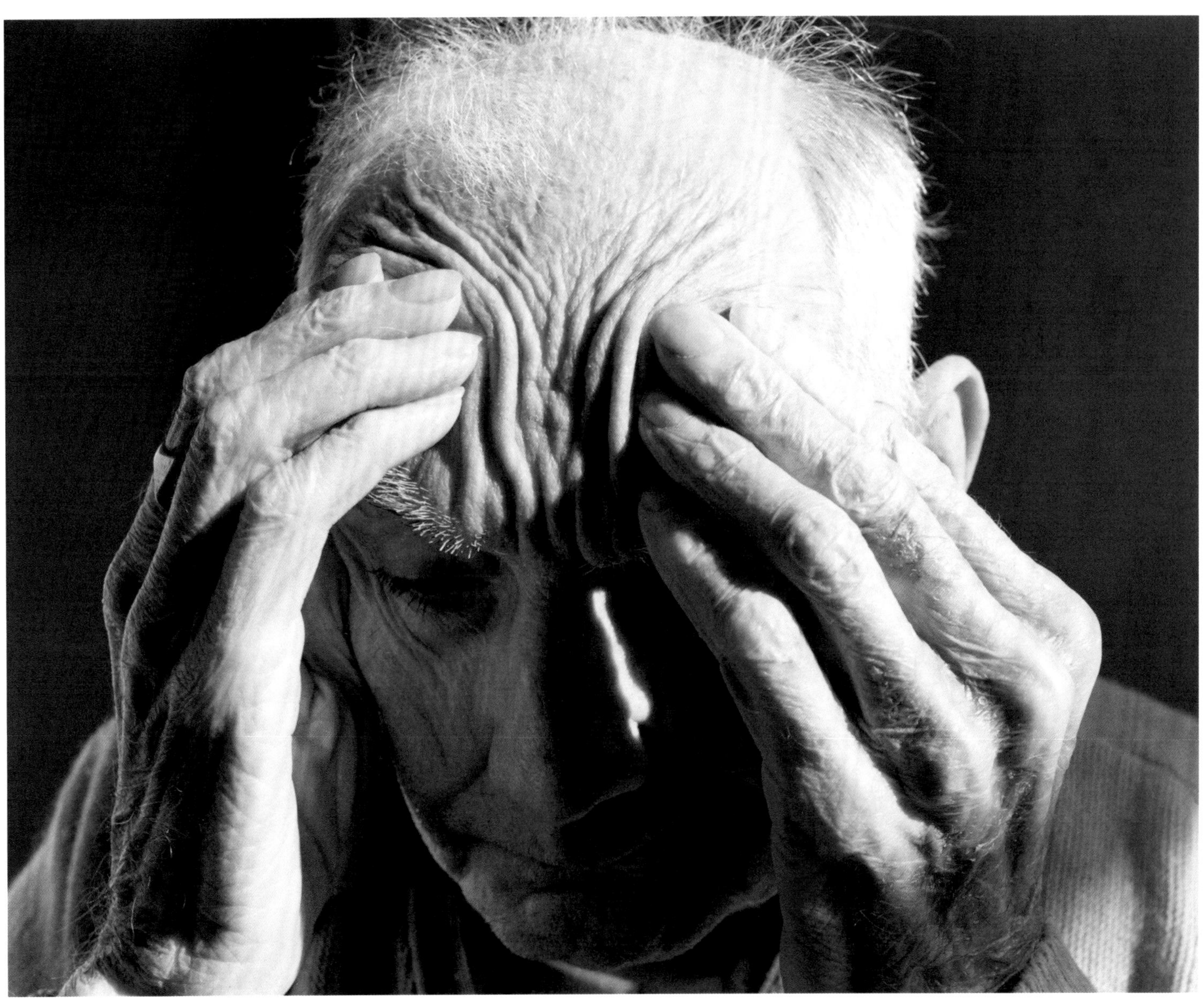

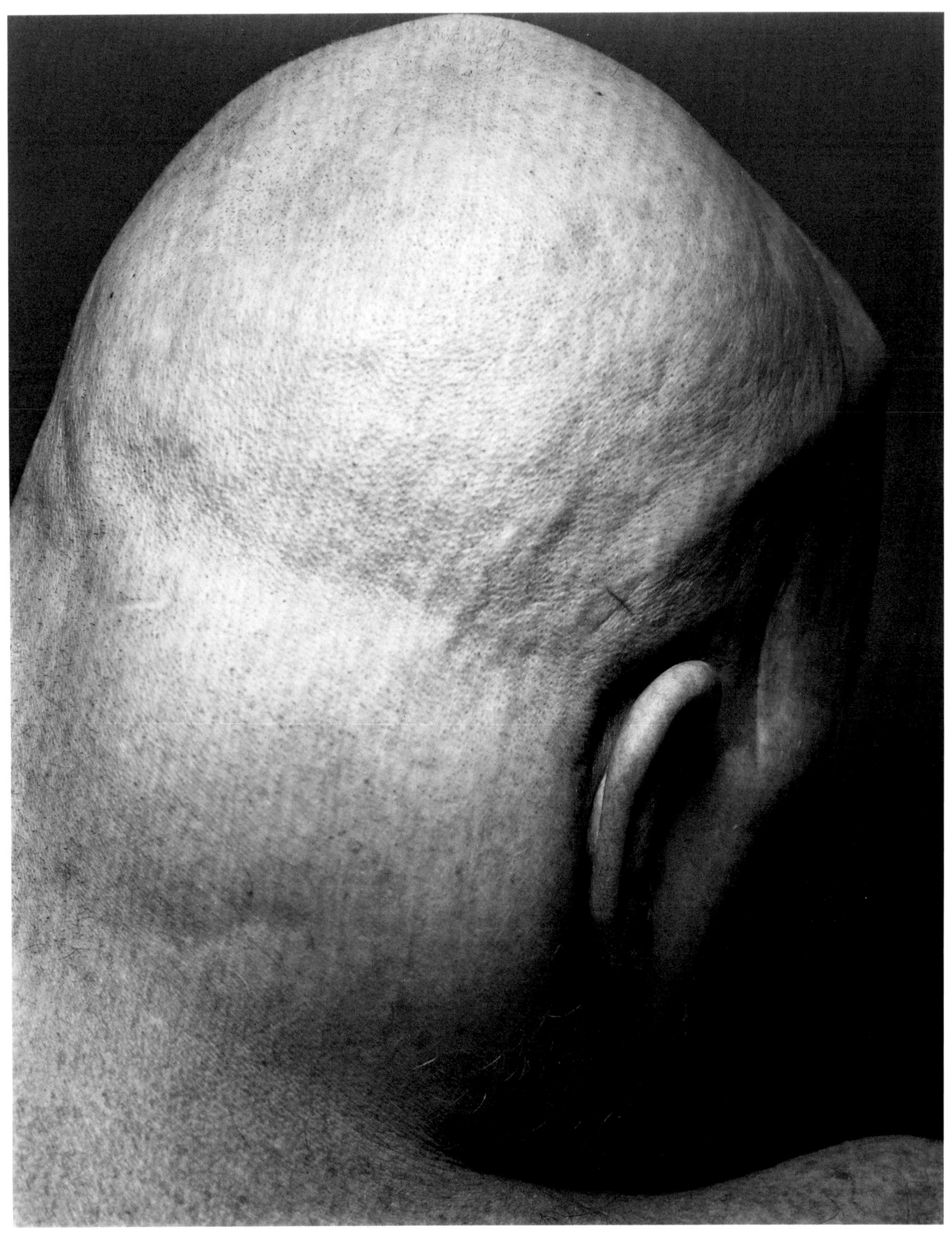

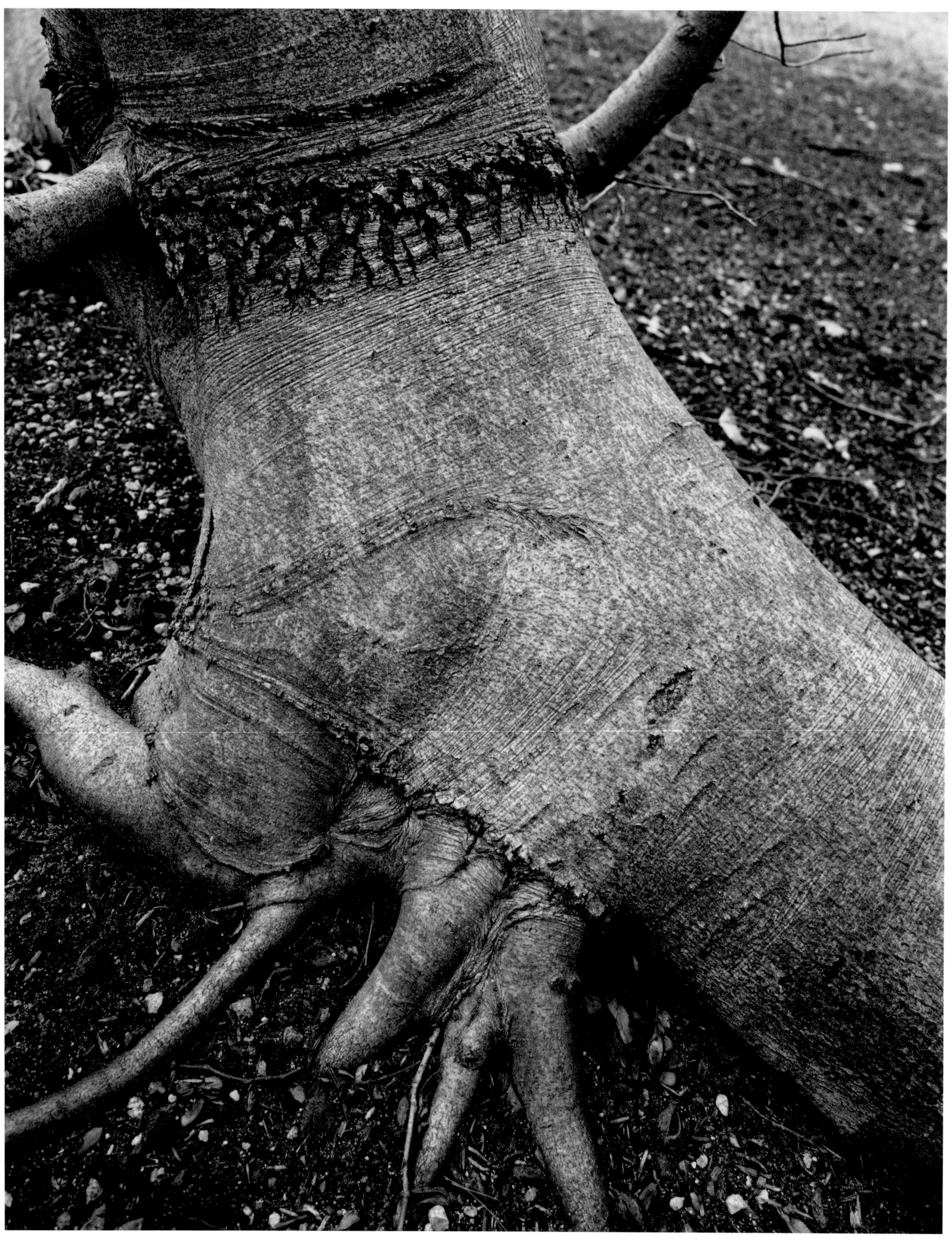

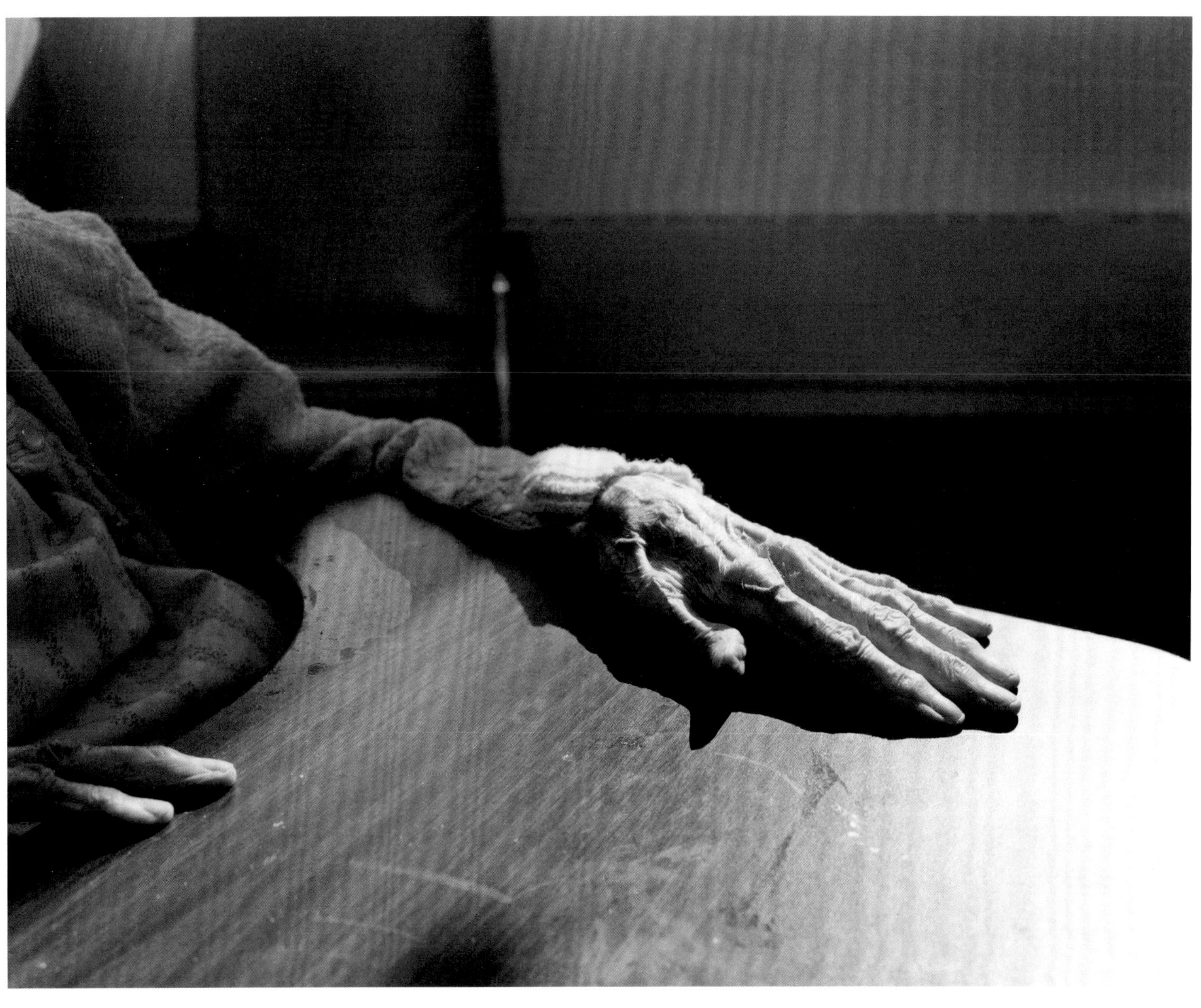

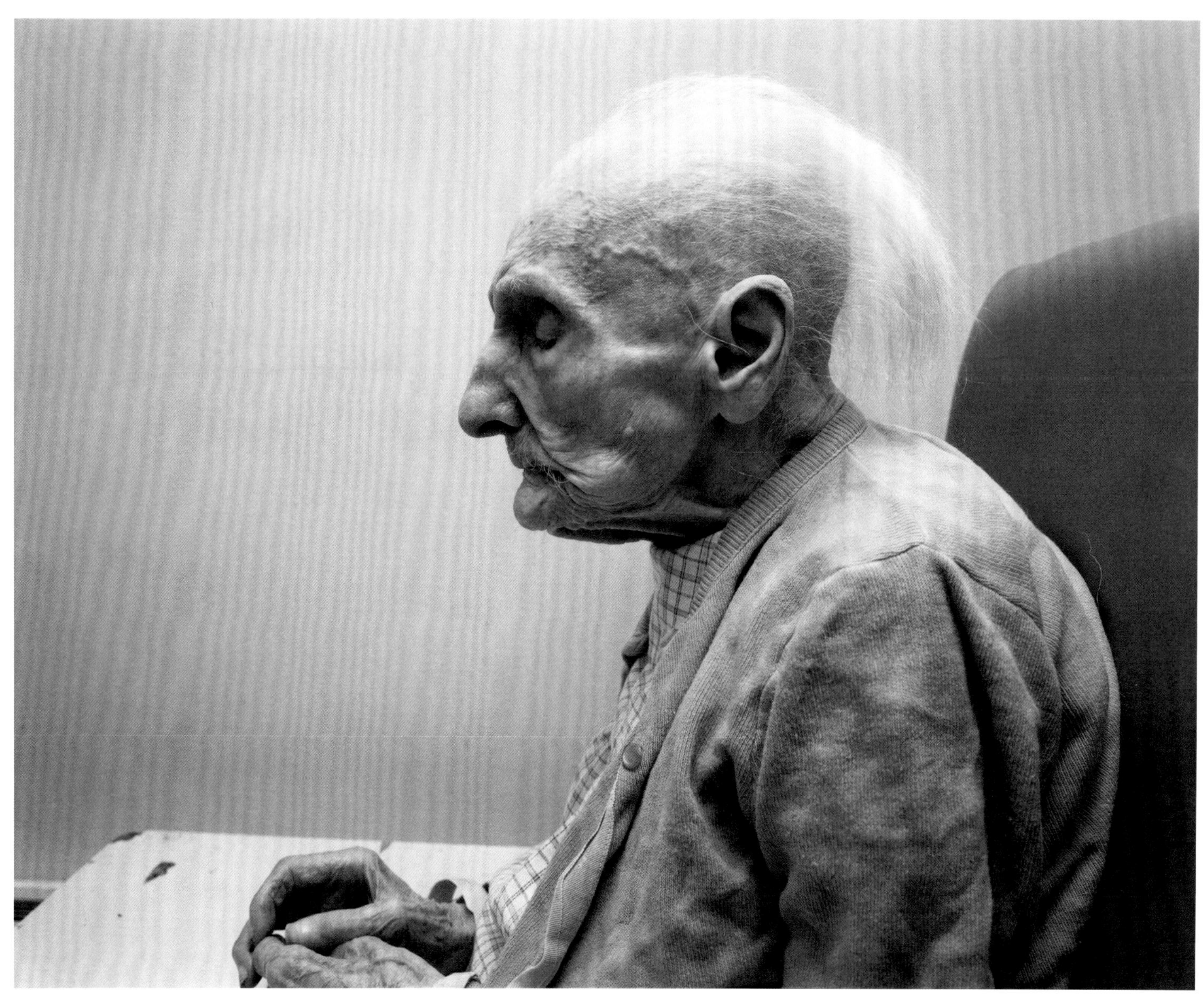

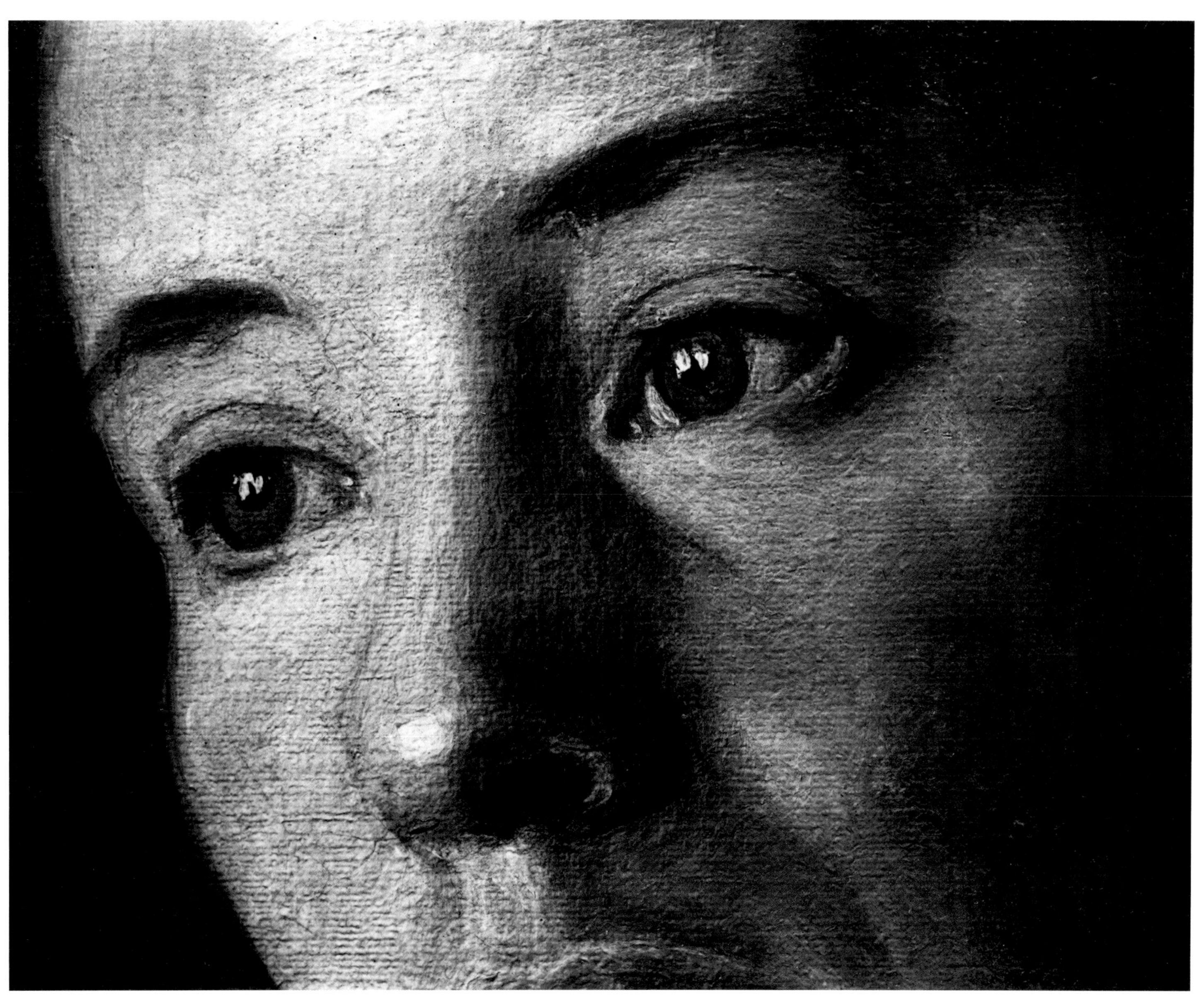

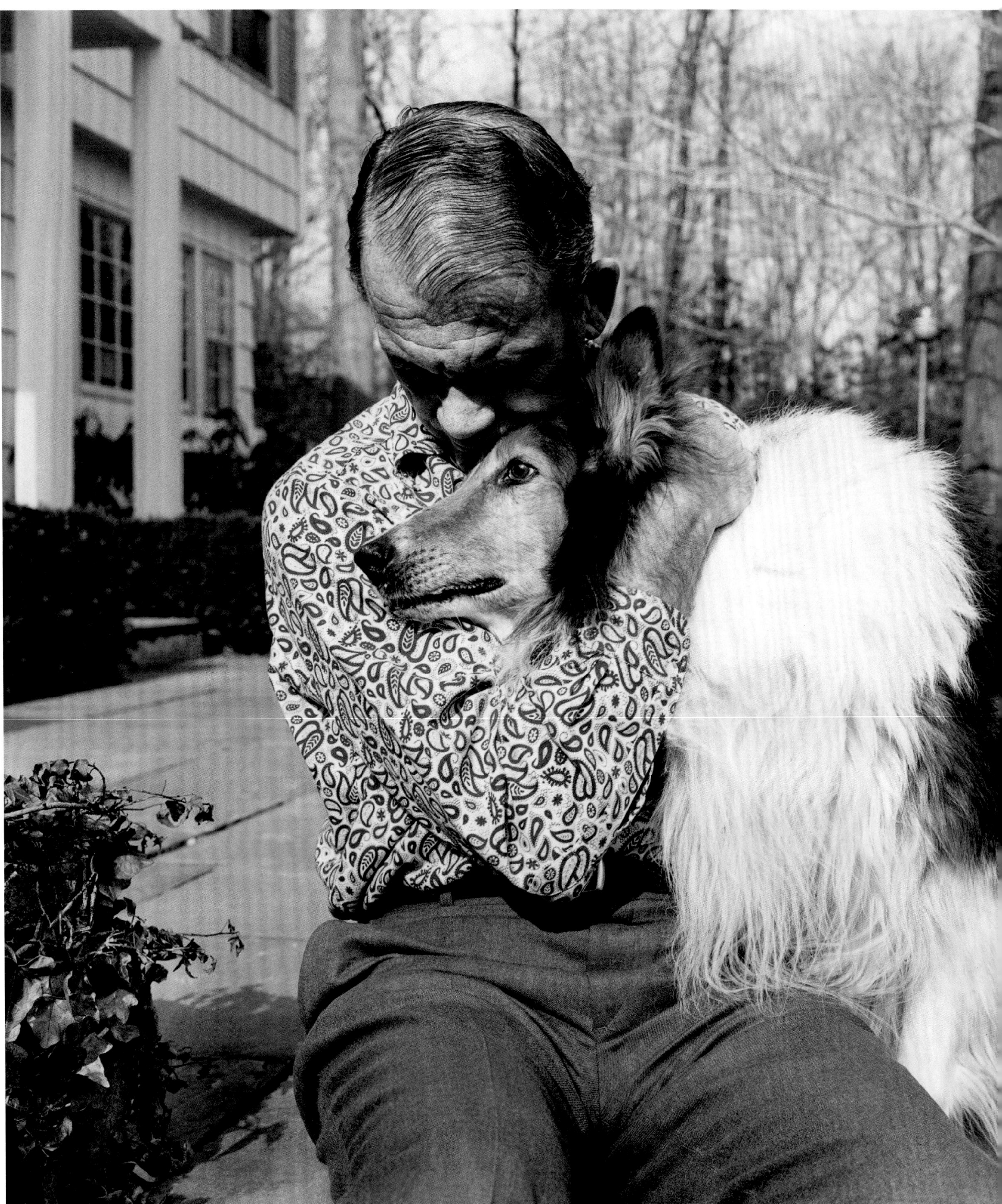

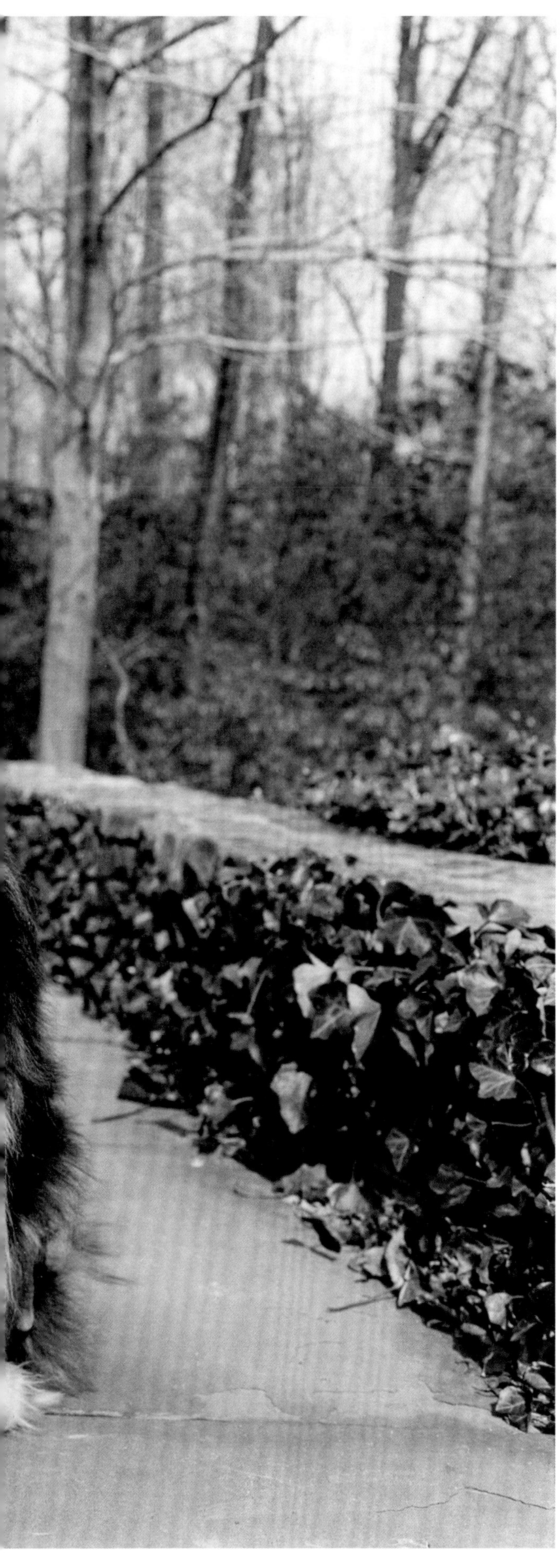

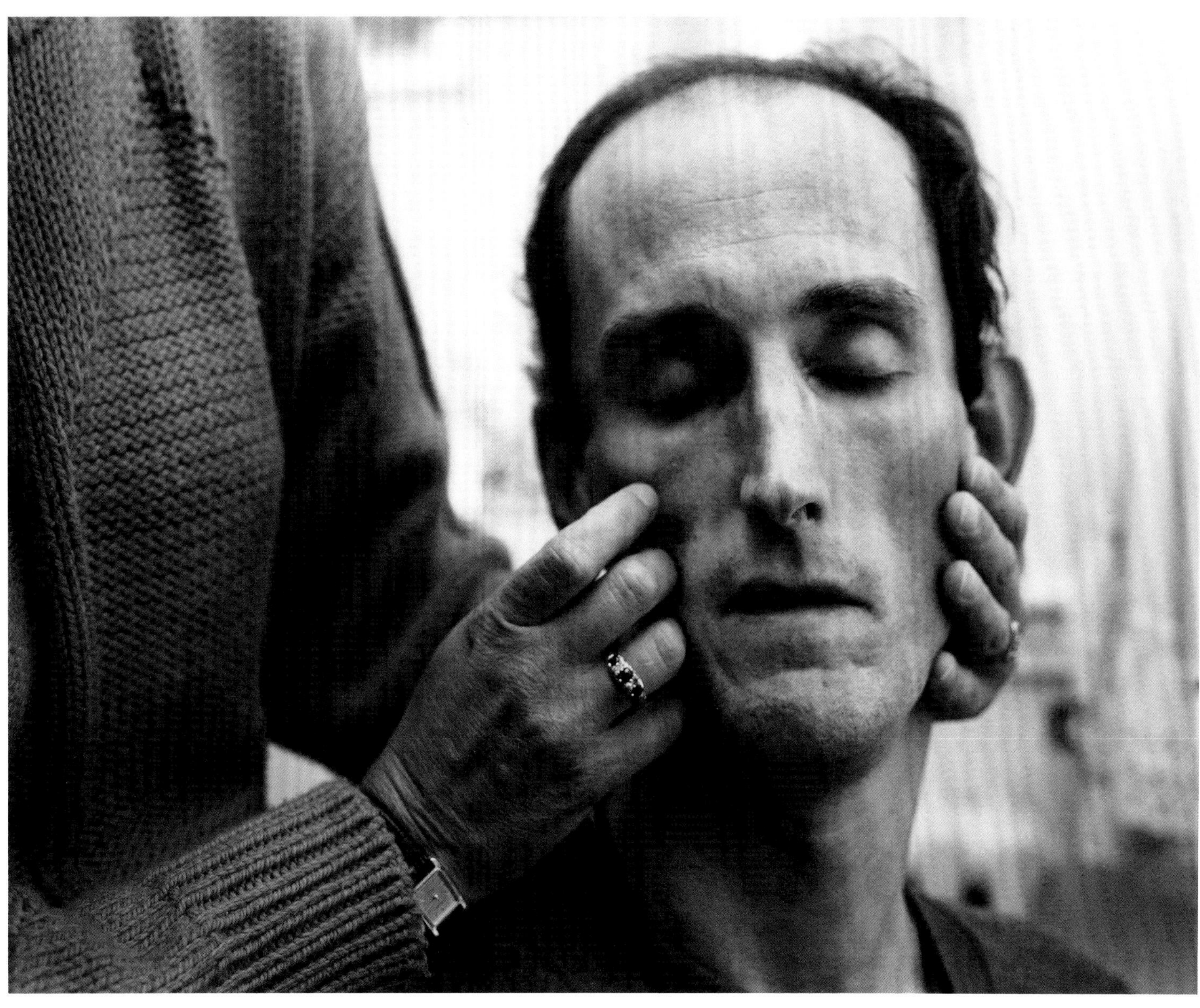

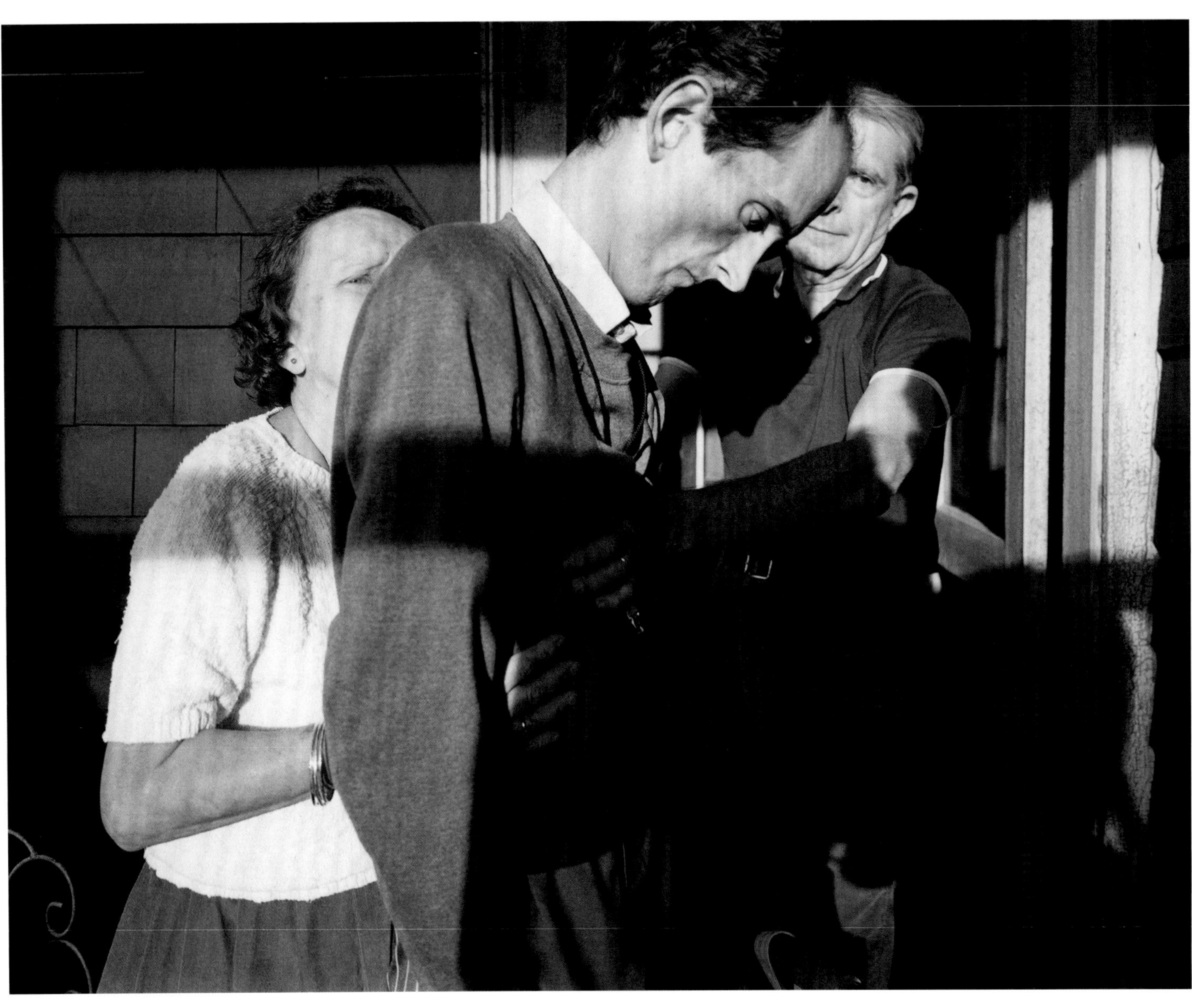

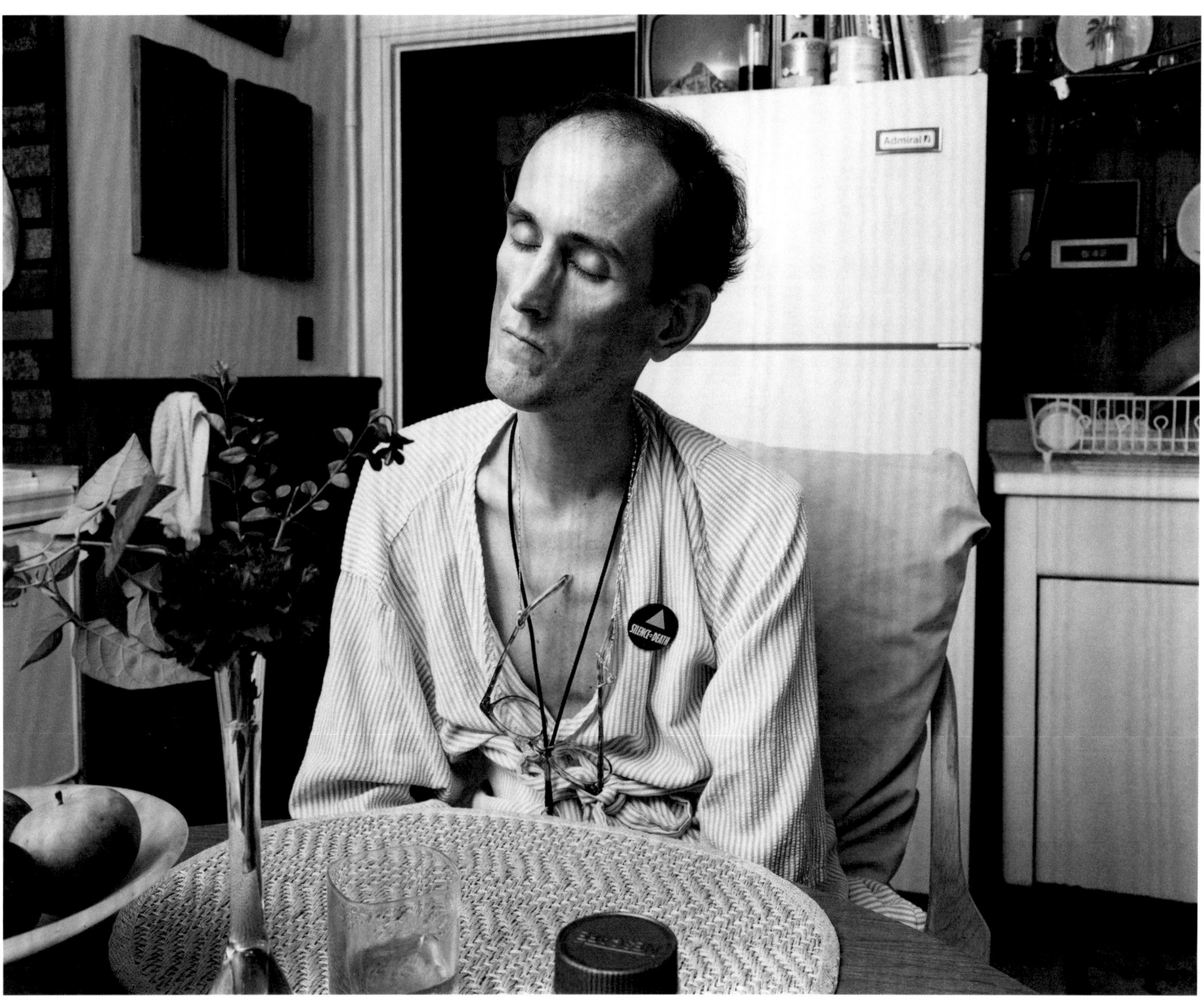
Admiral
SILENCE=DEATH

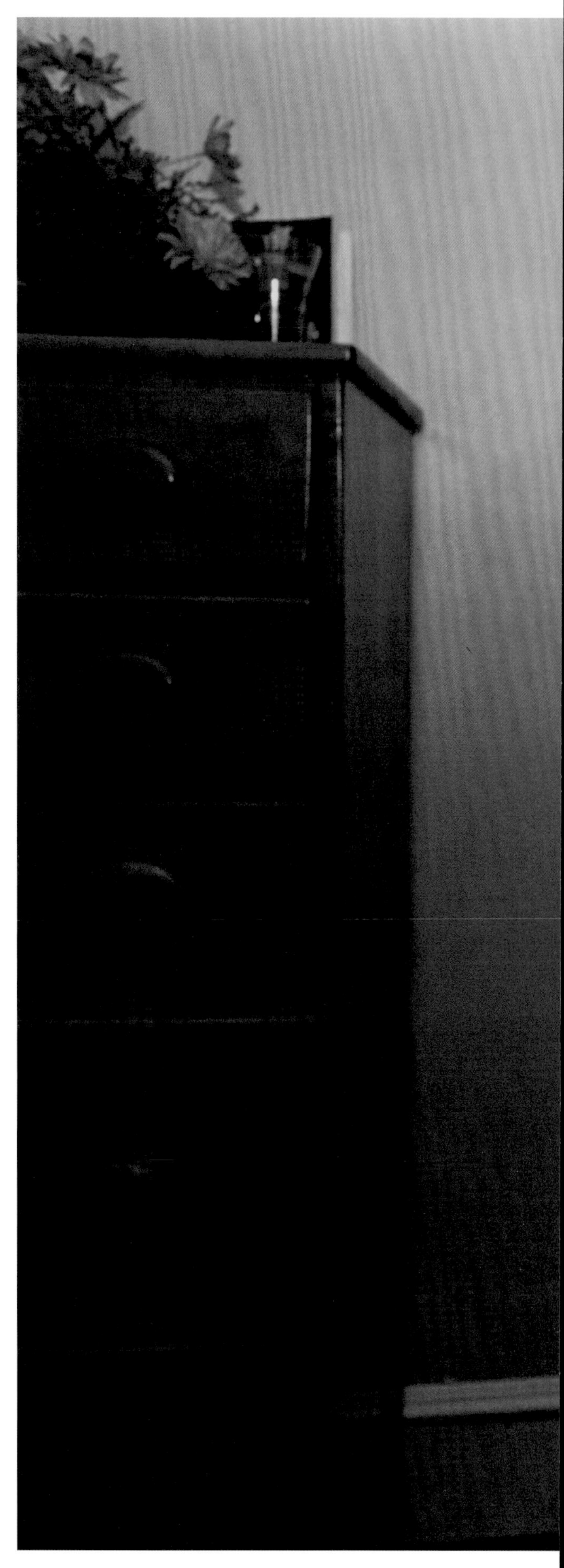

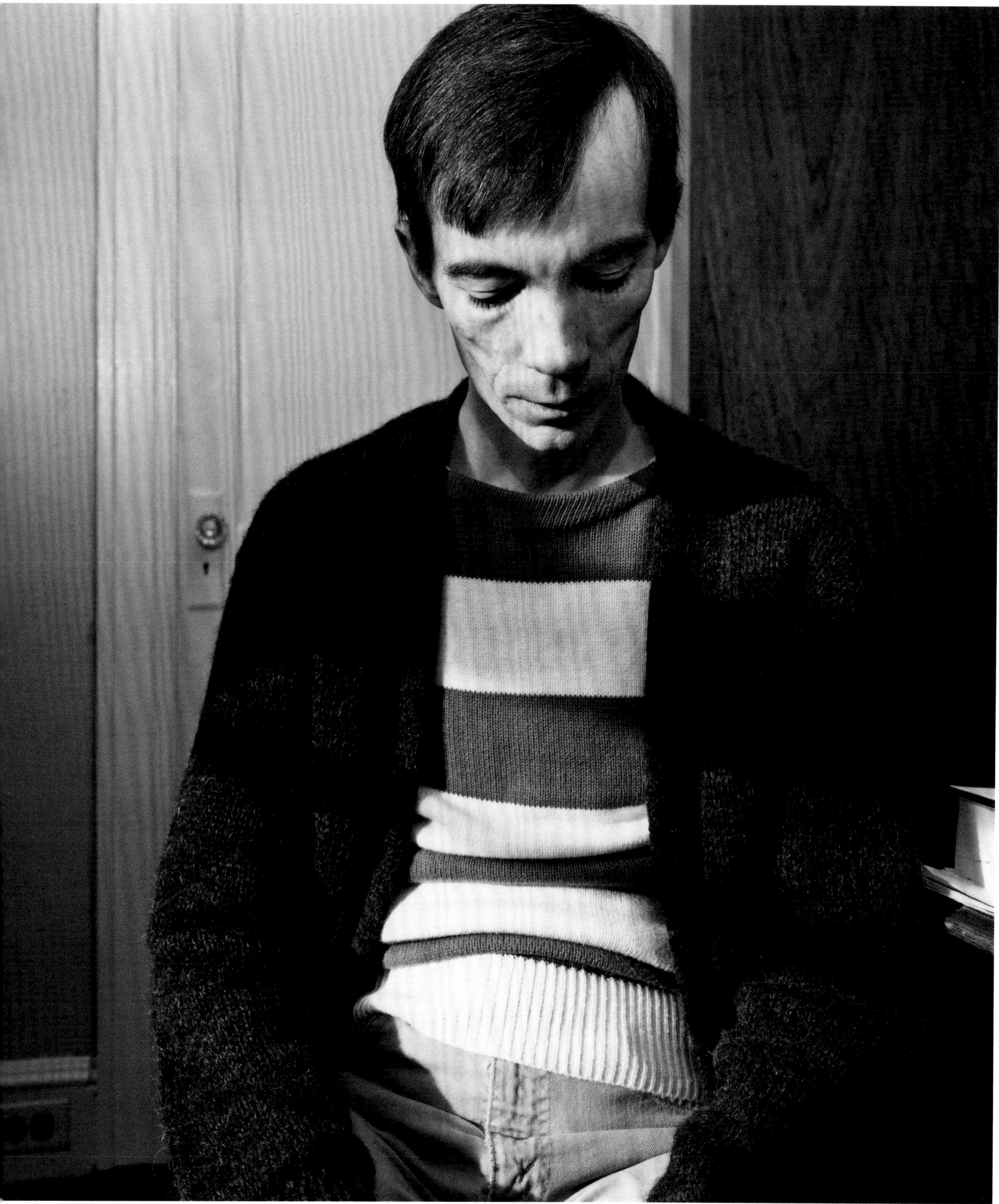

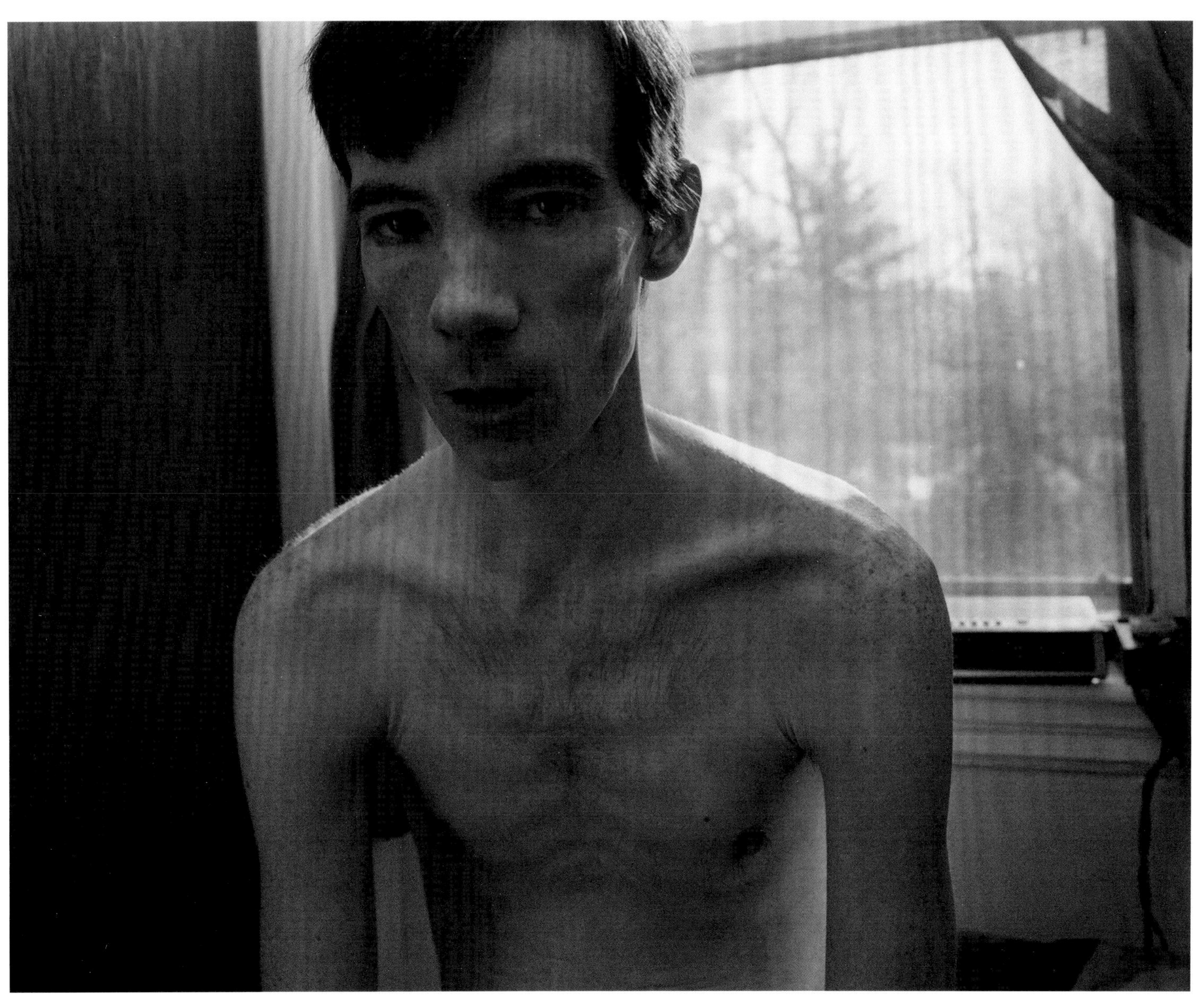

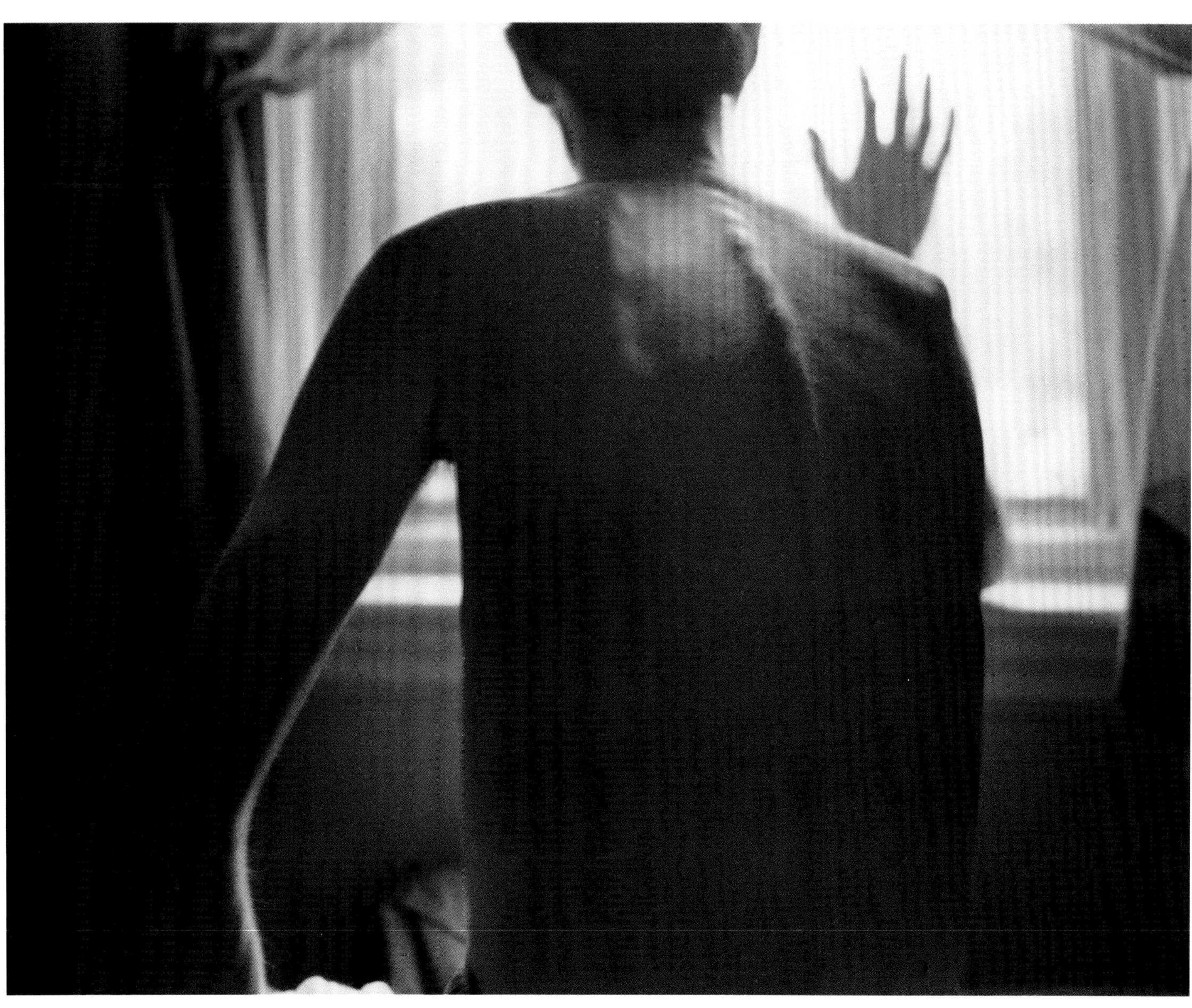

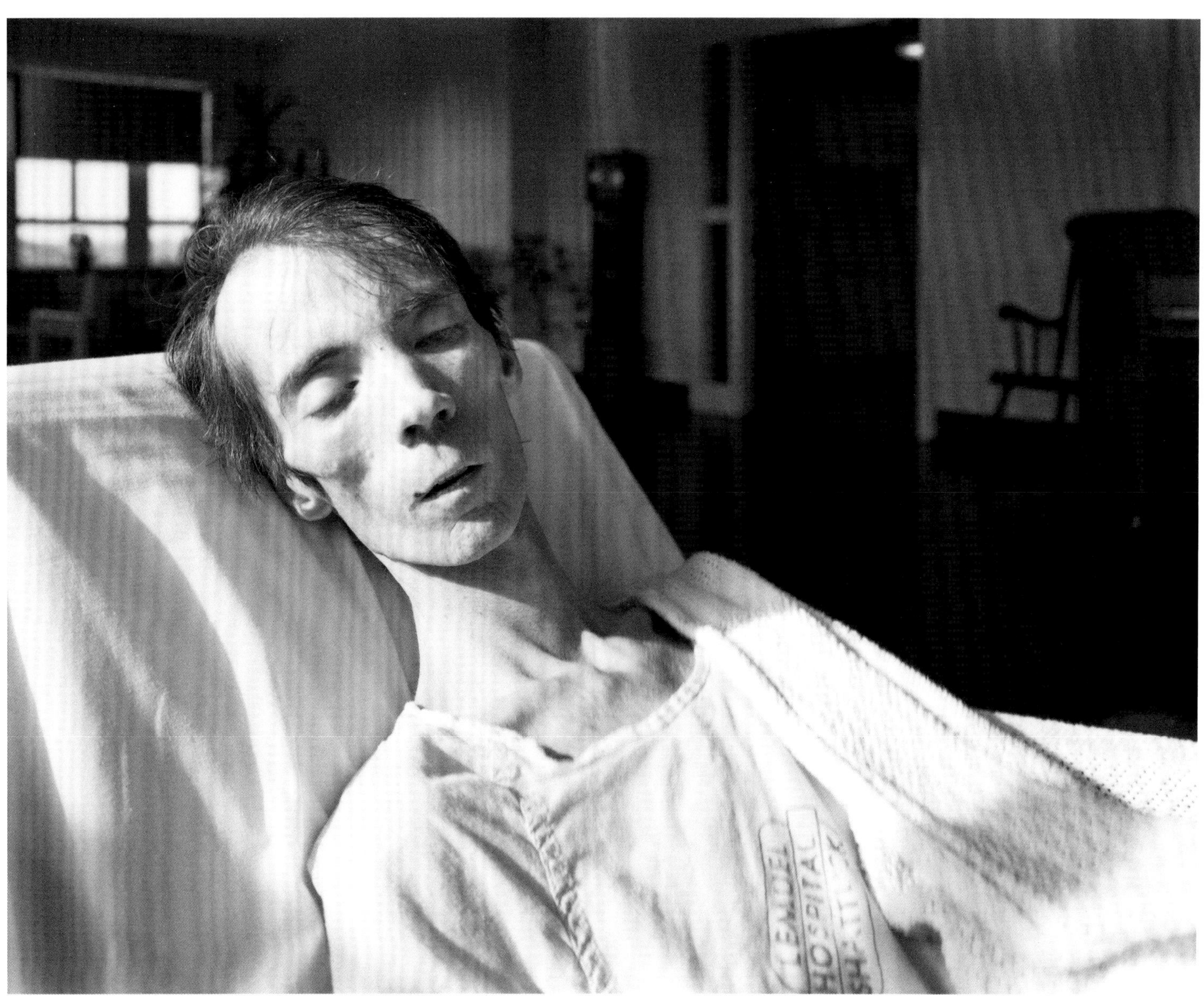
HOSPITAL

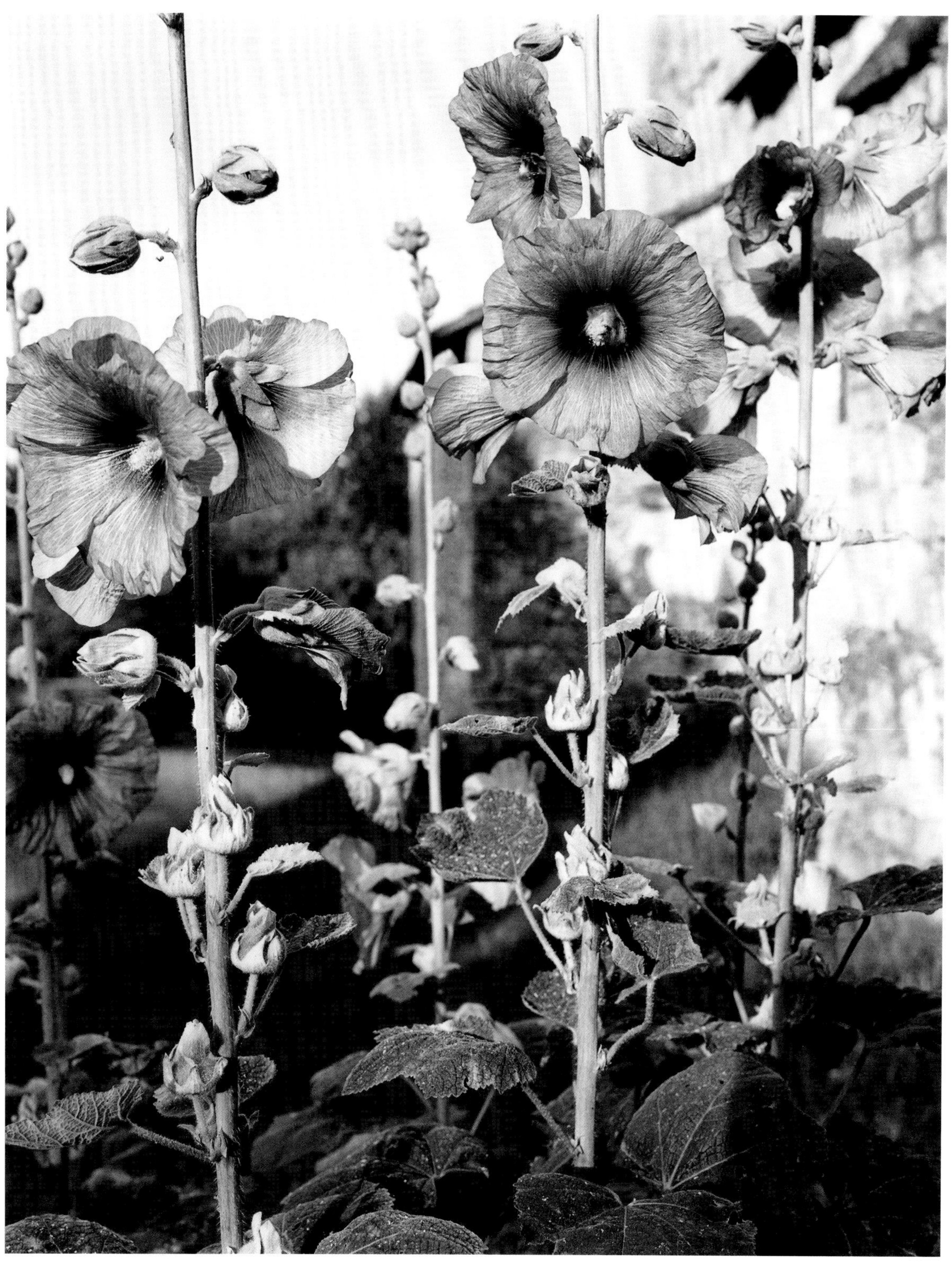

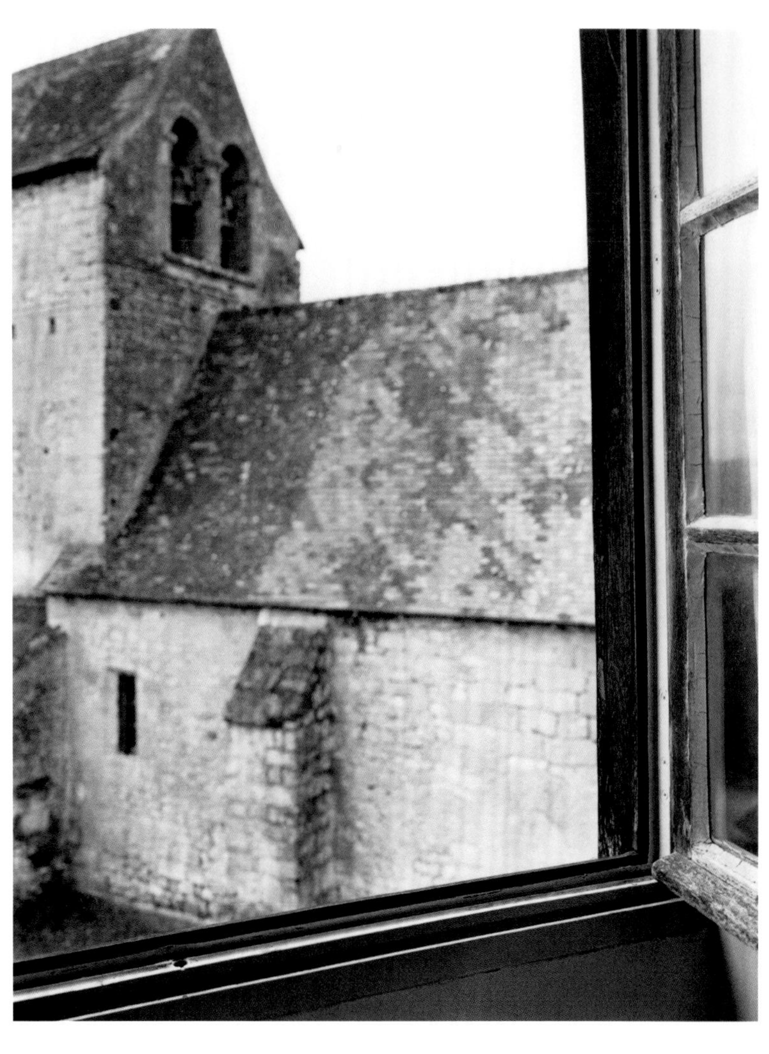

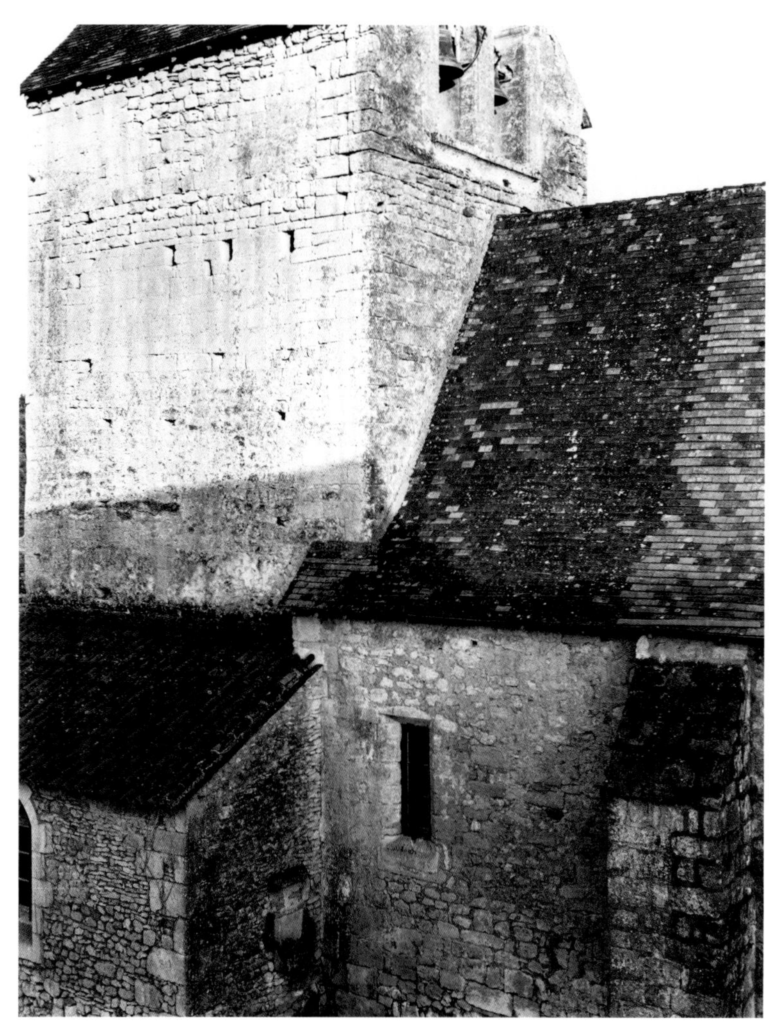

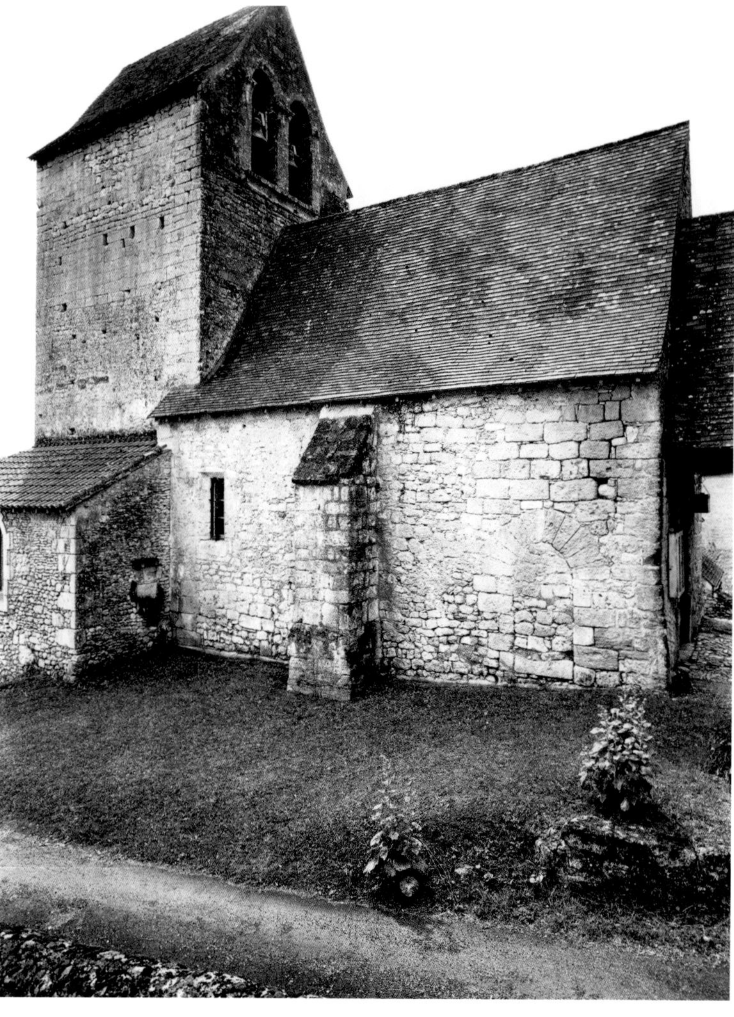

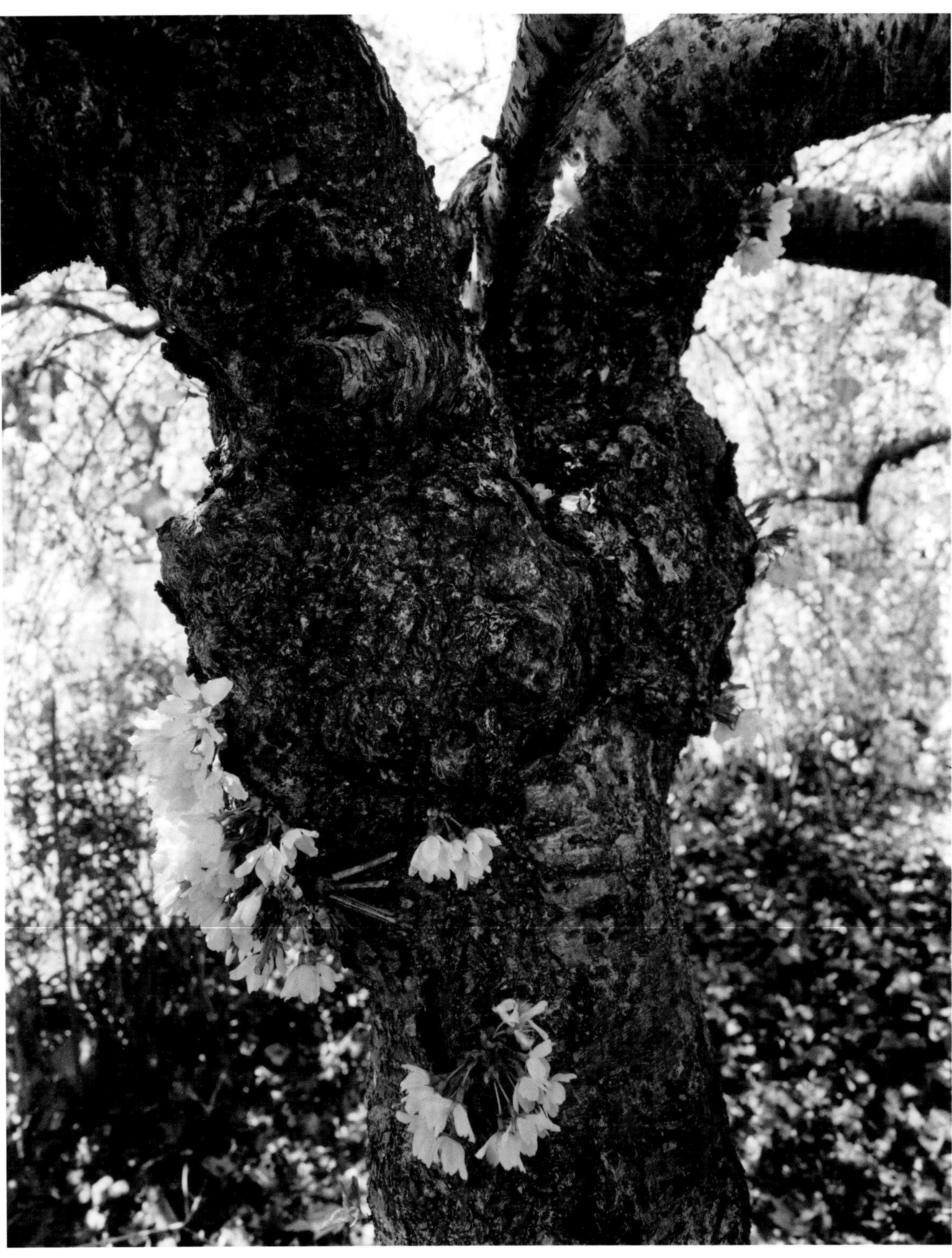

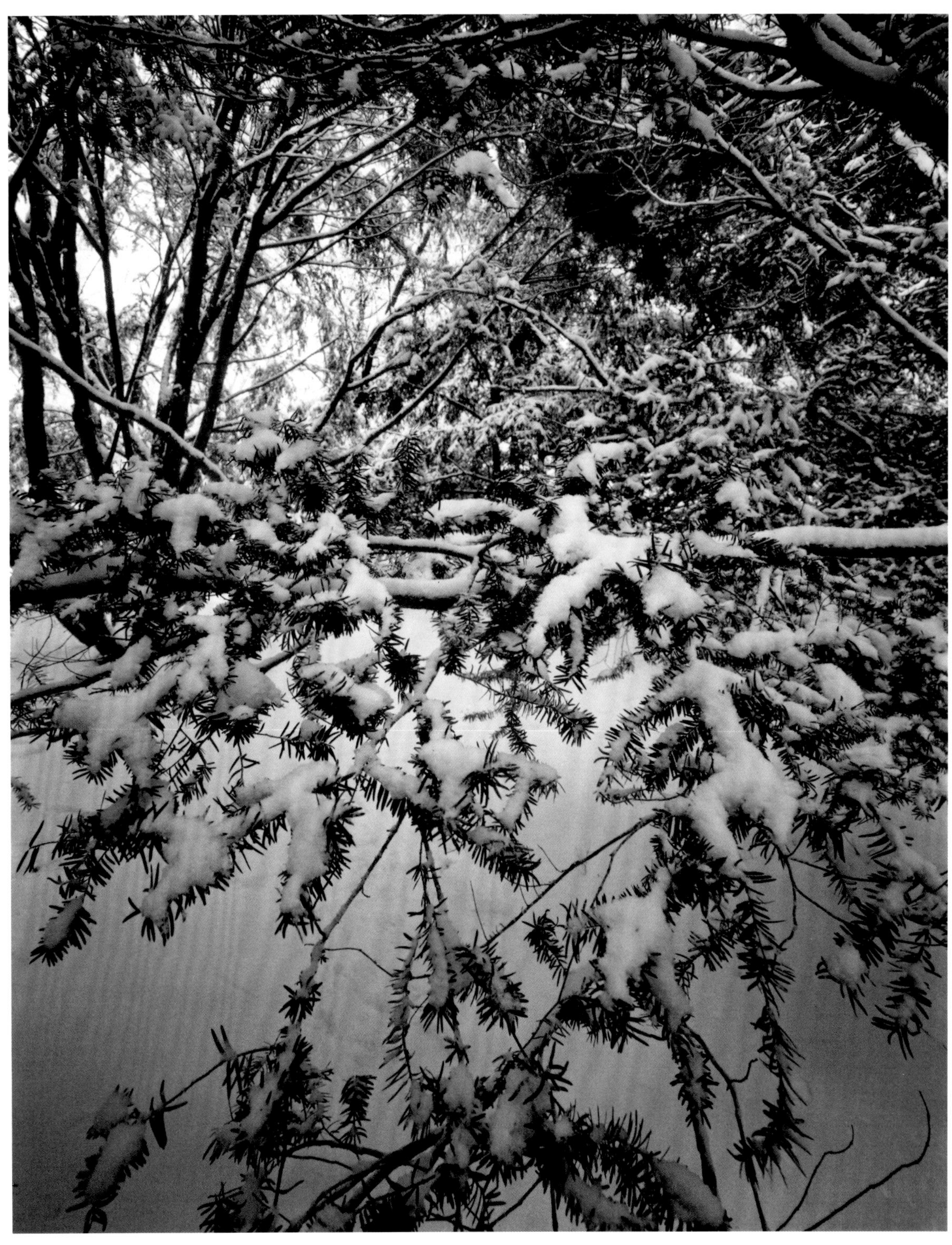

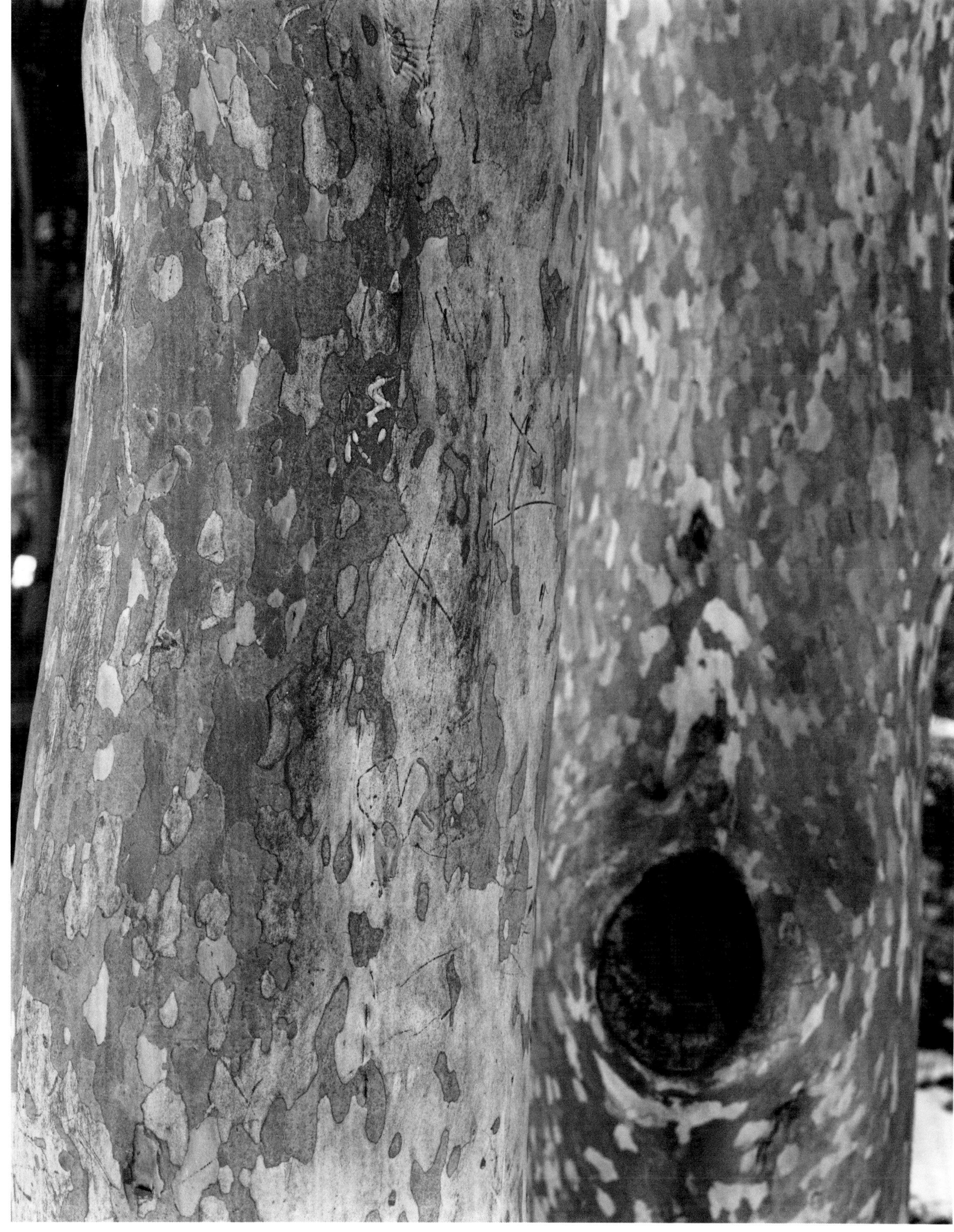

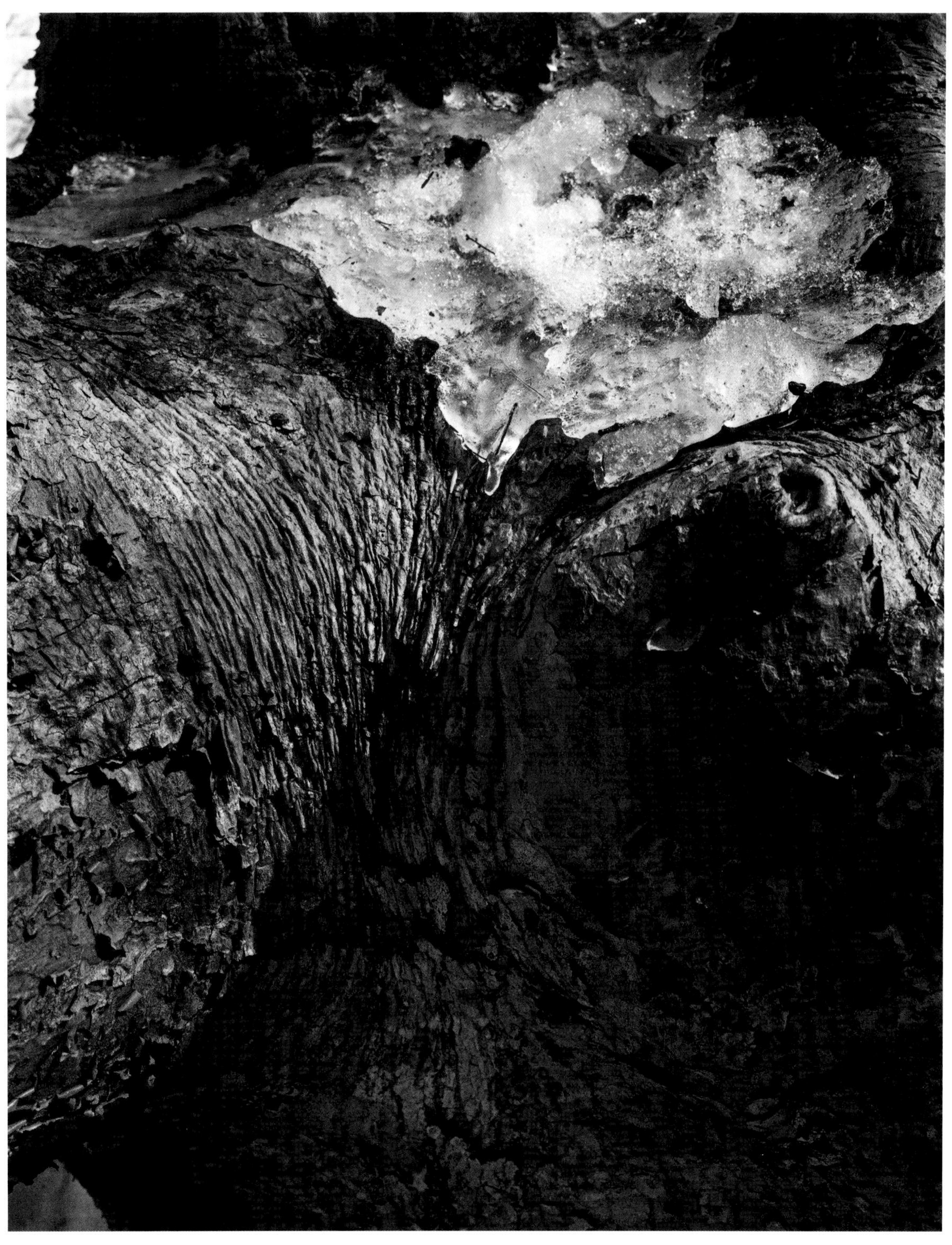

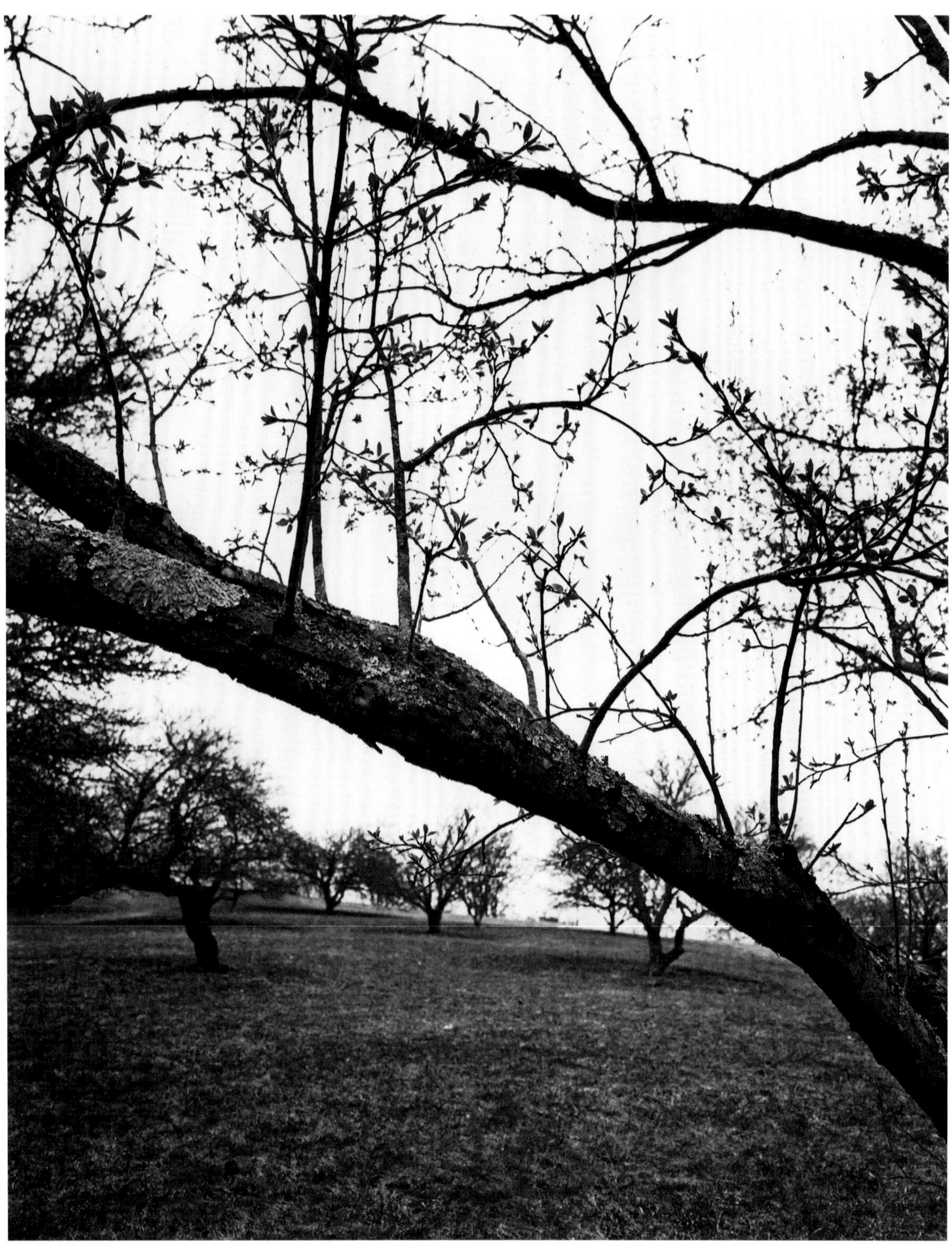

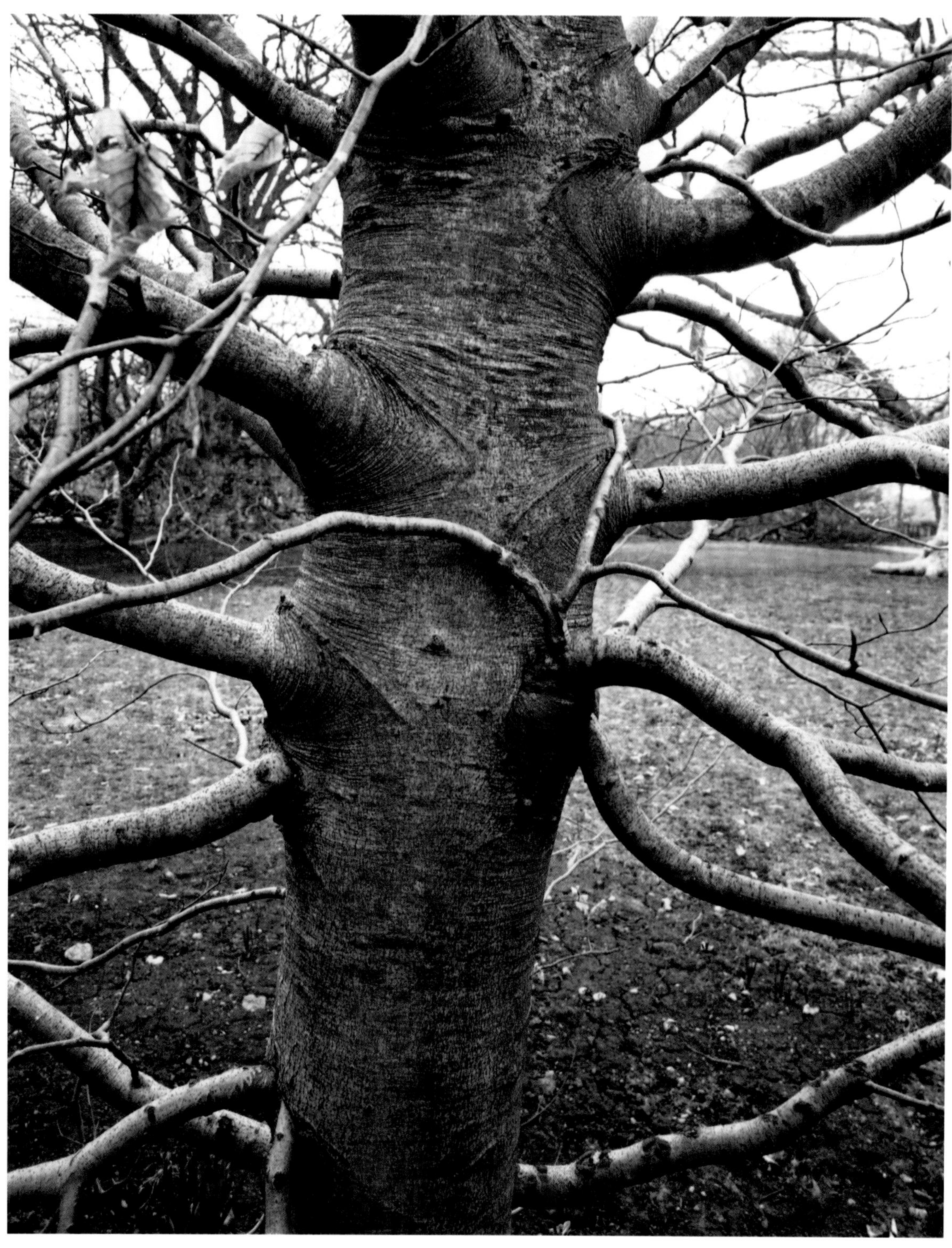

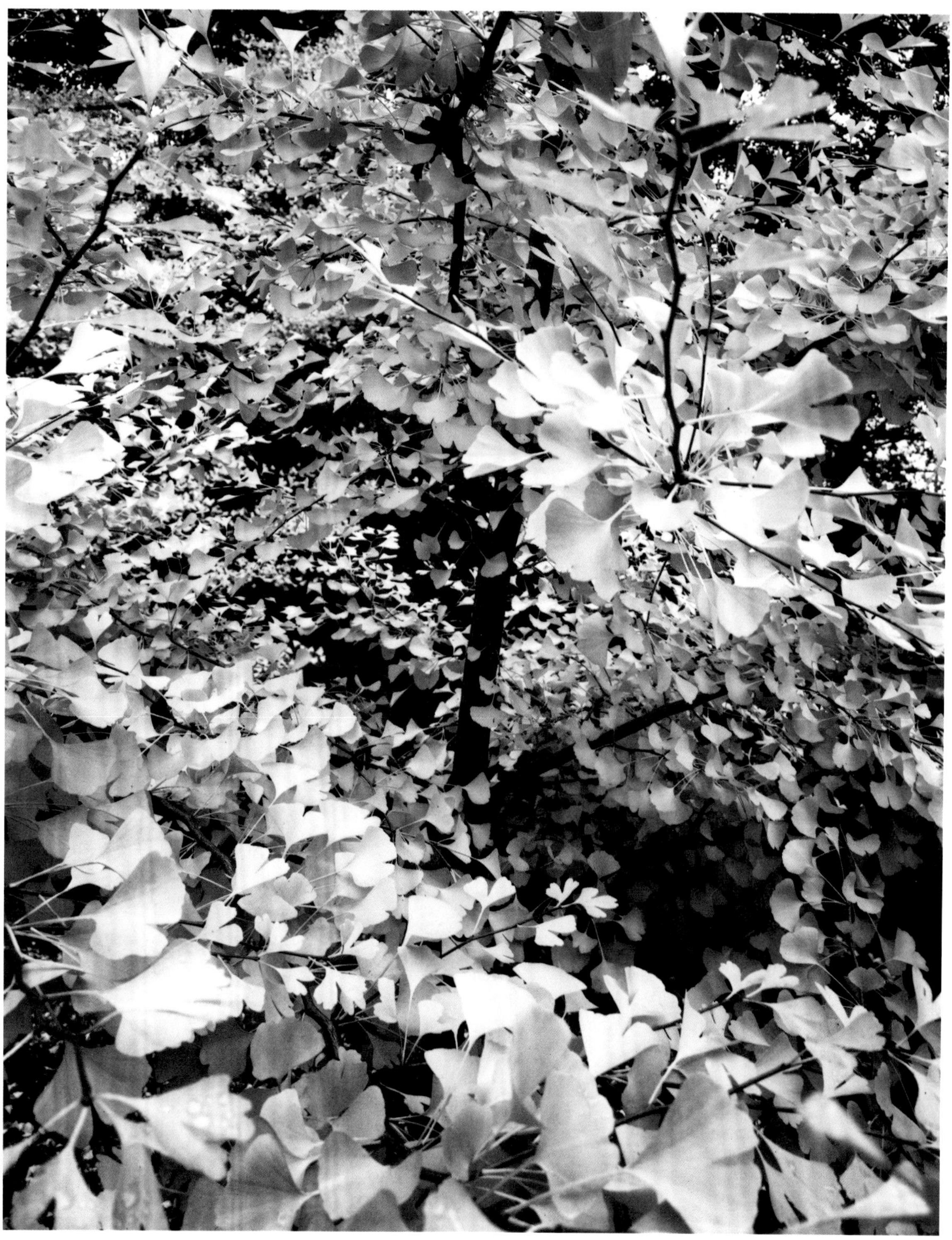

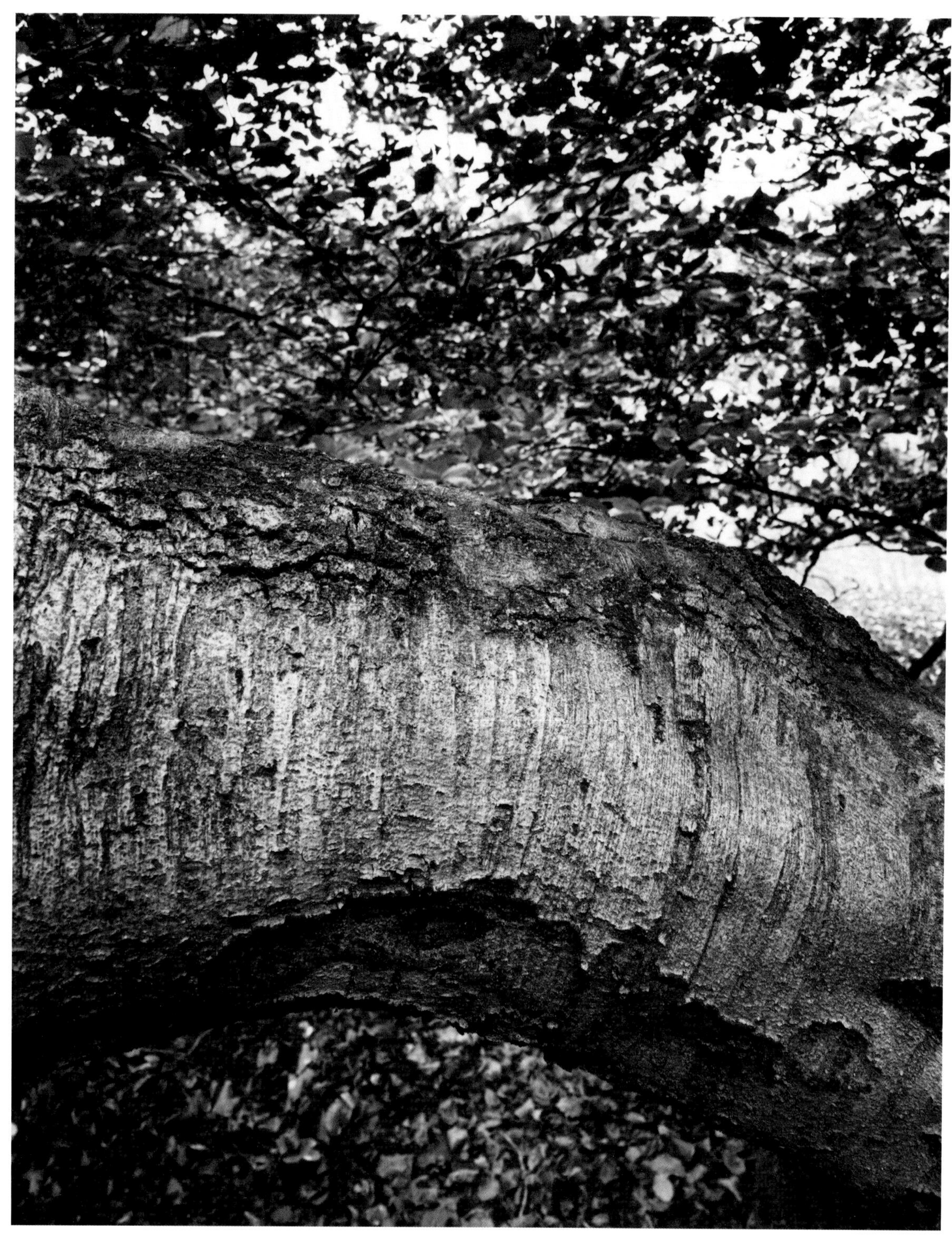

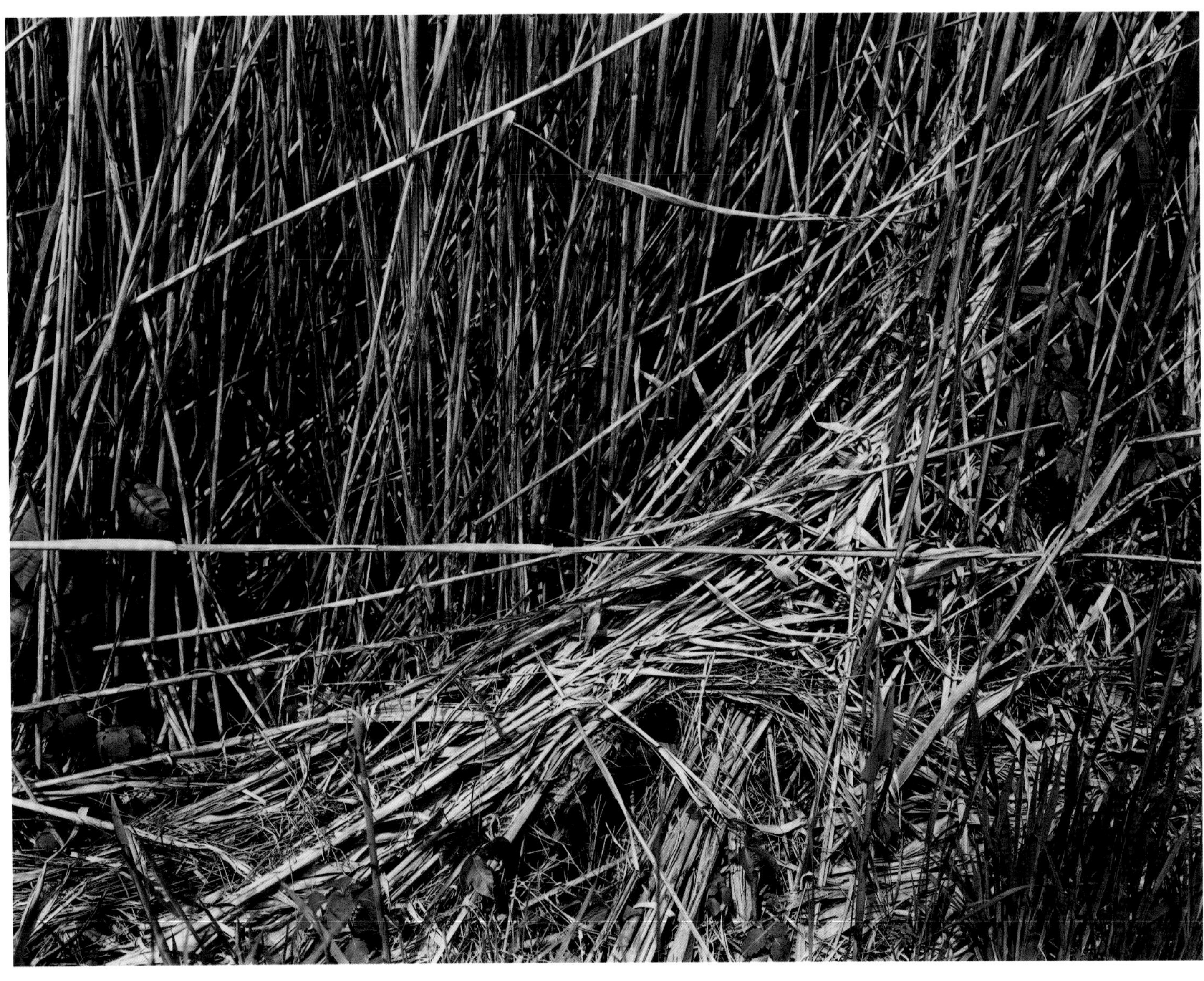

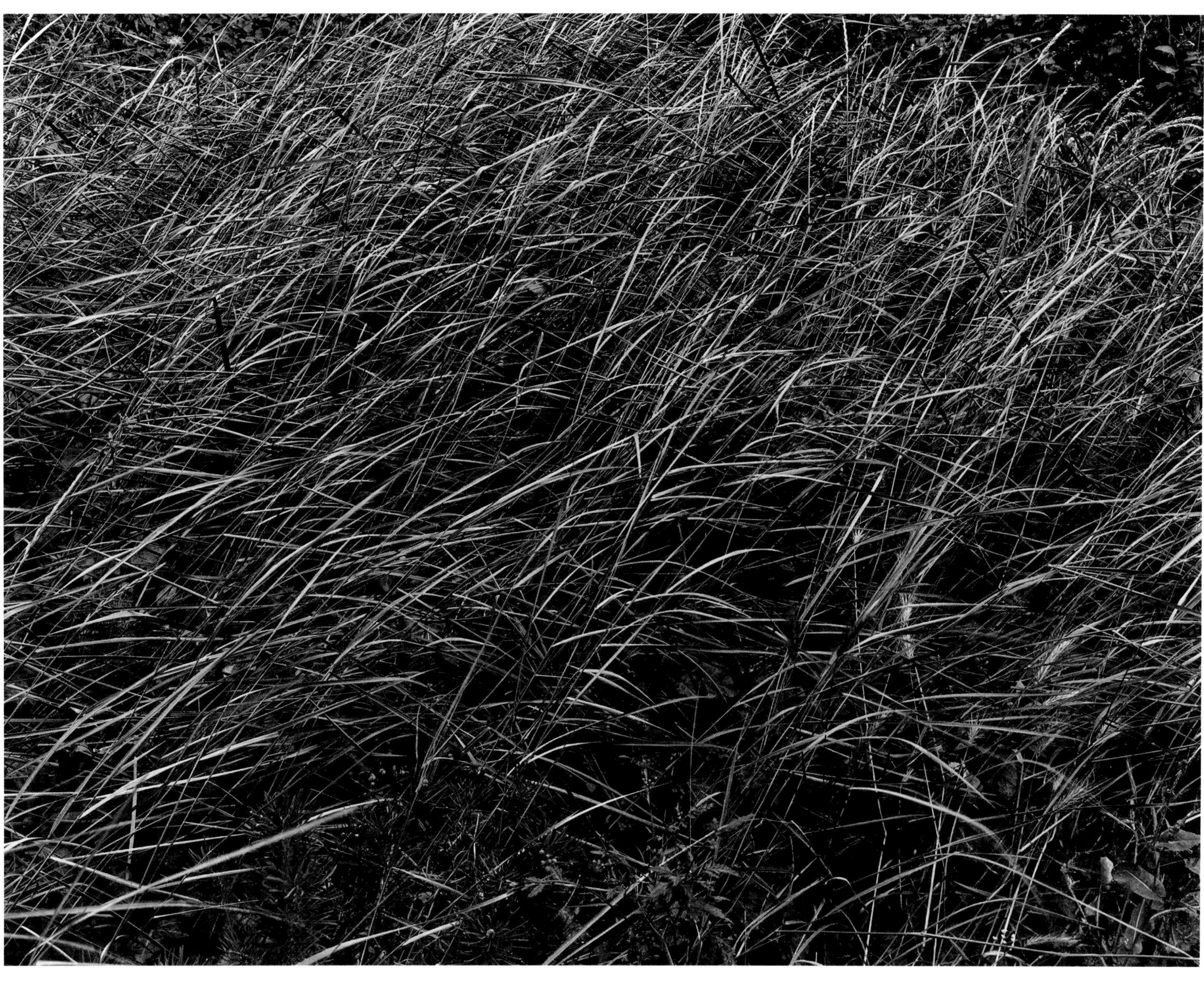

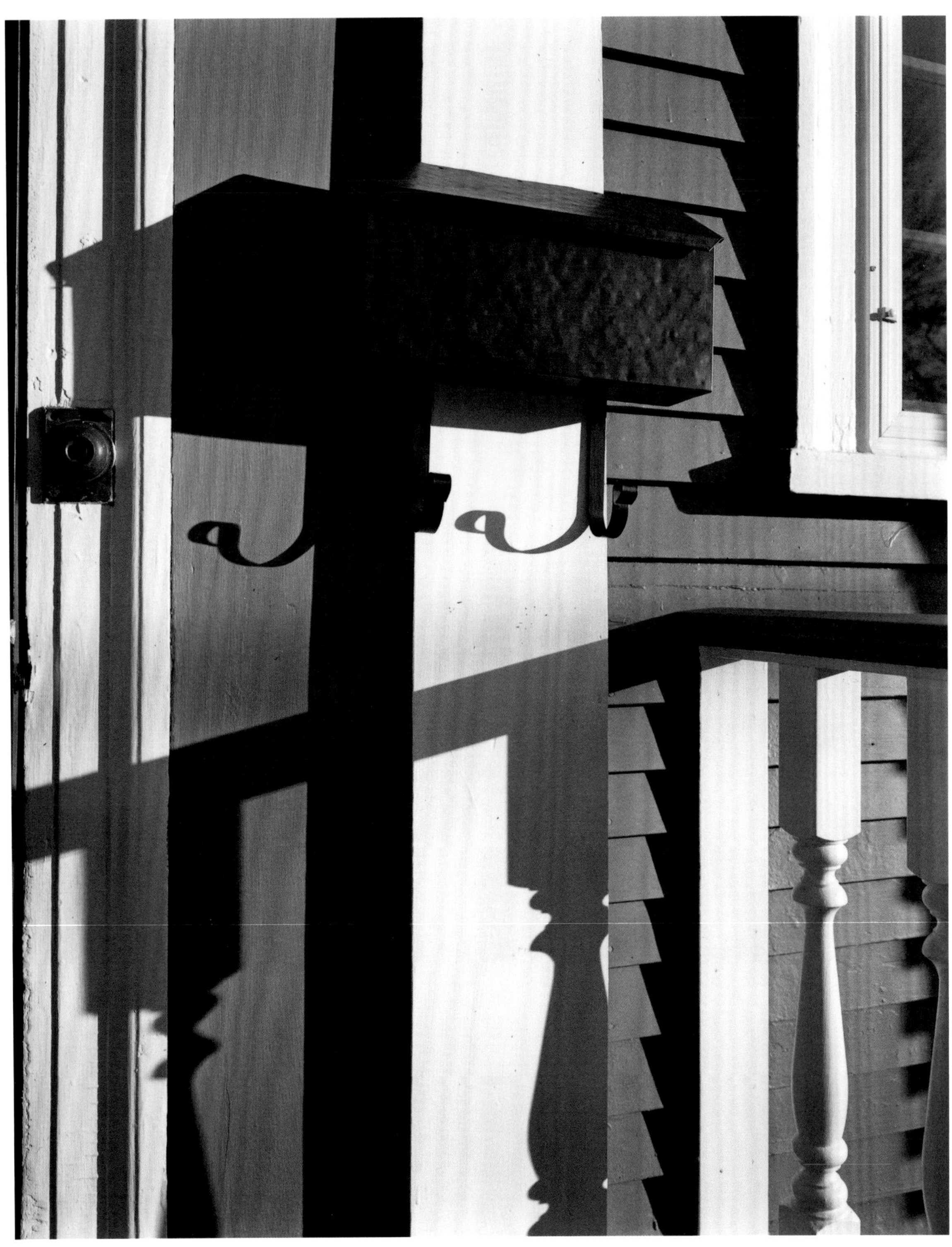

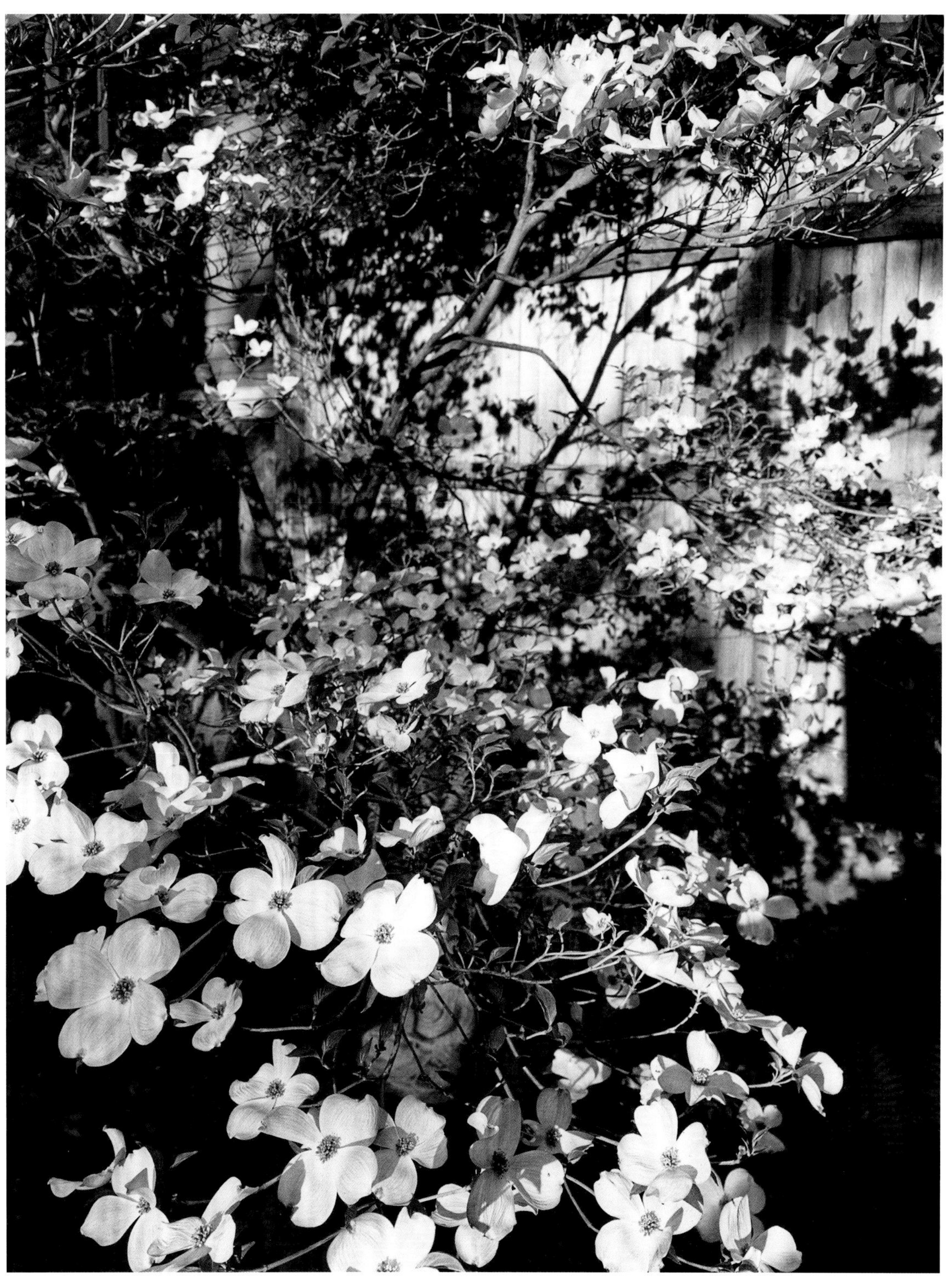

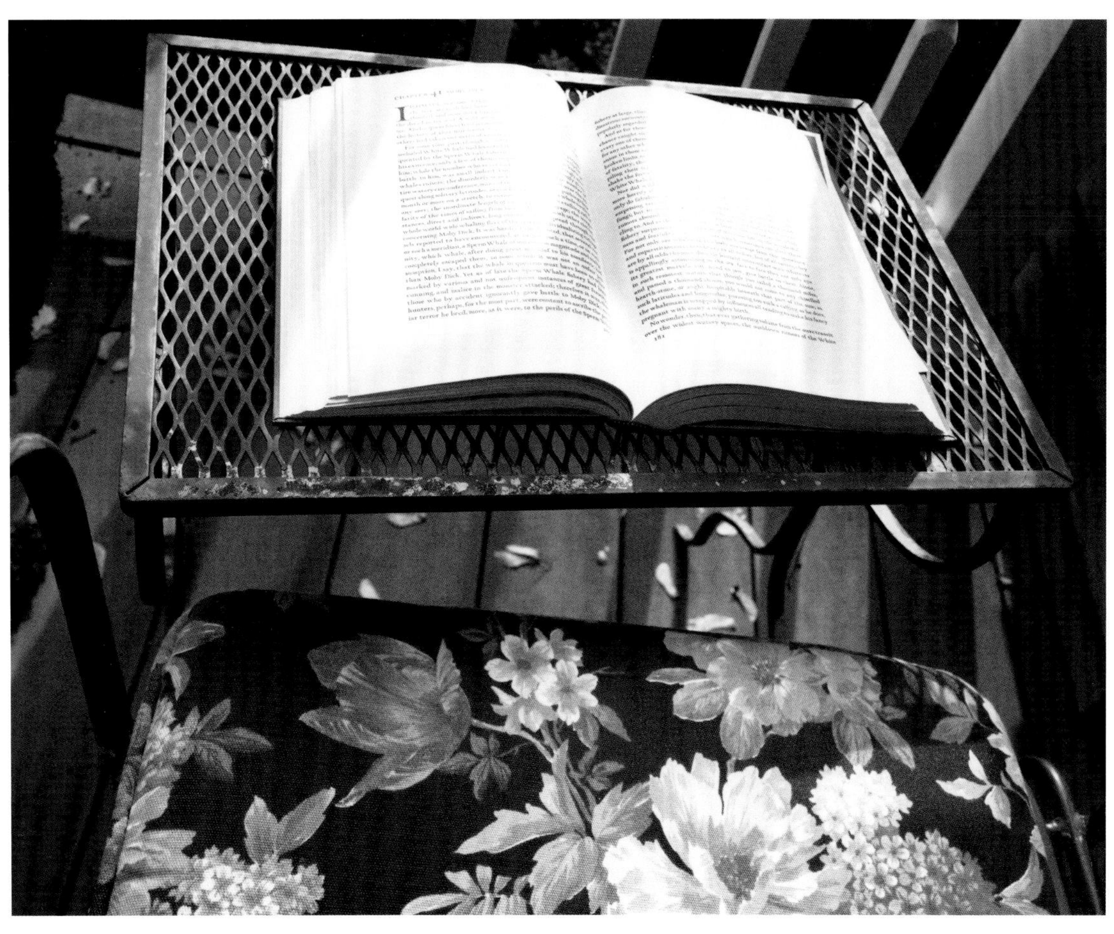

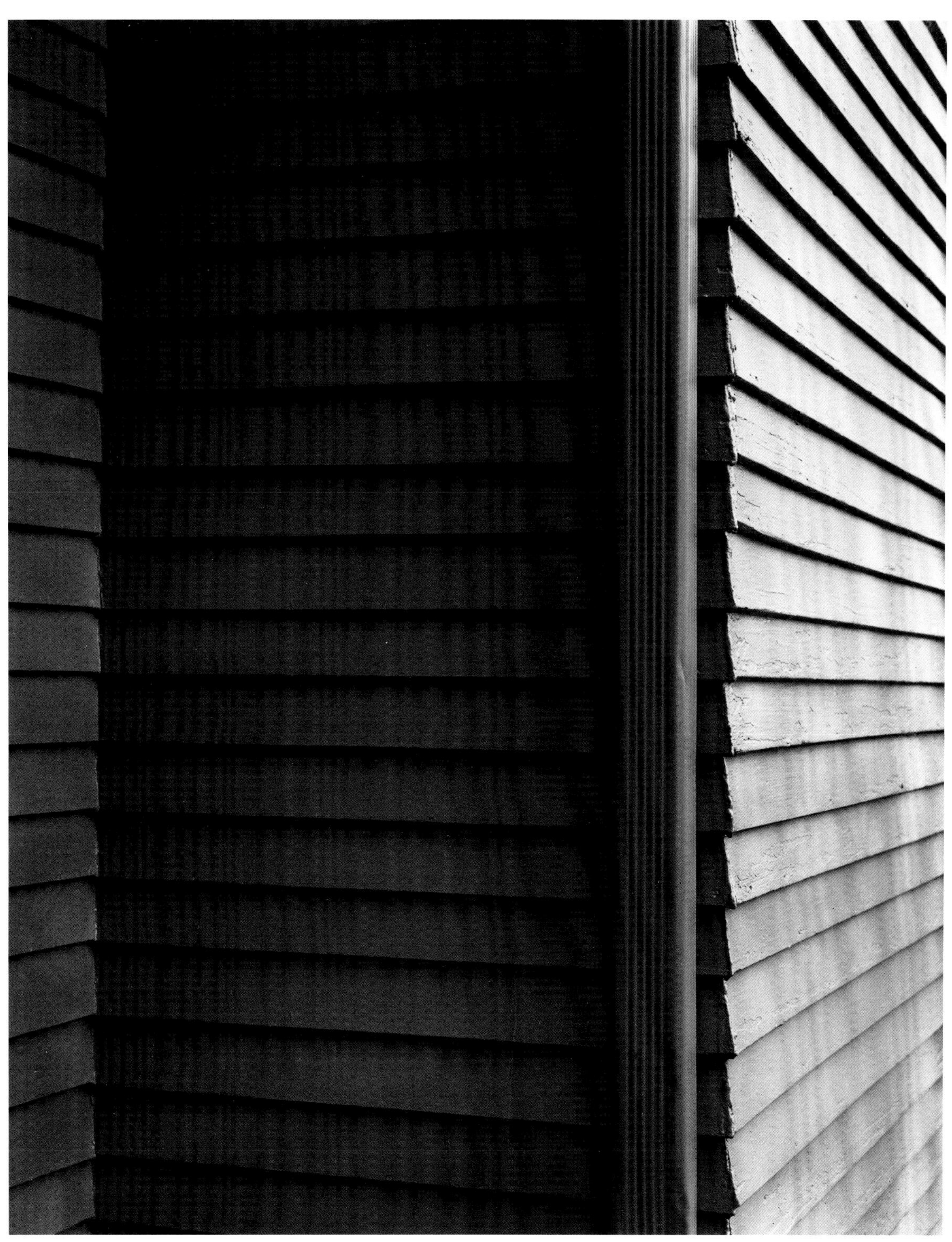

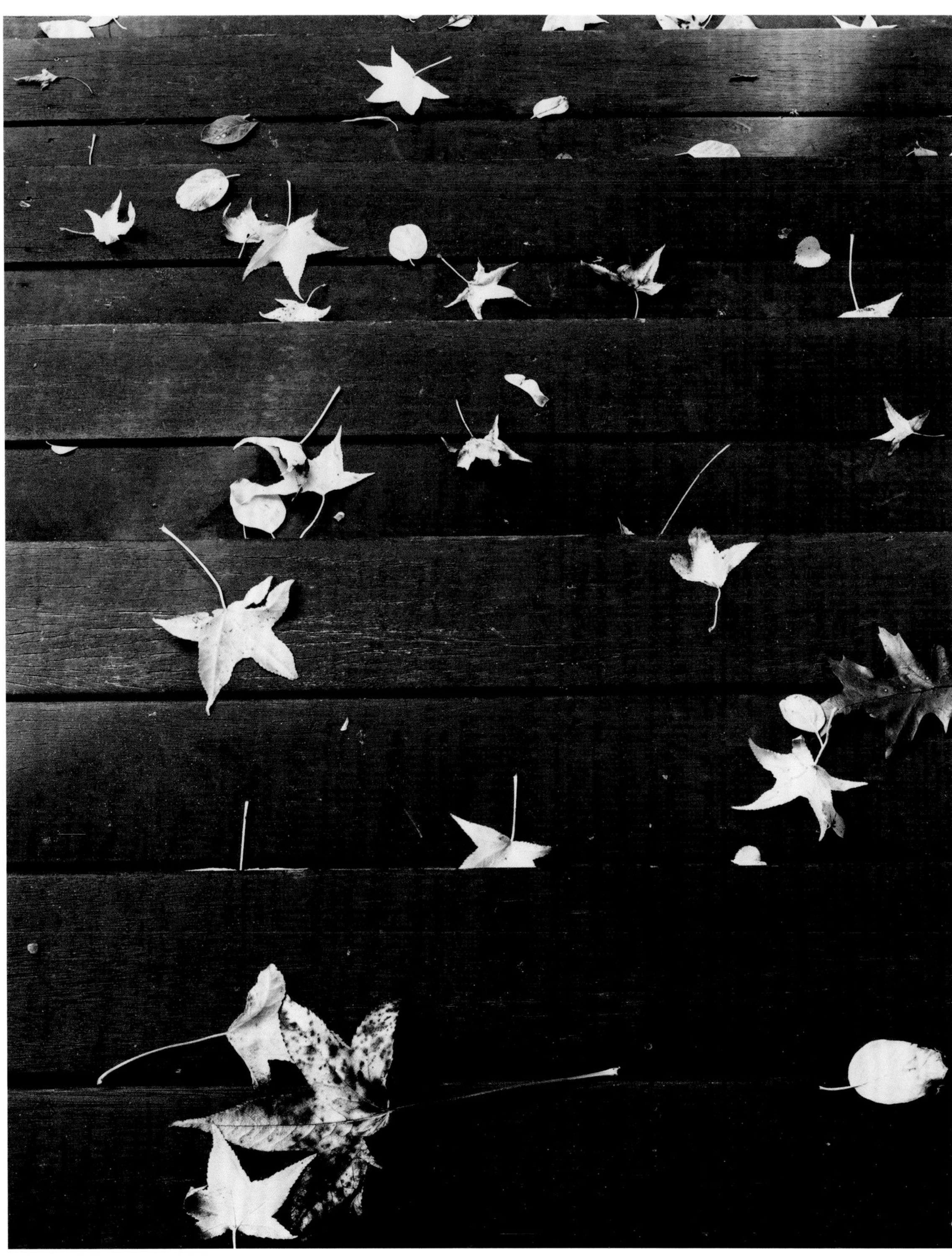

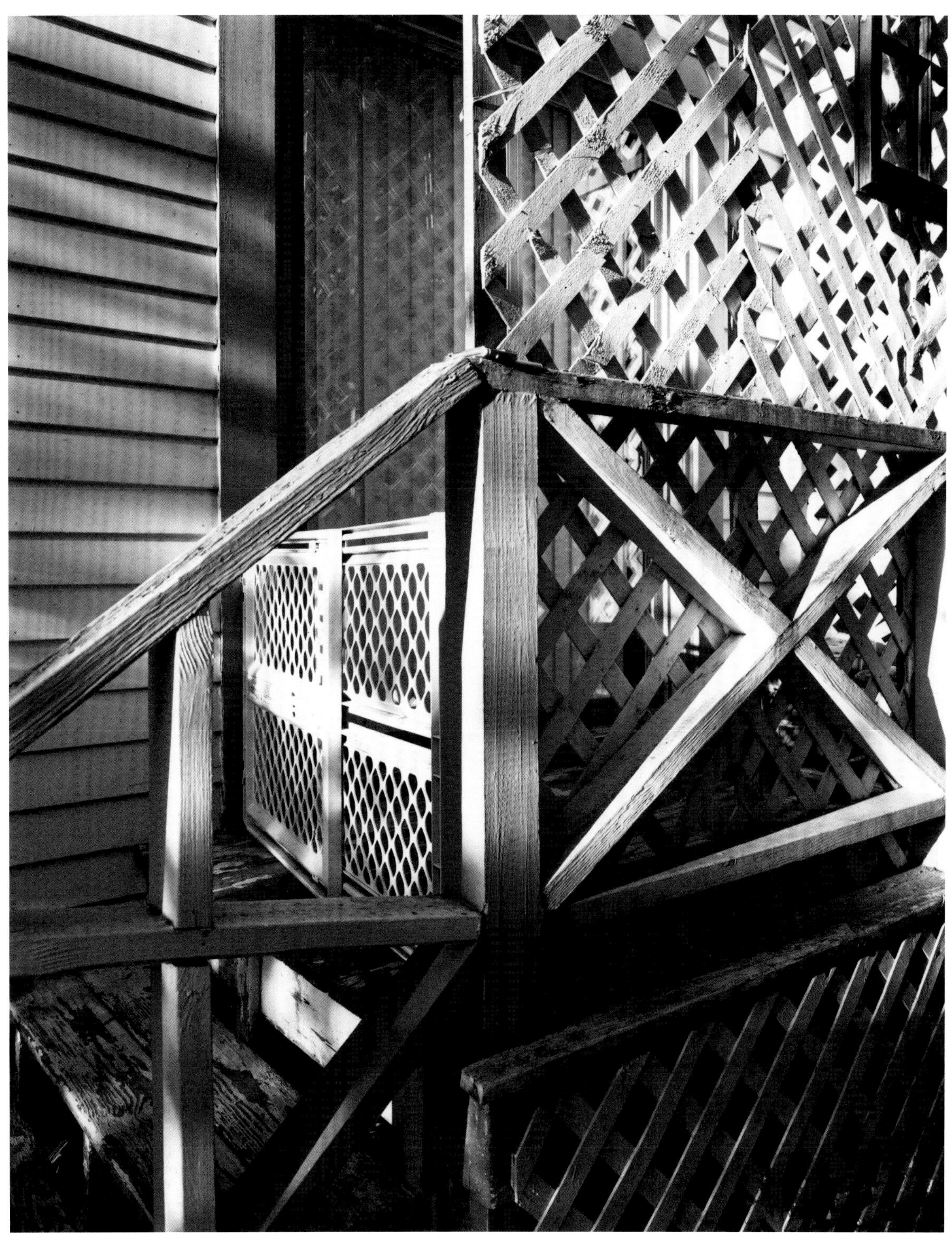

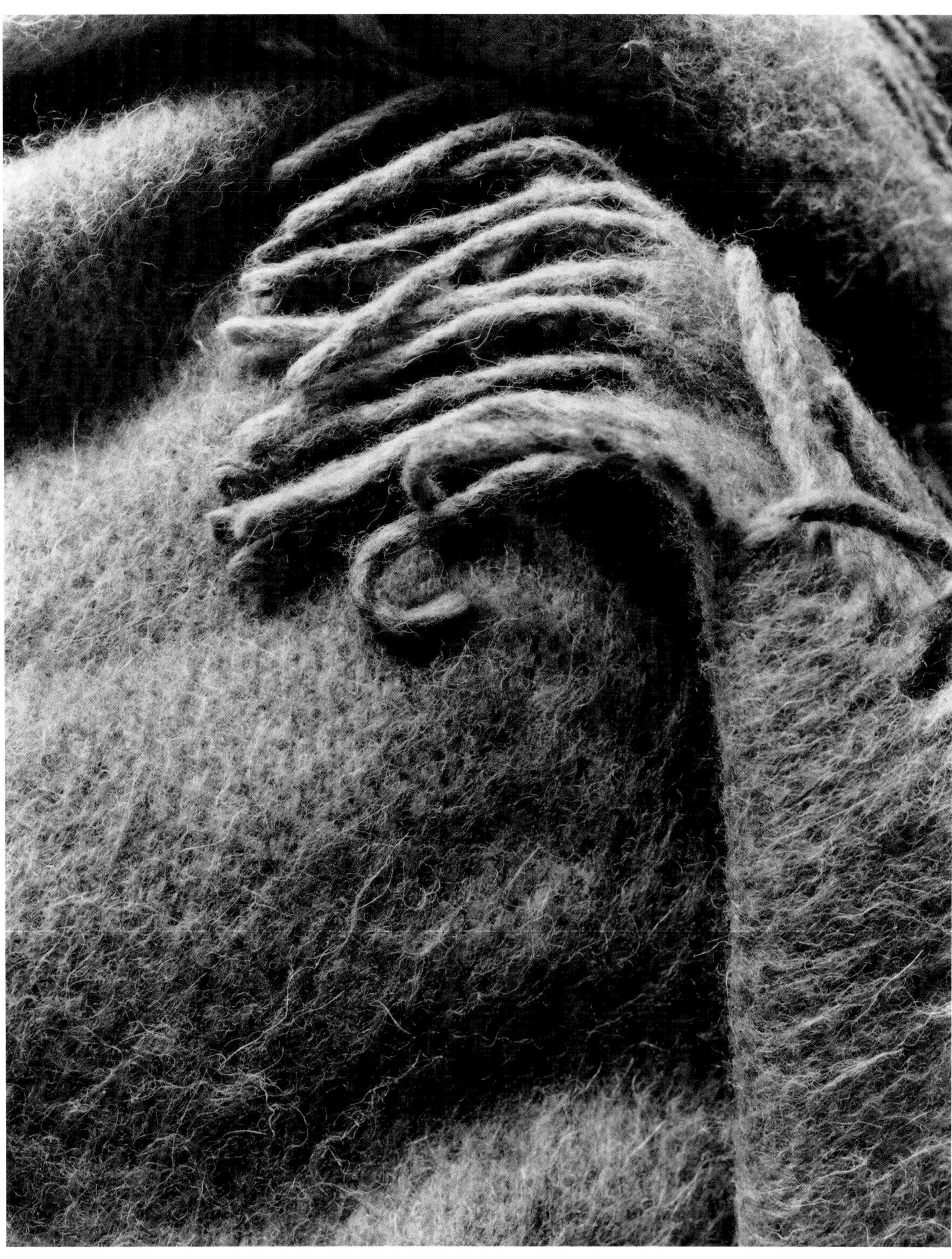

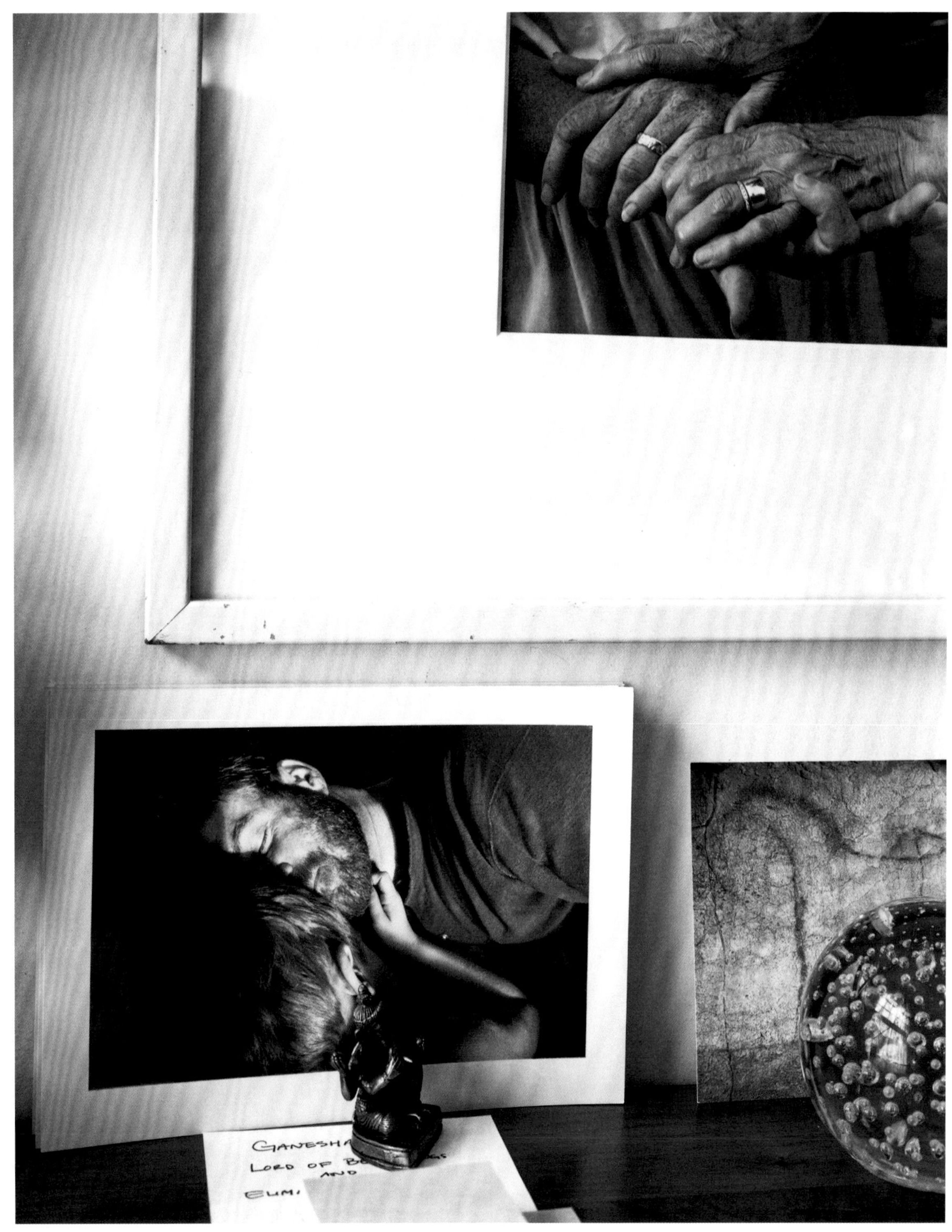
GANESHA
LORD OF
AND

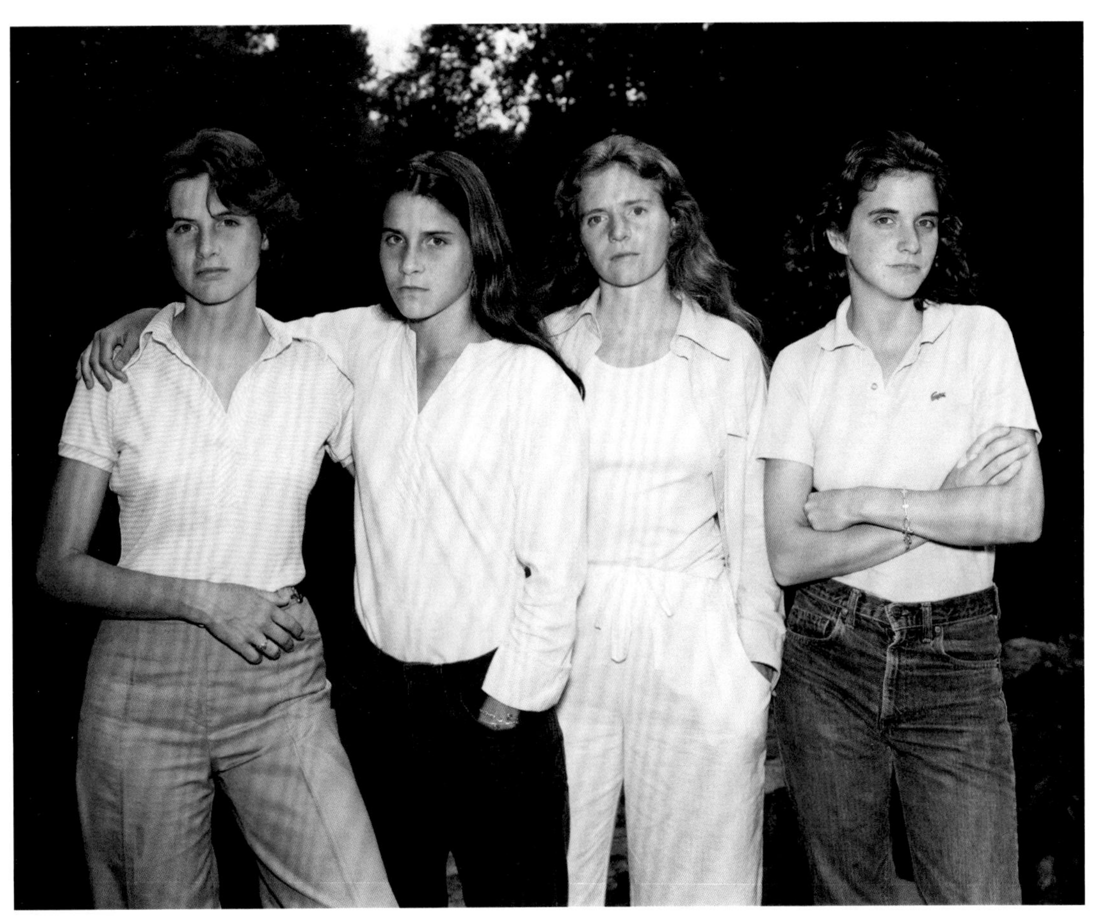

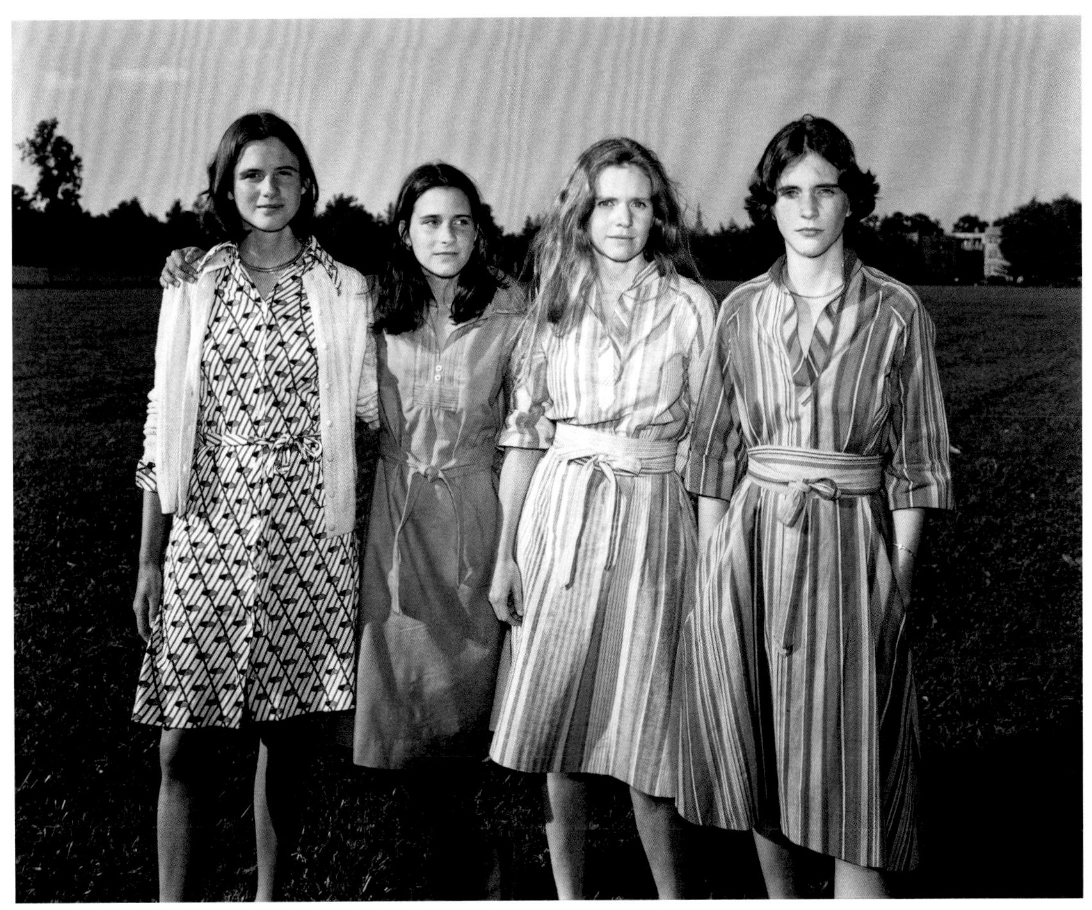

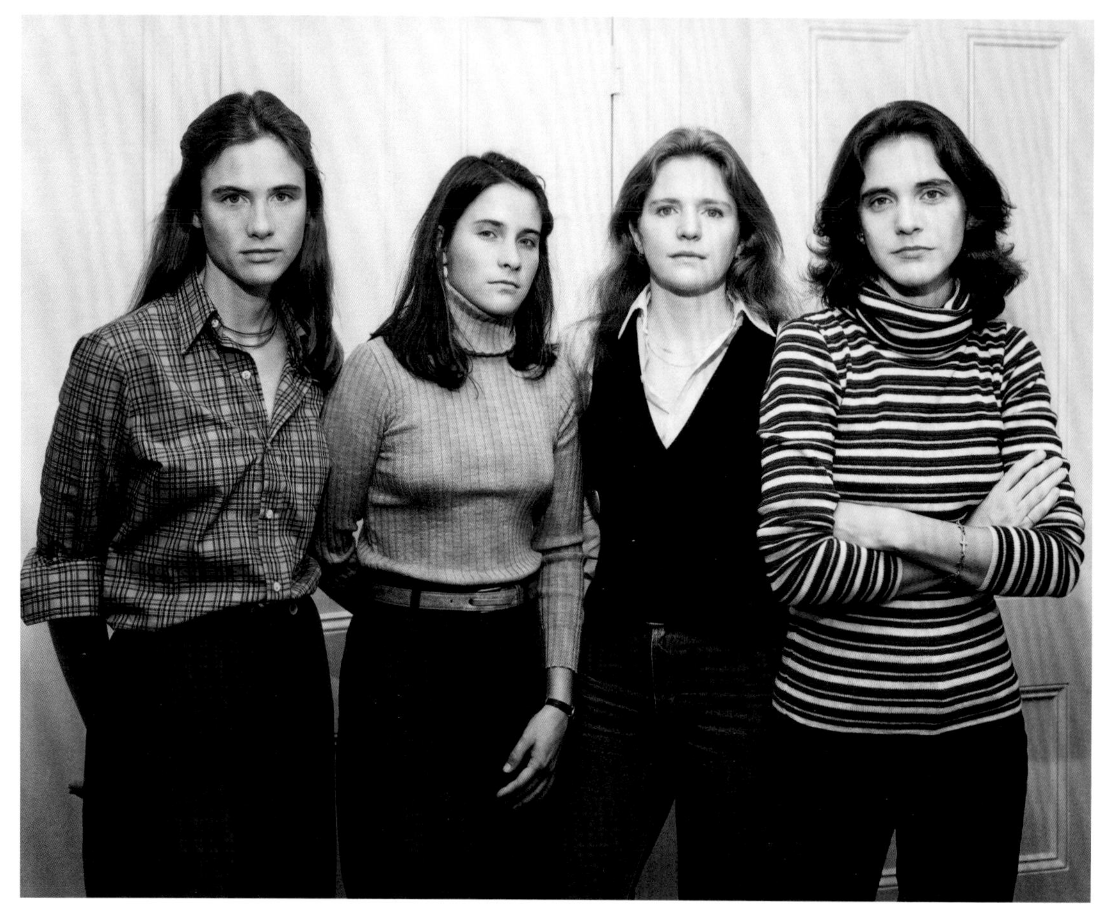

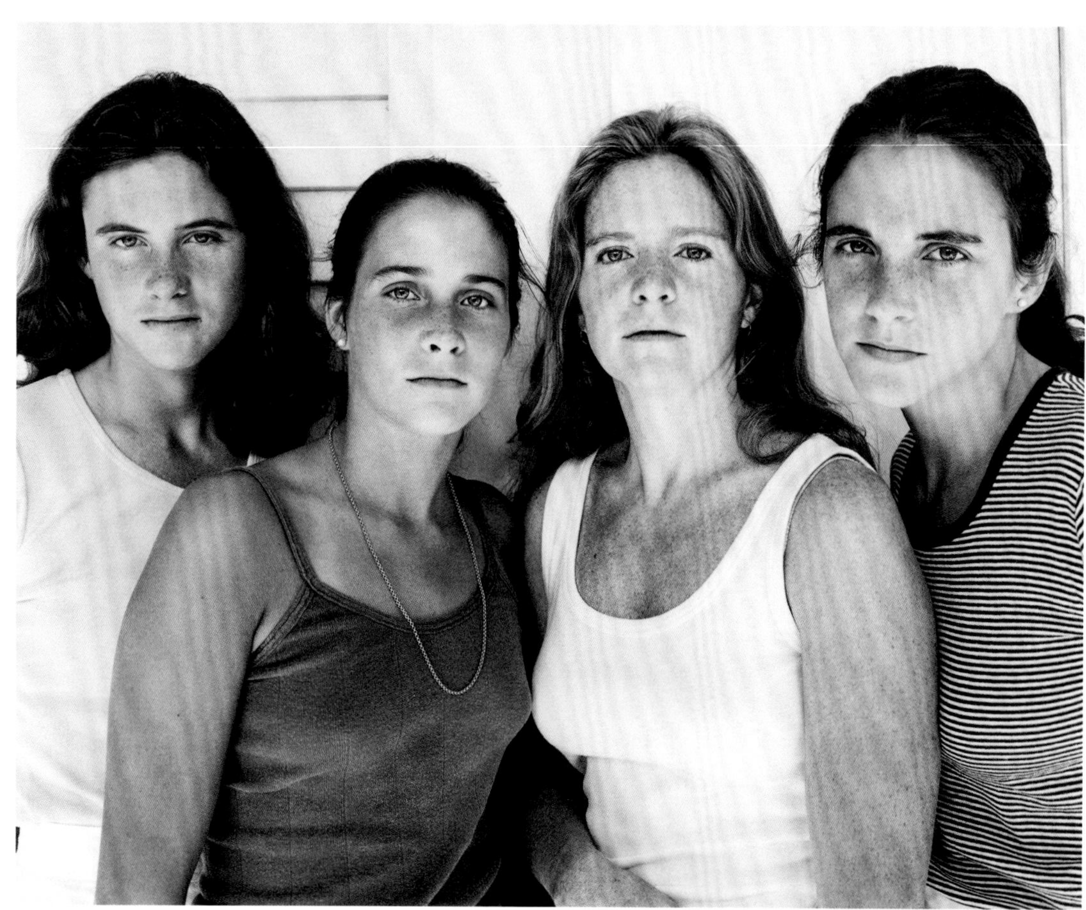

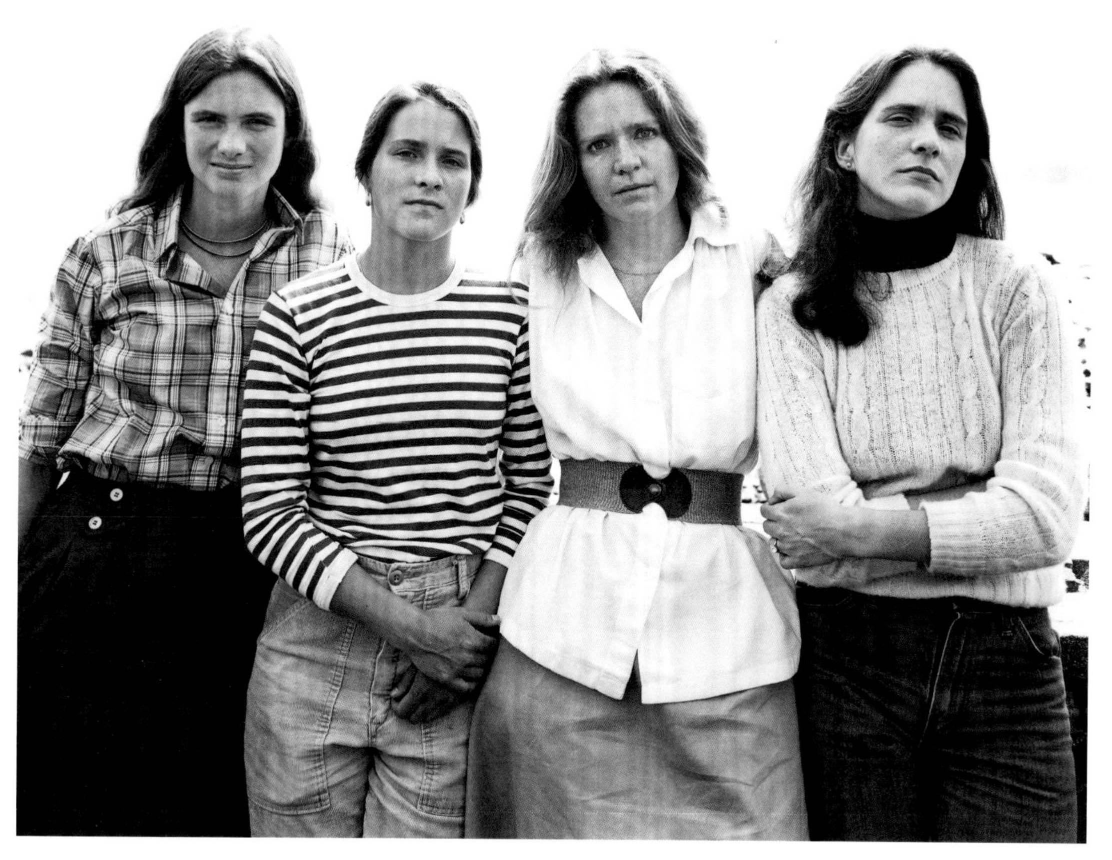

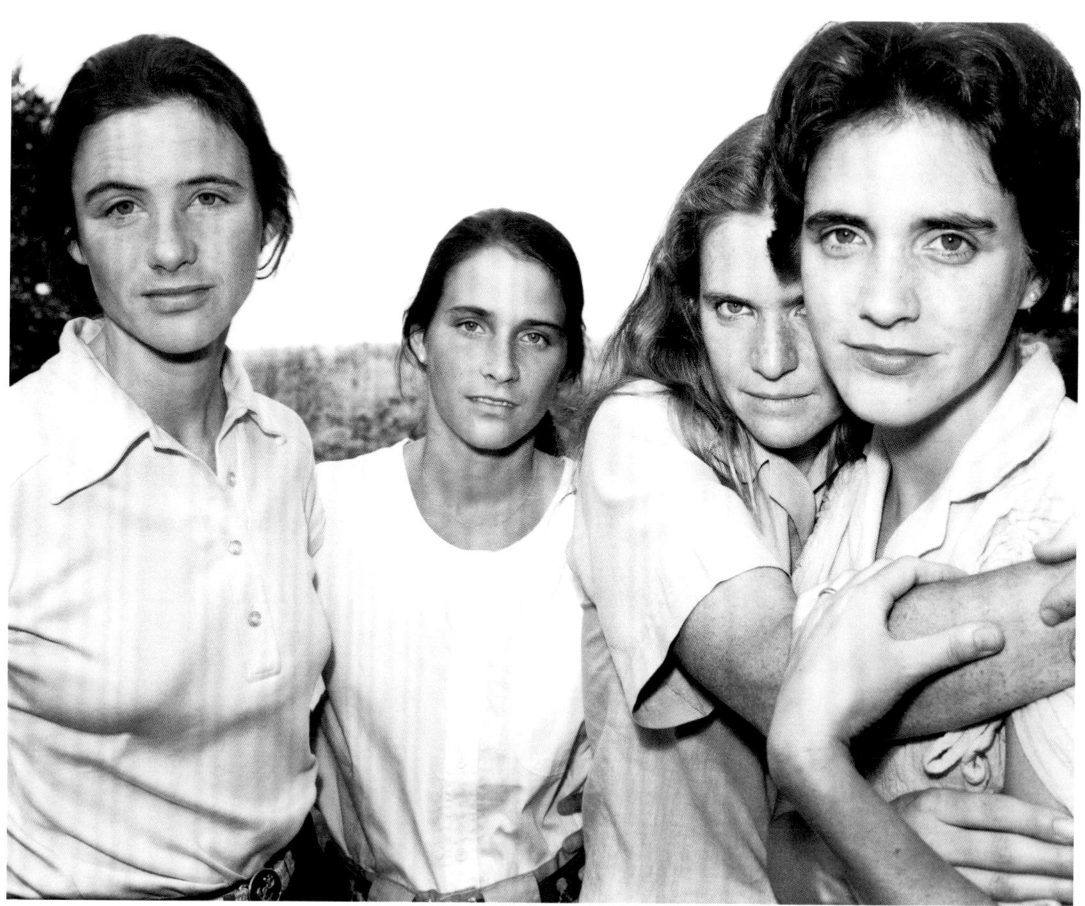

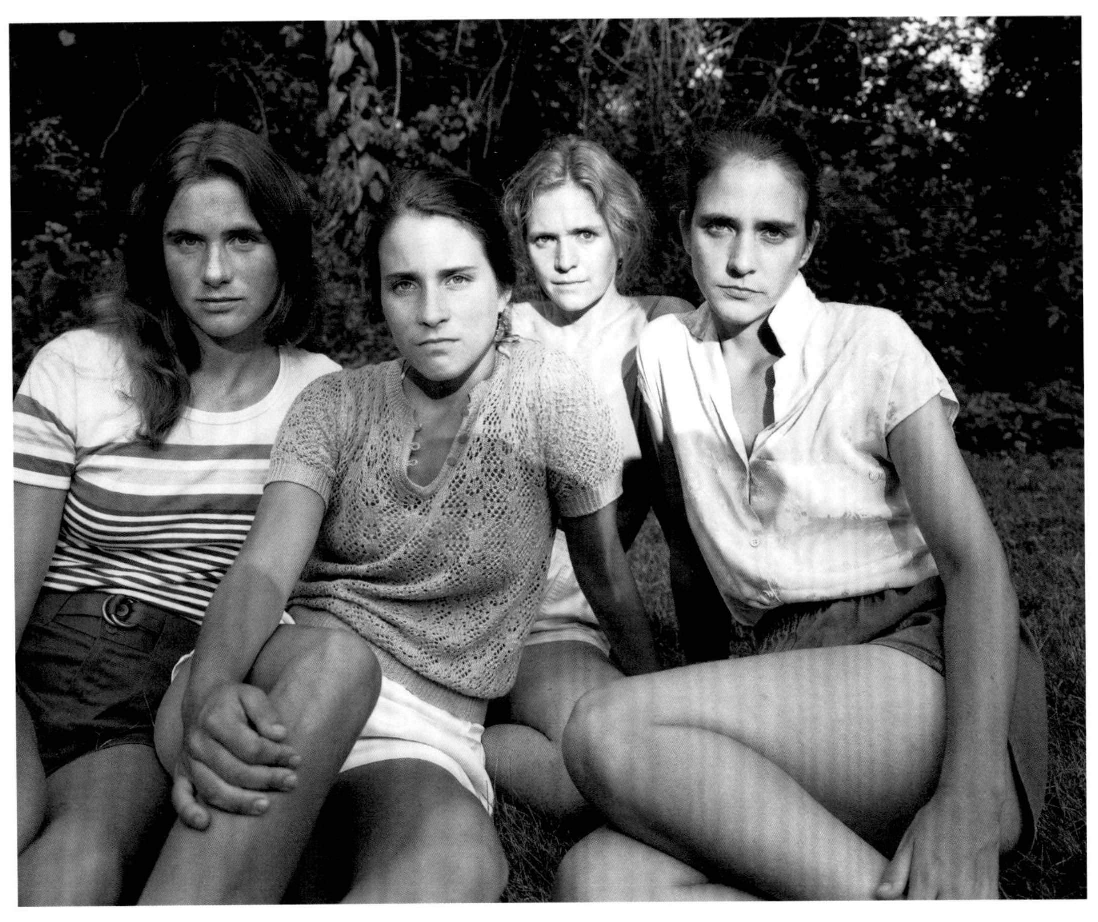

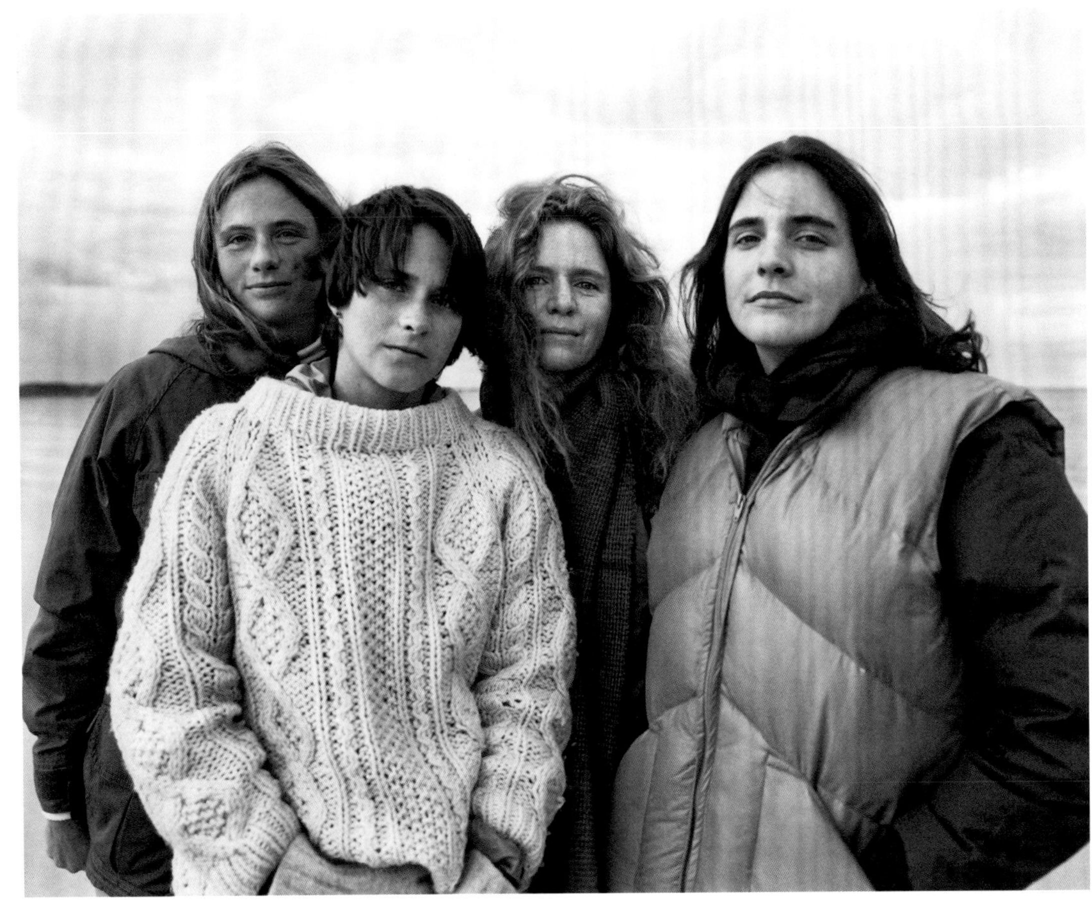

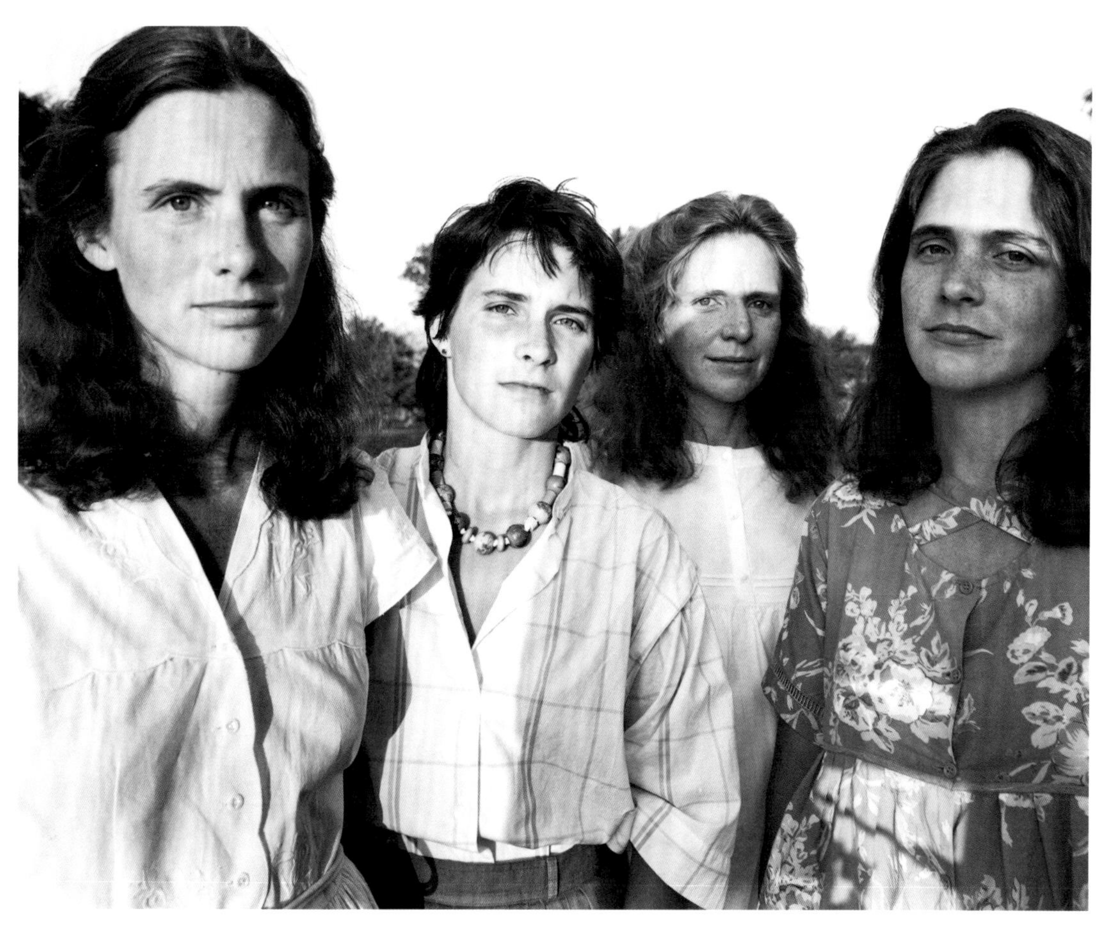

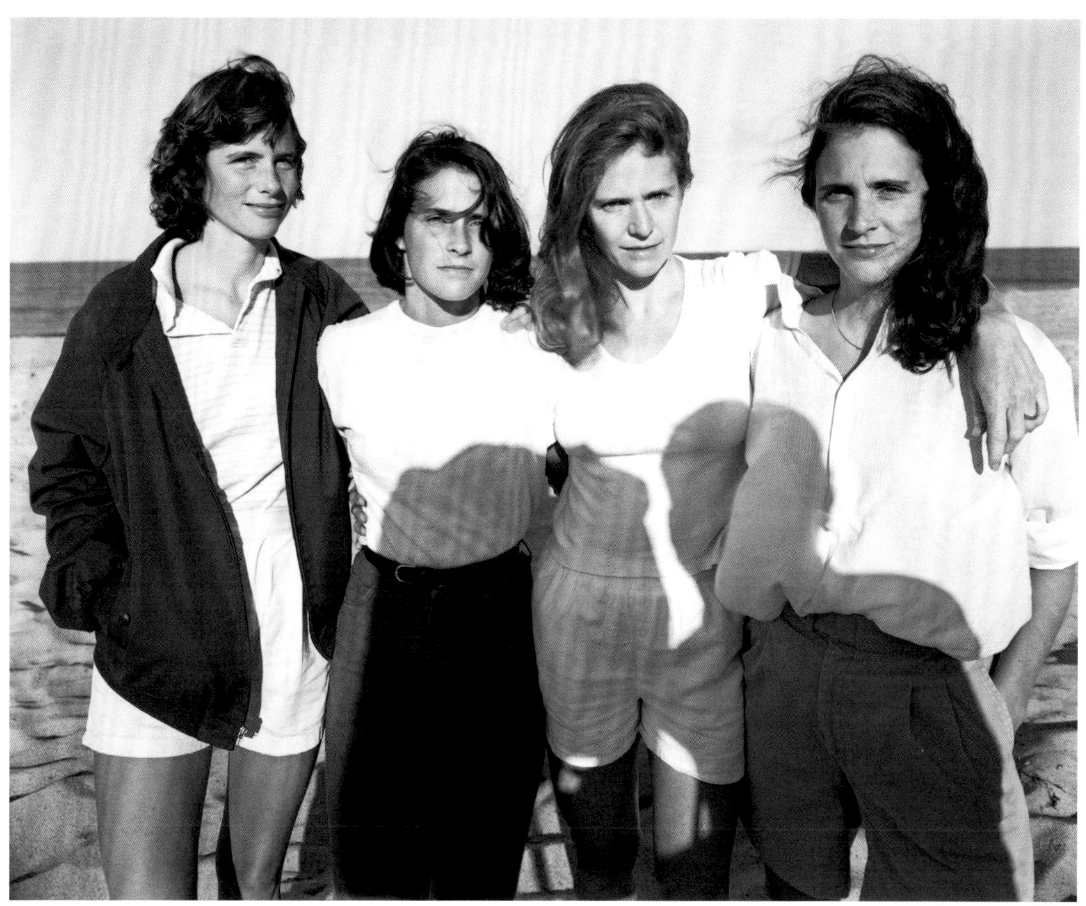

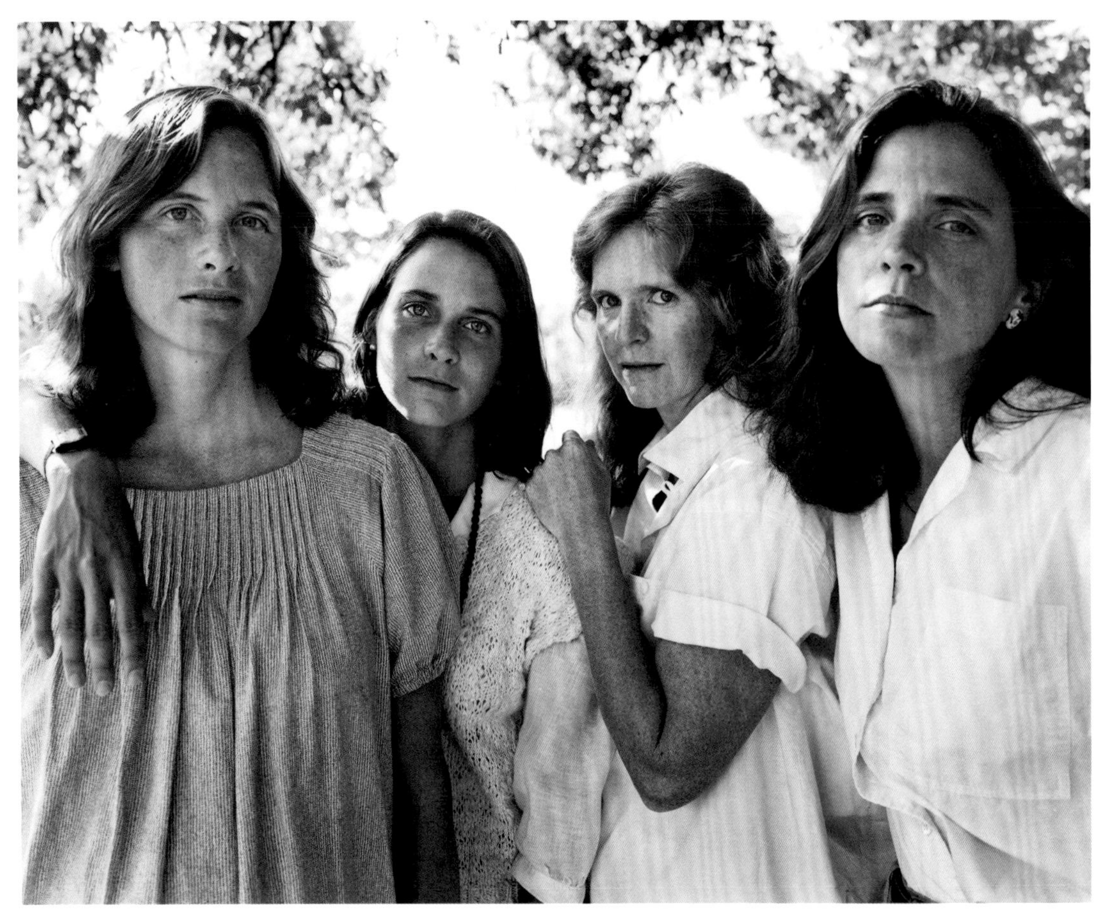

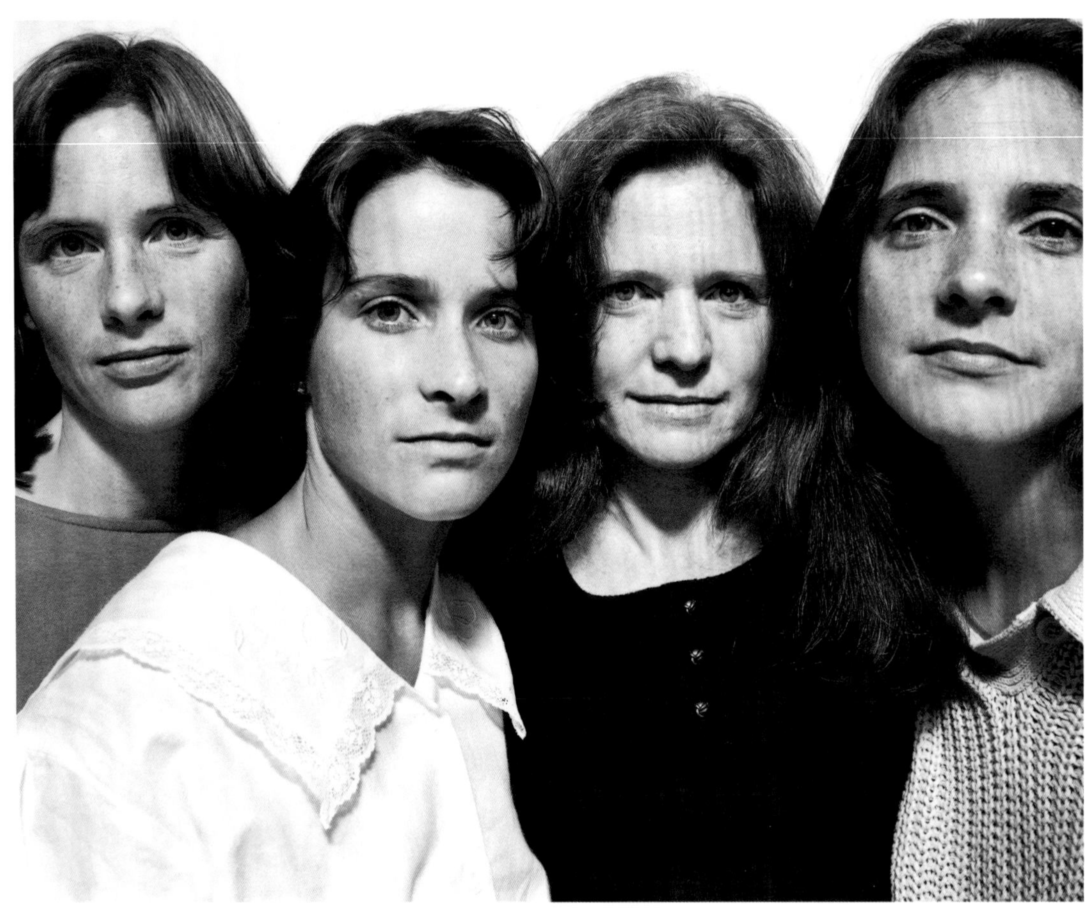

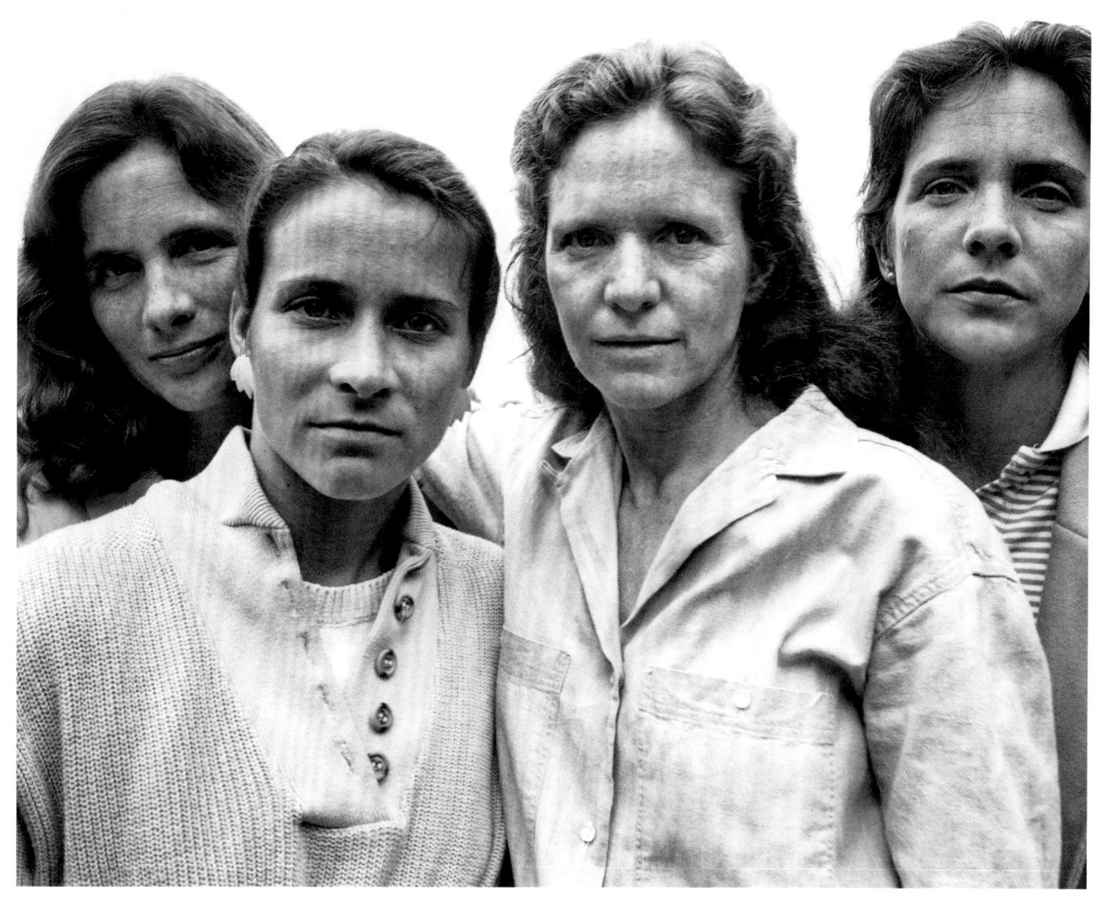

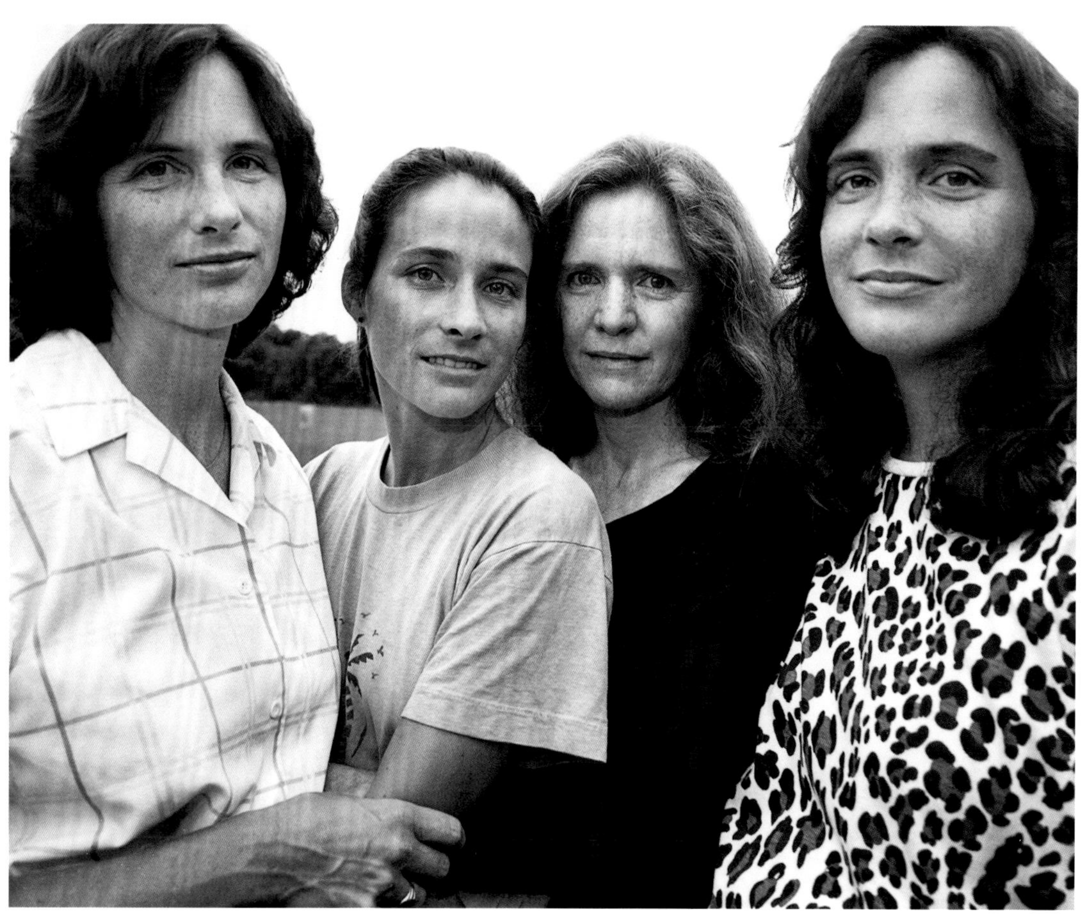

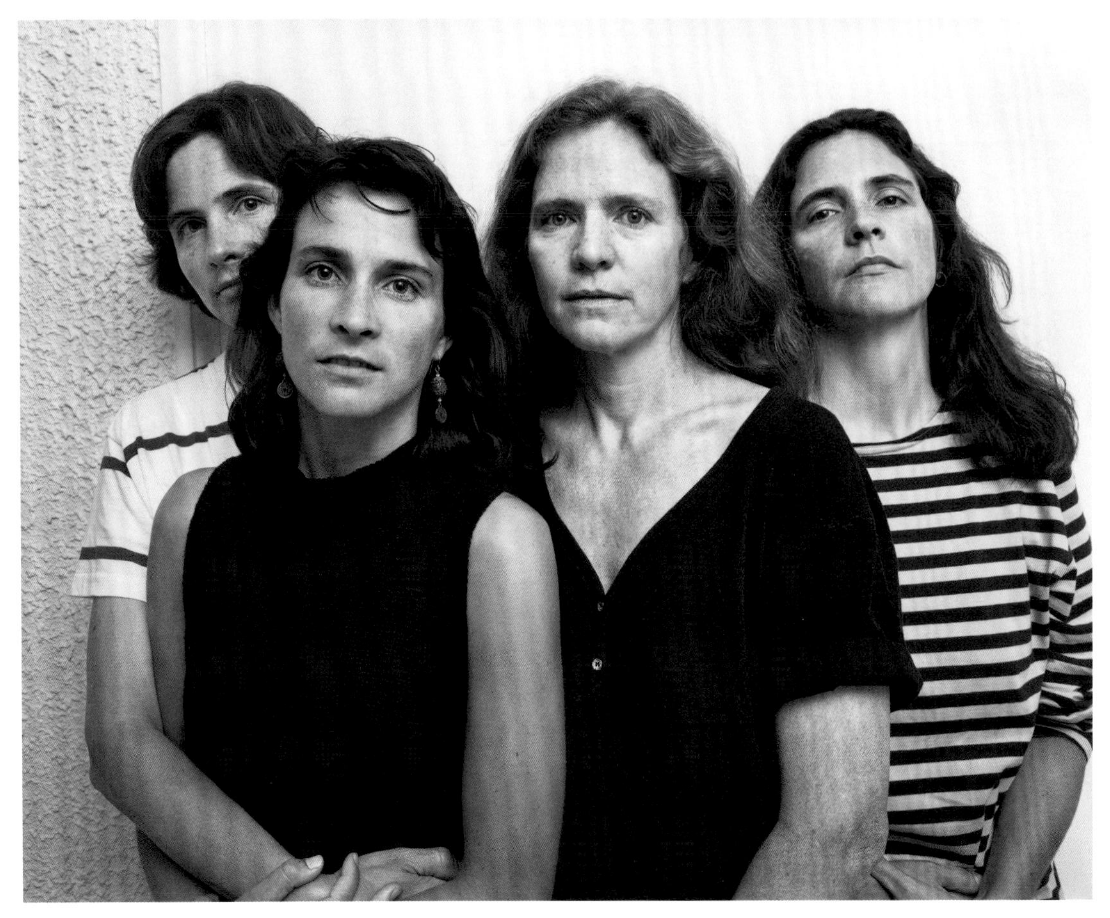

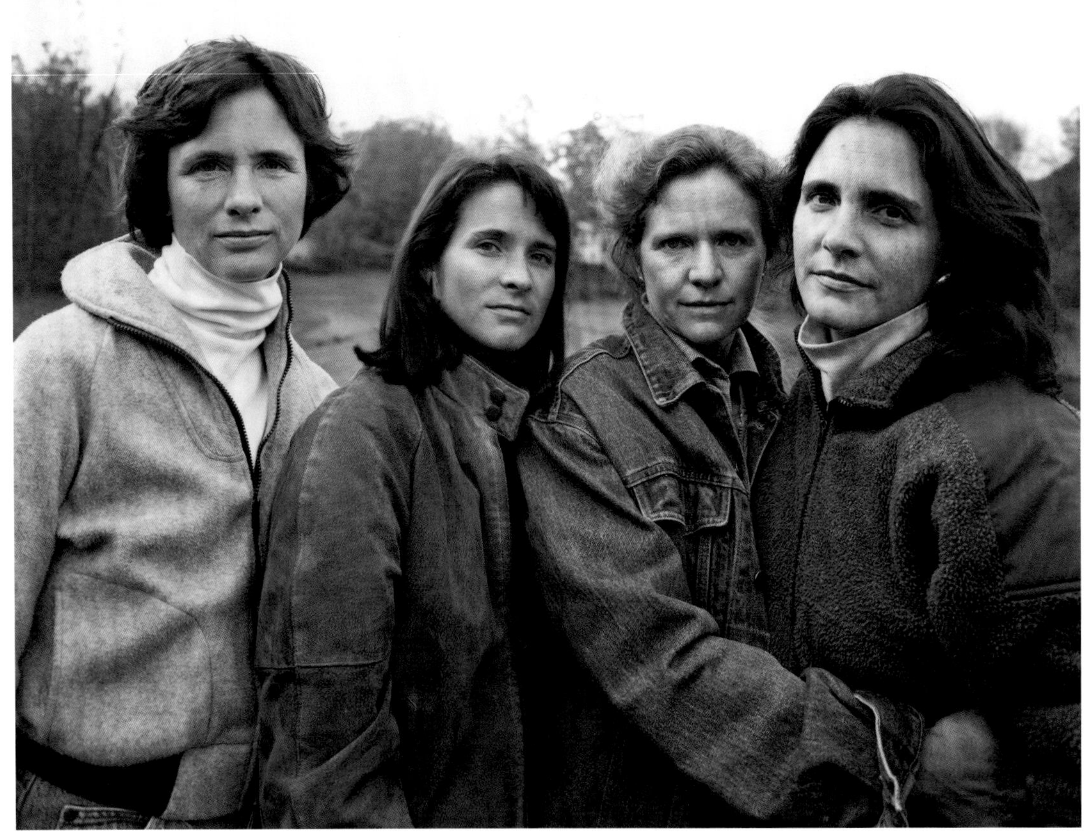

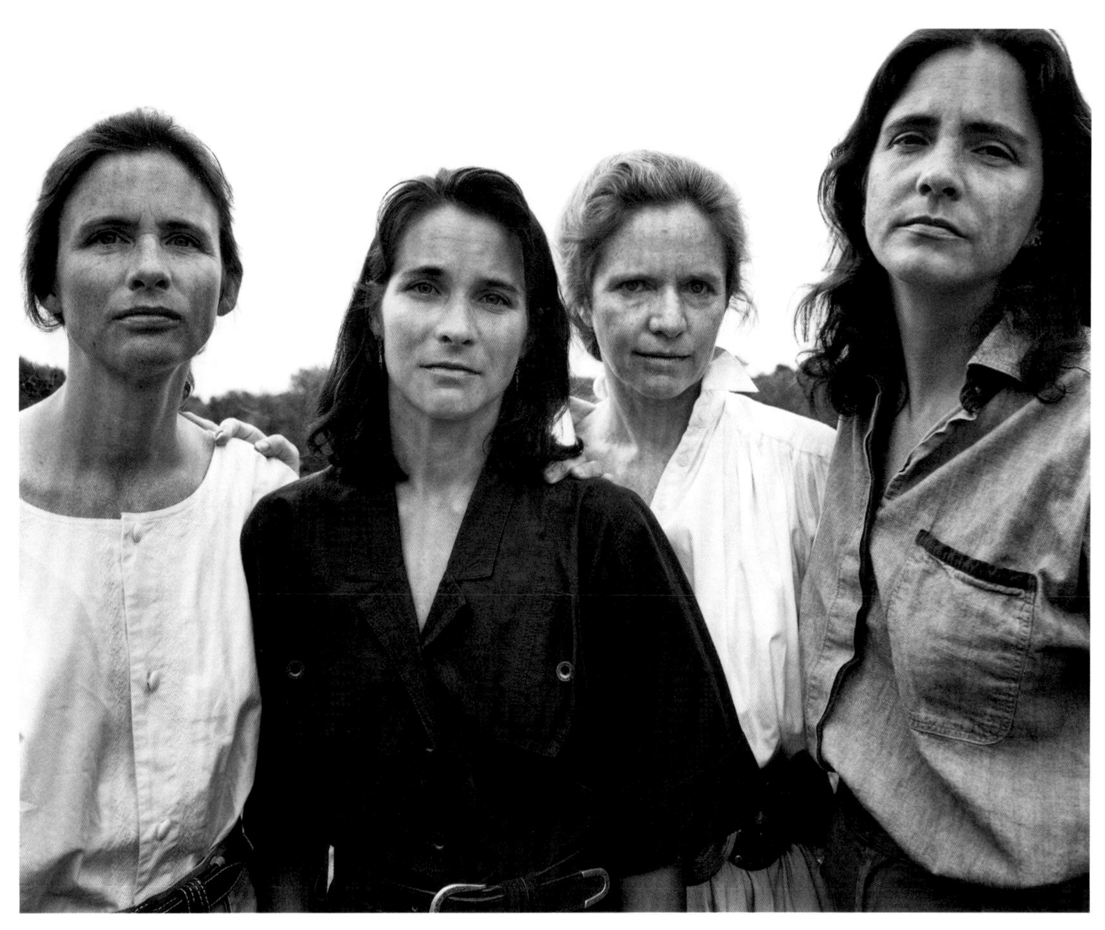

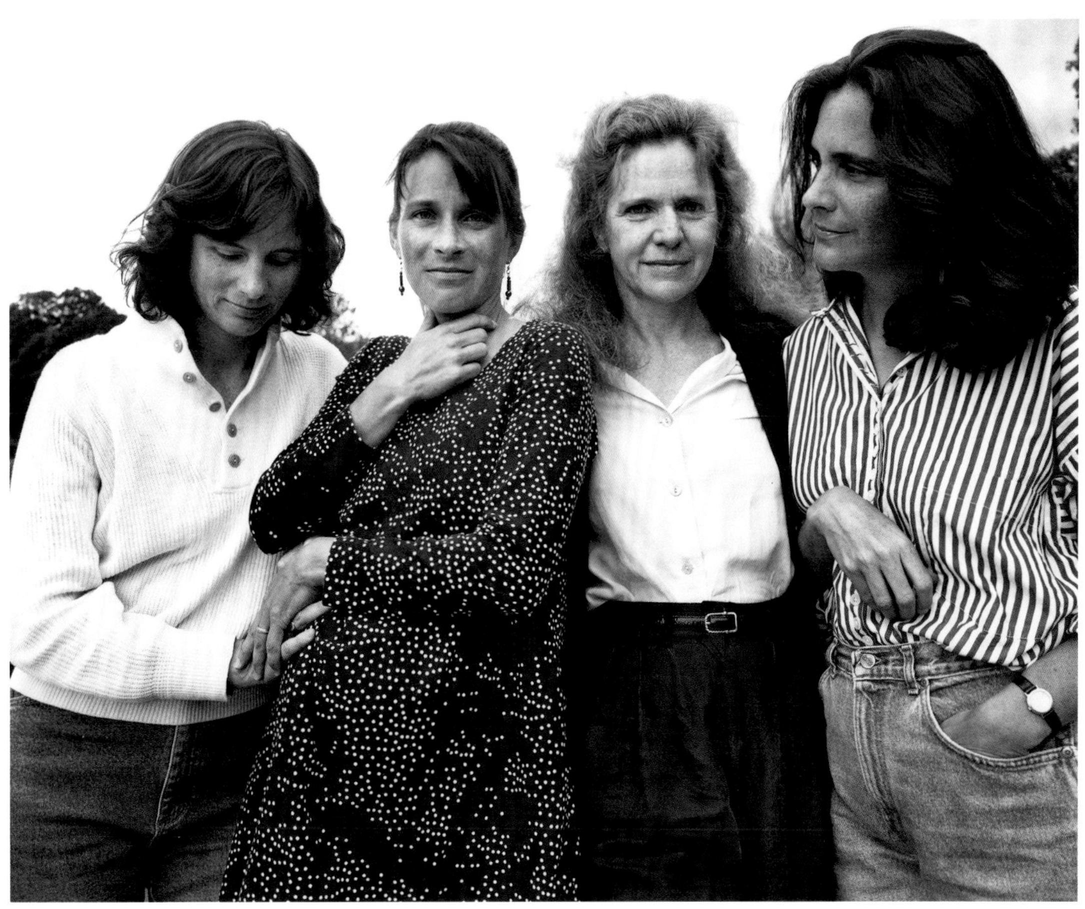

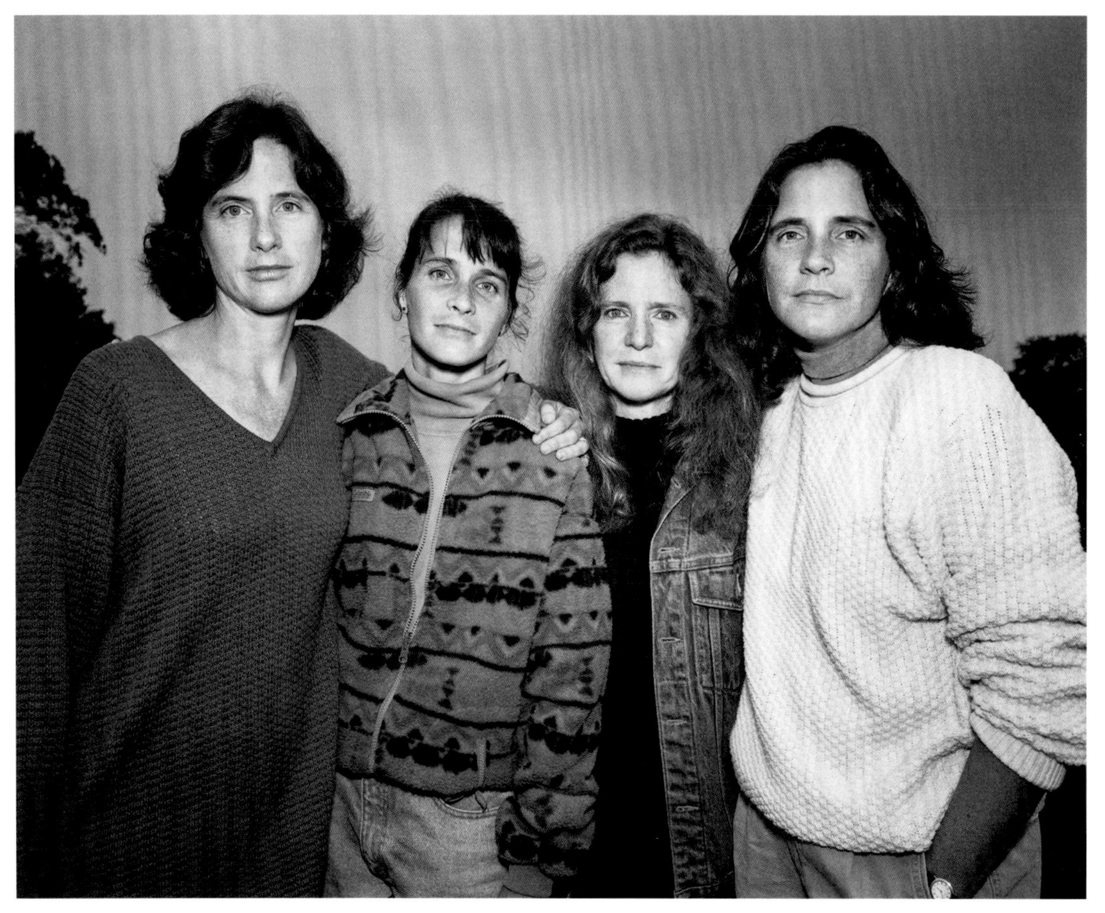

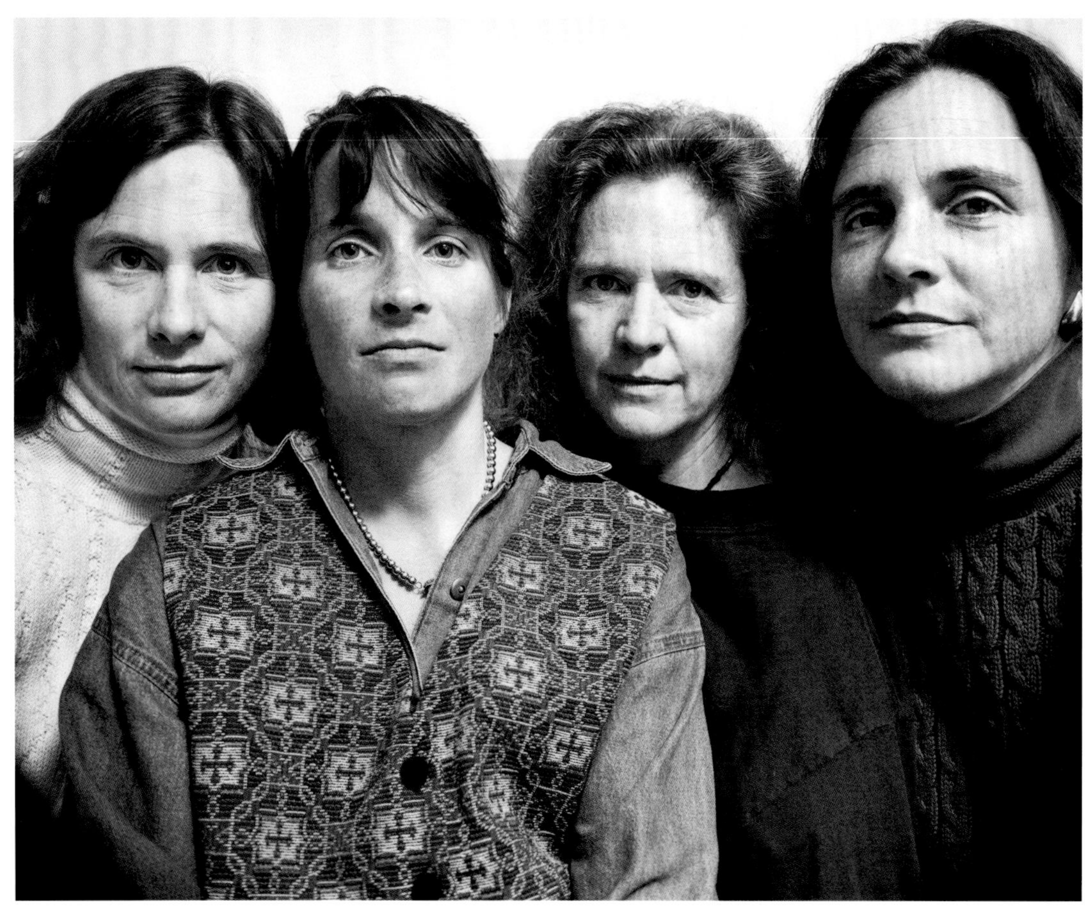

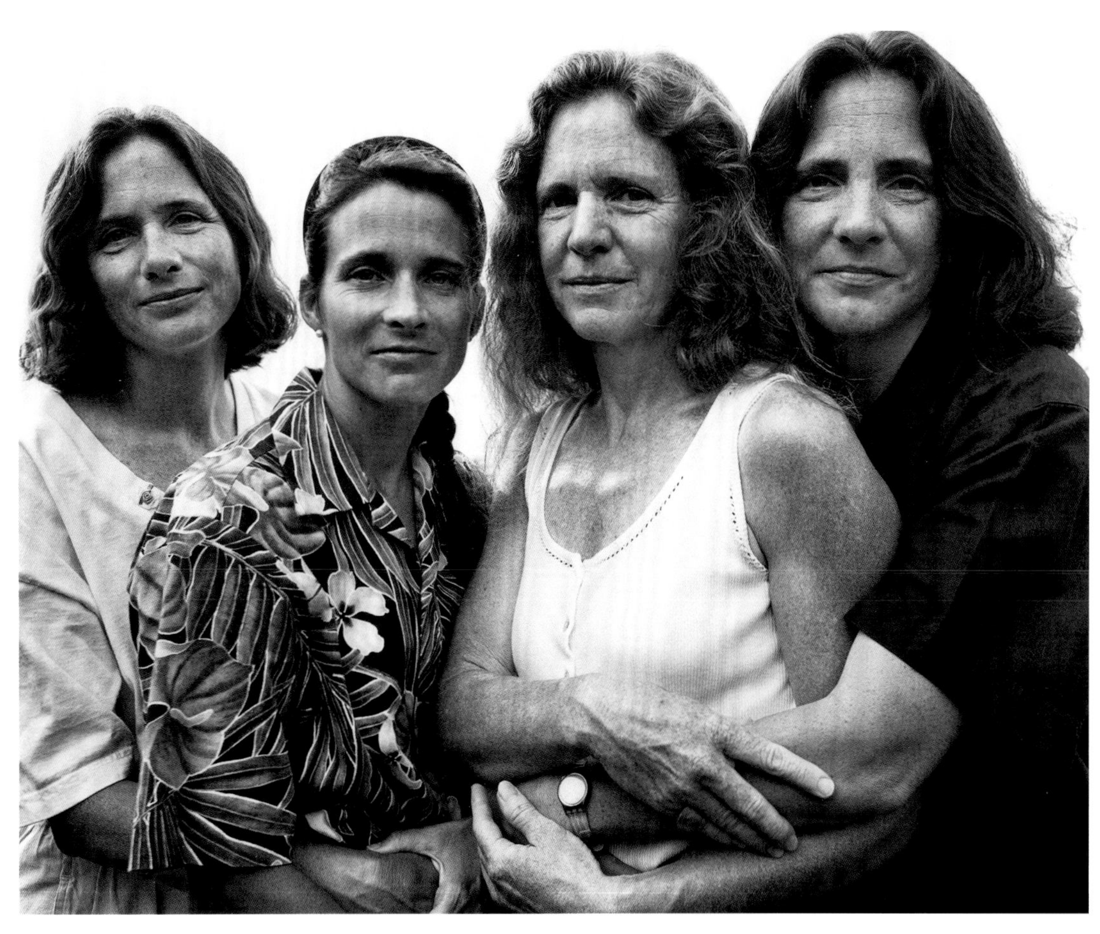

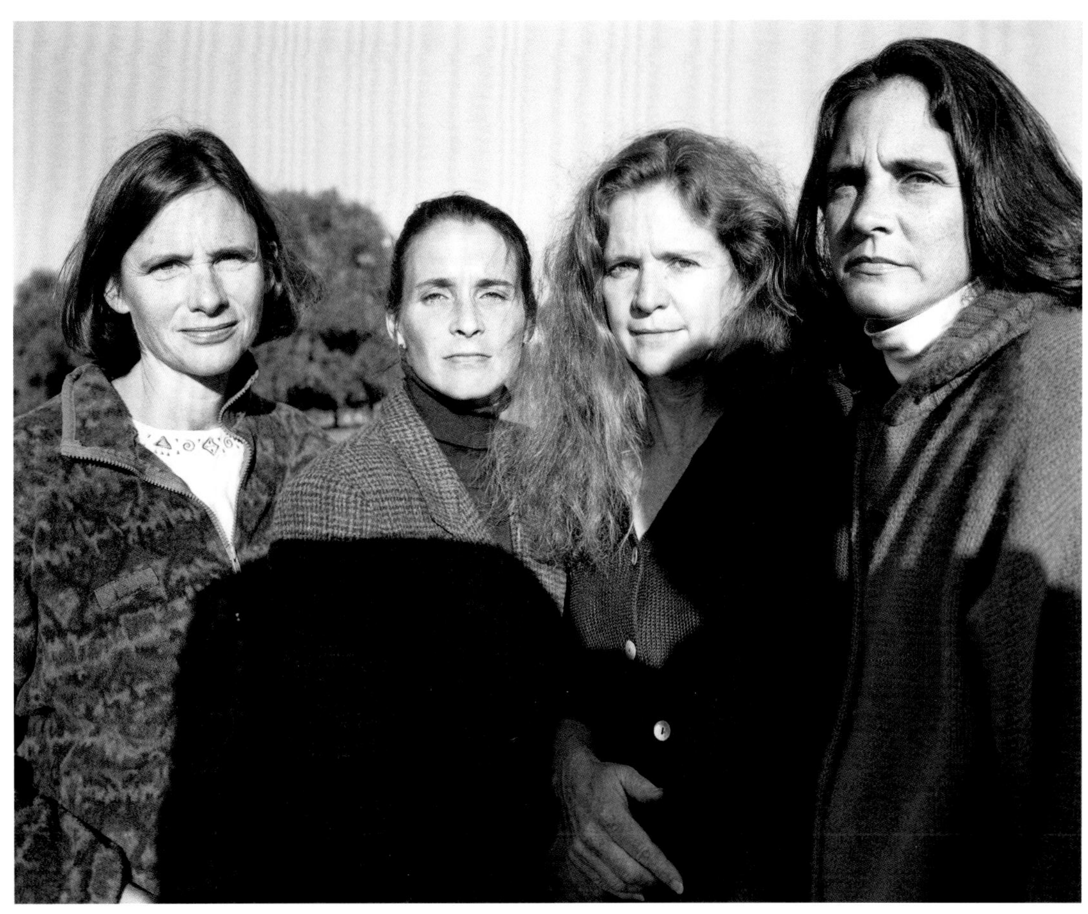

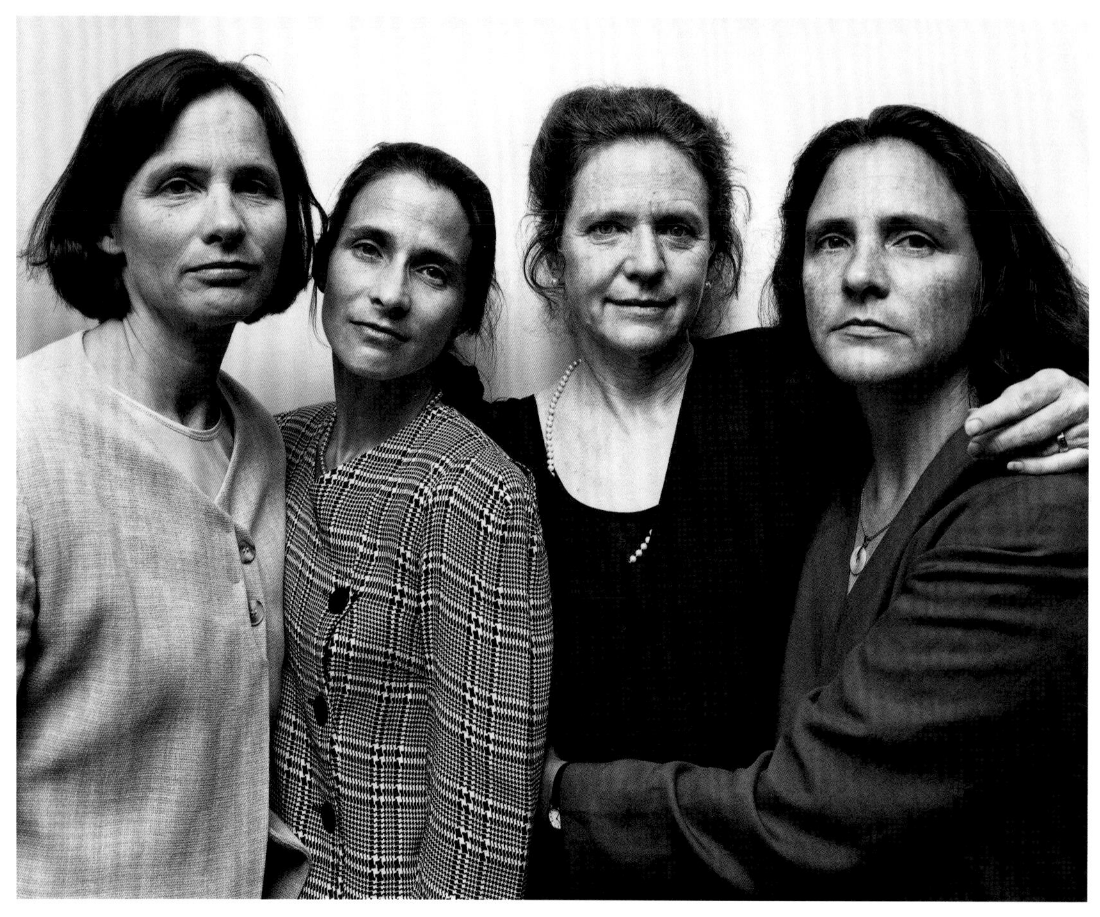

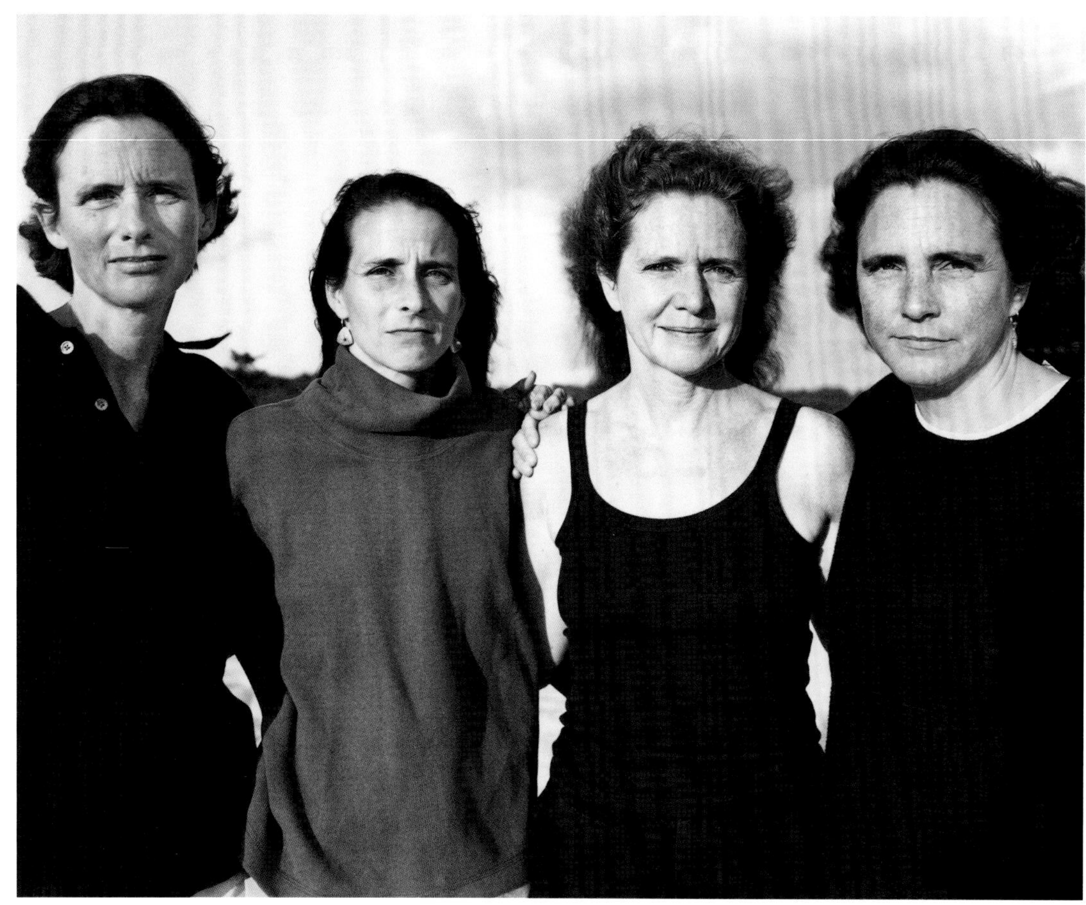

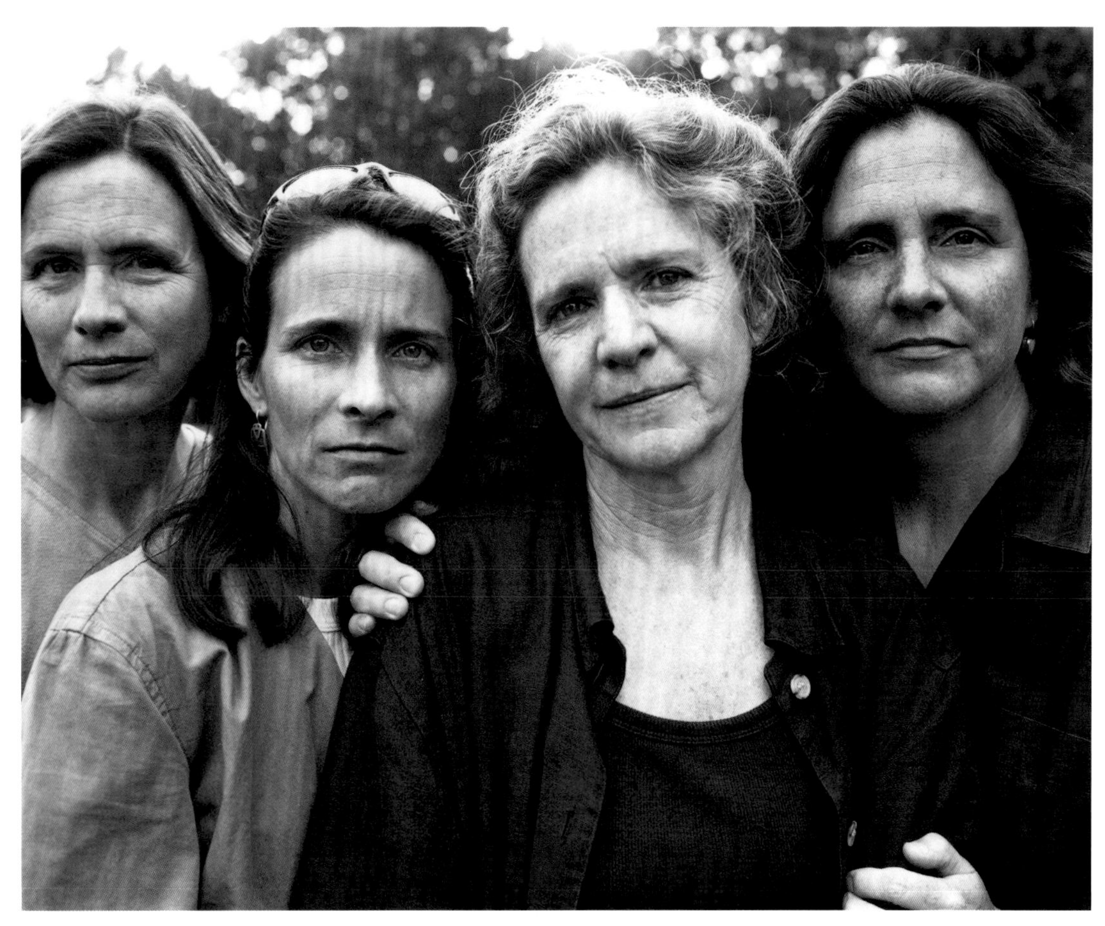

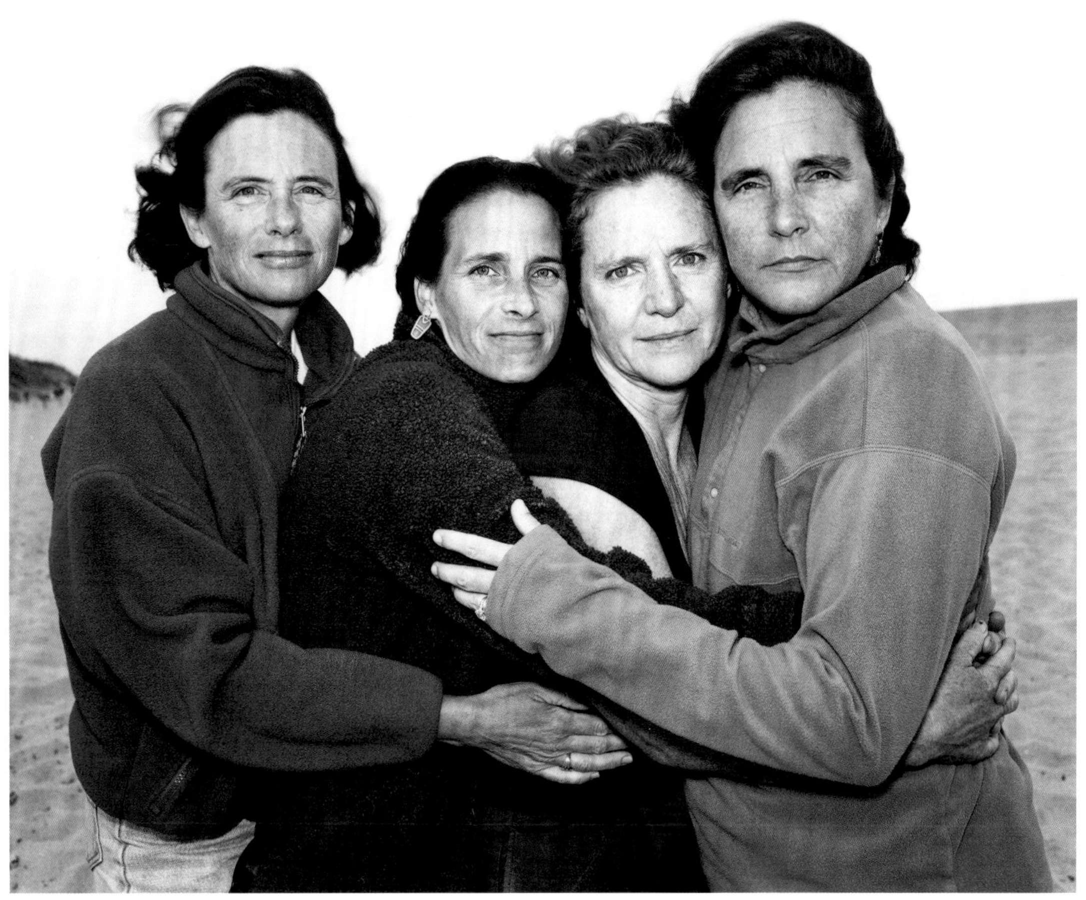

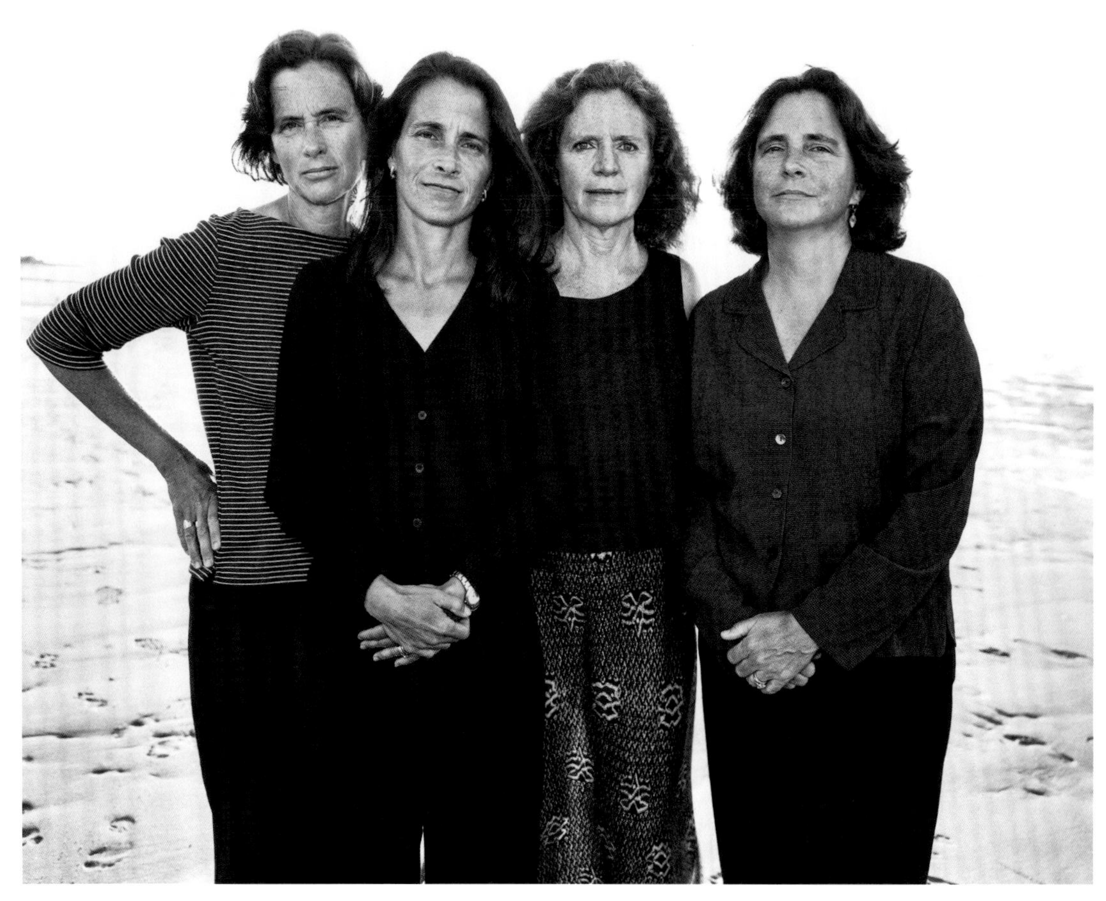

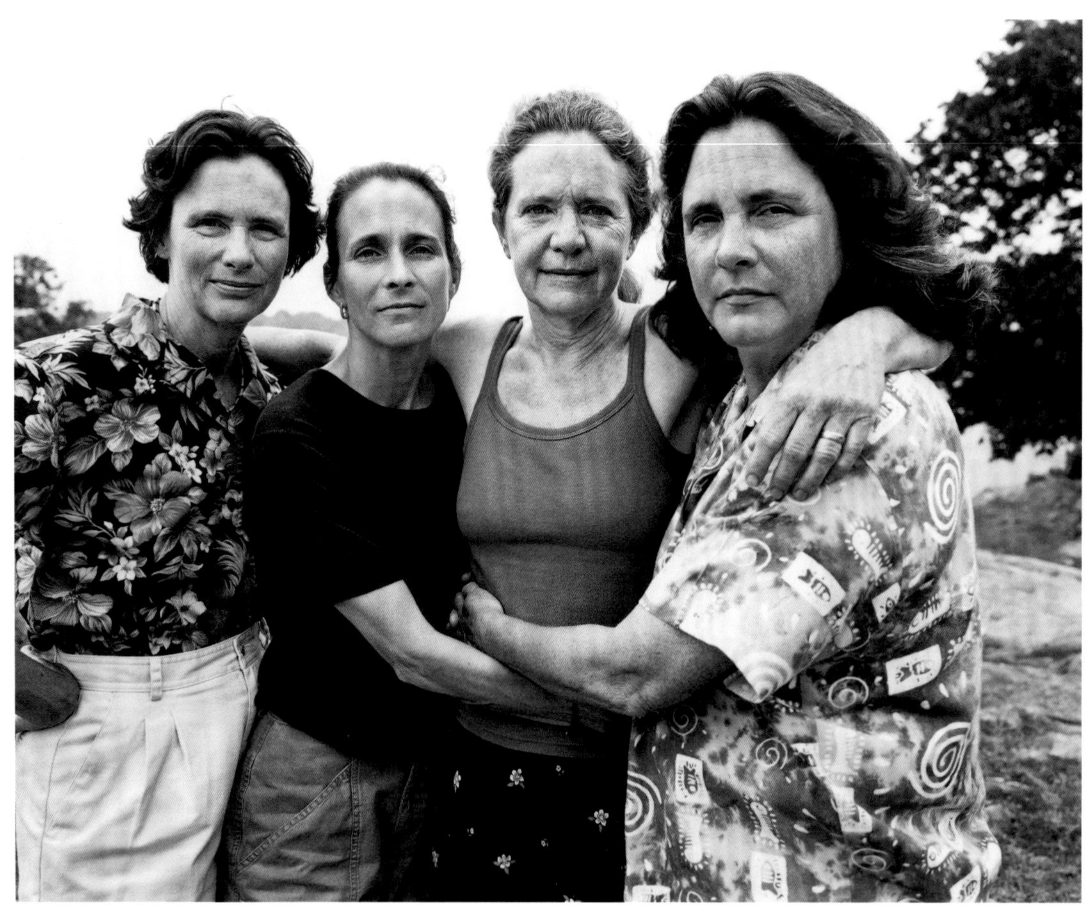

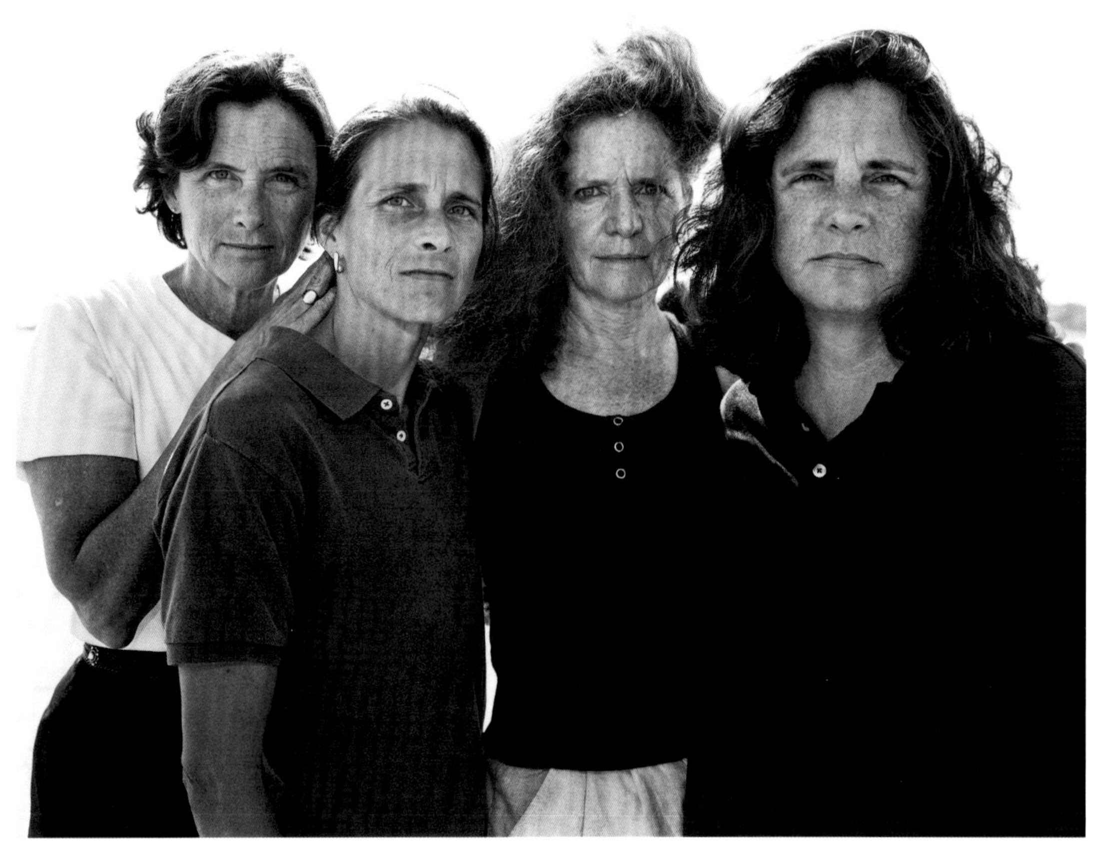

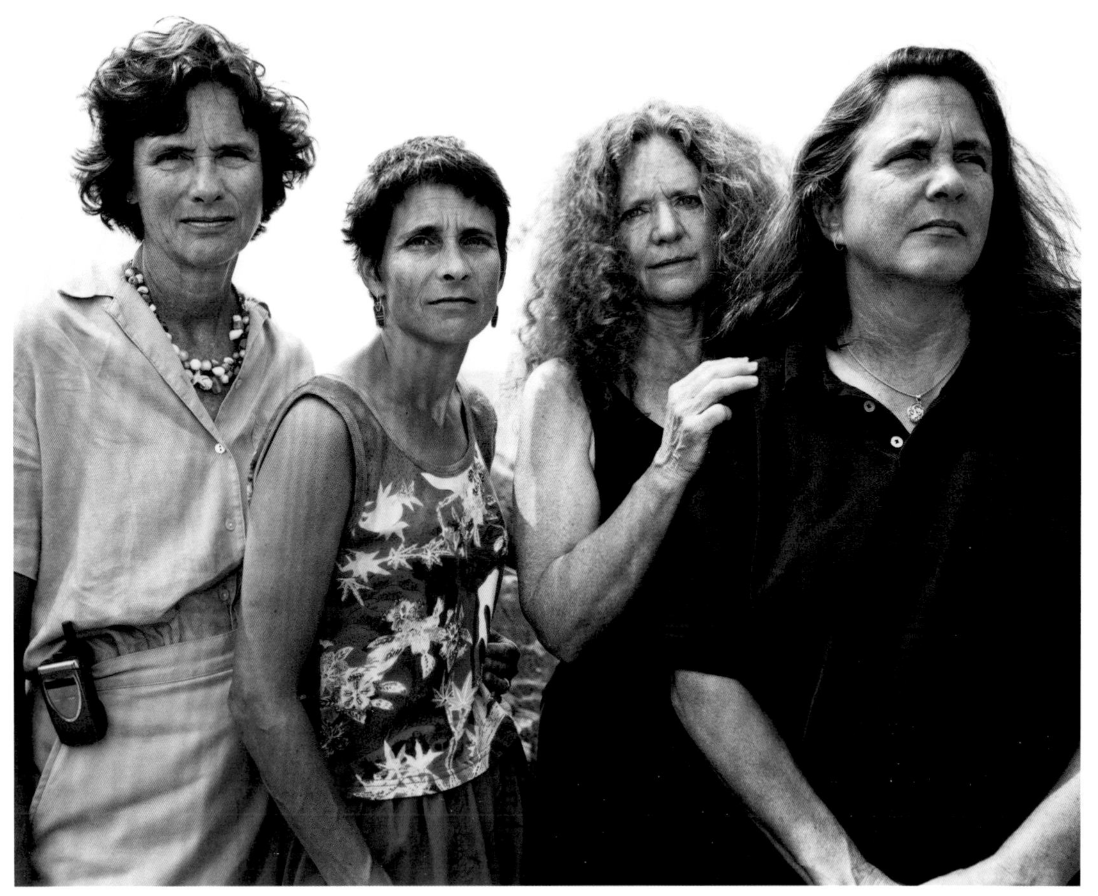

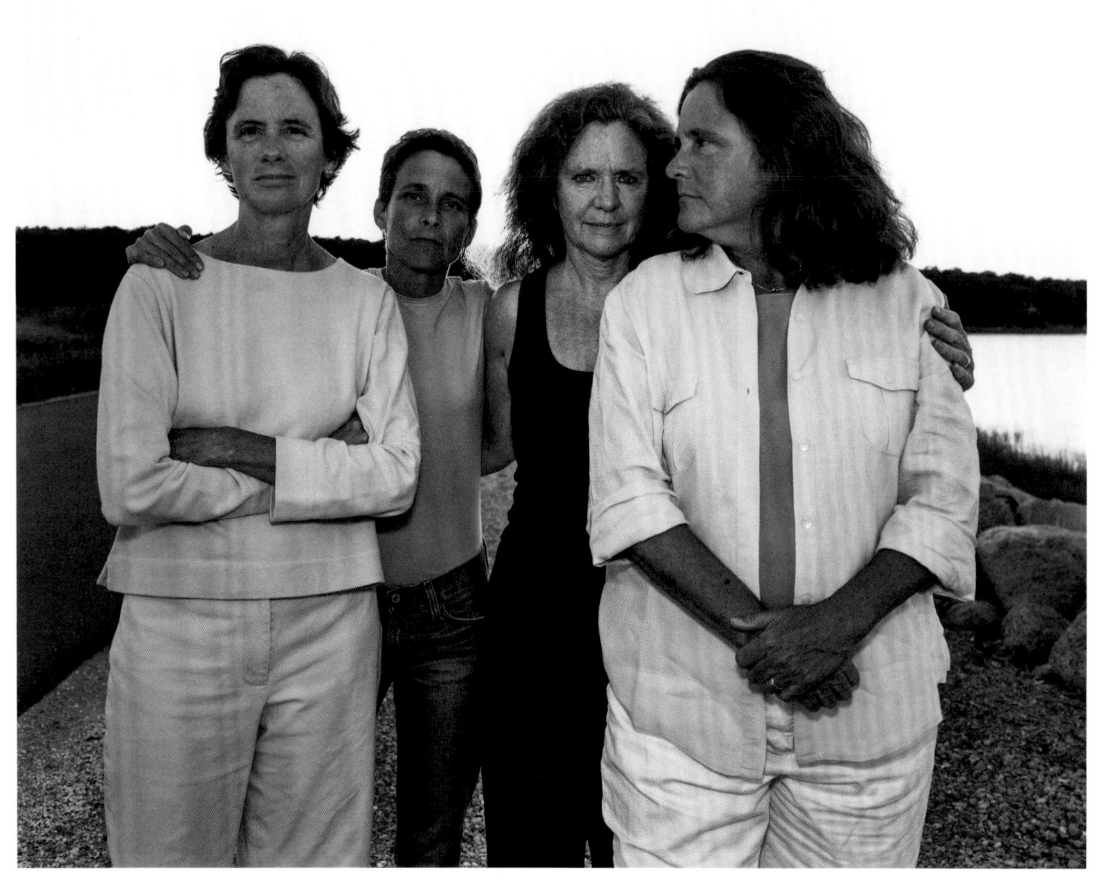

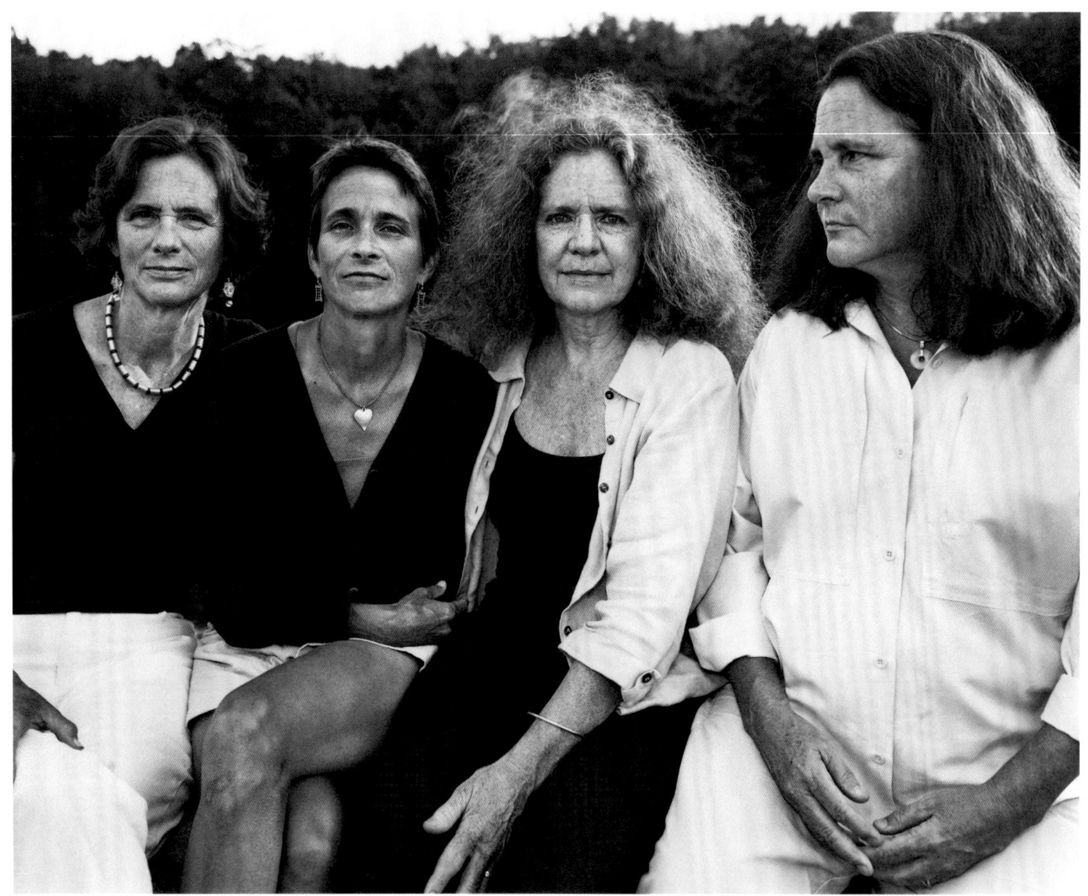

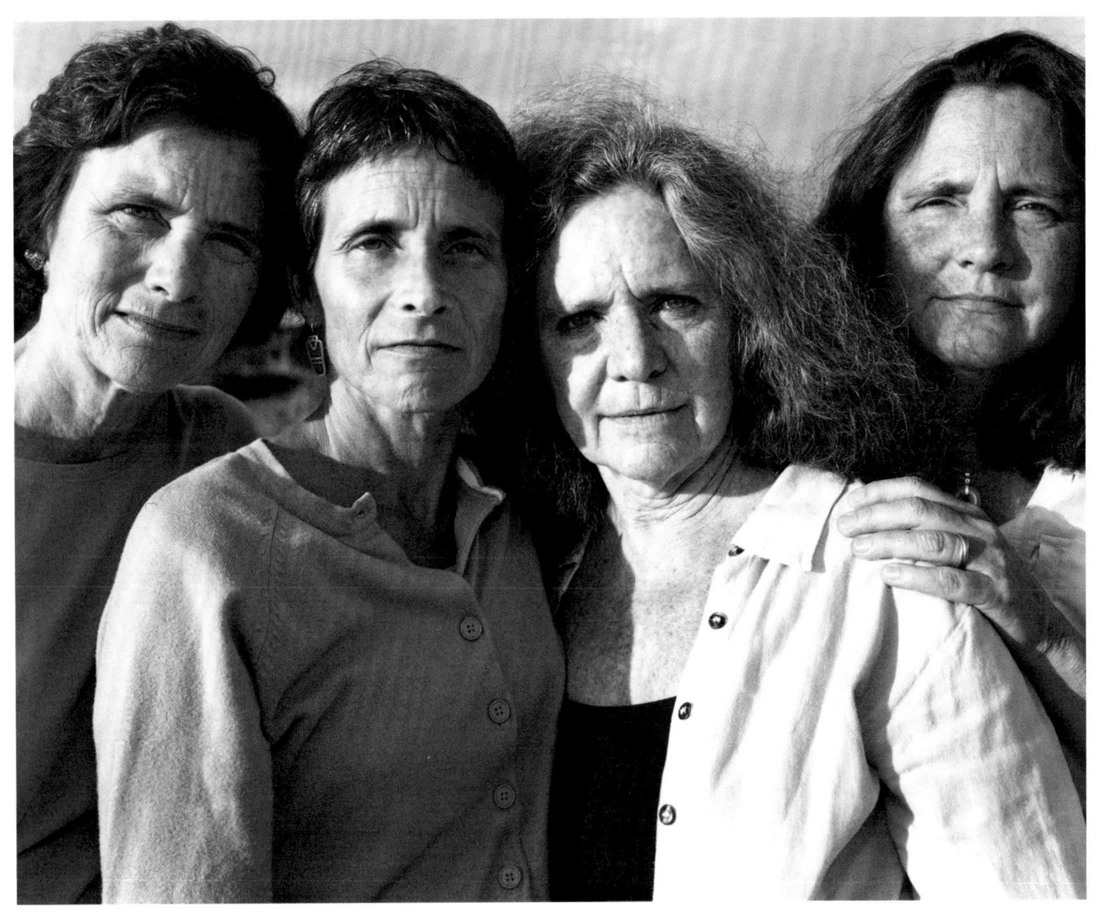

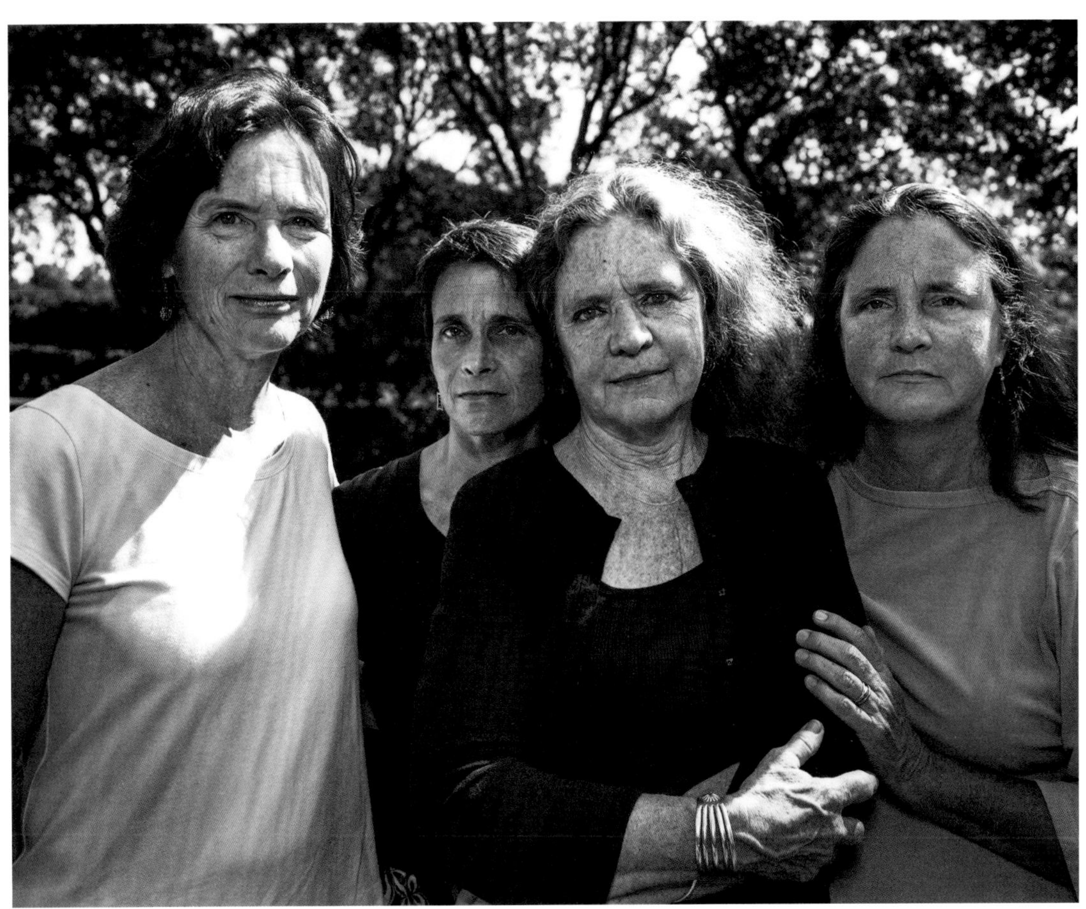

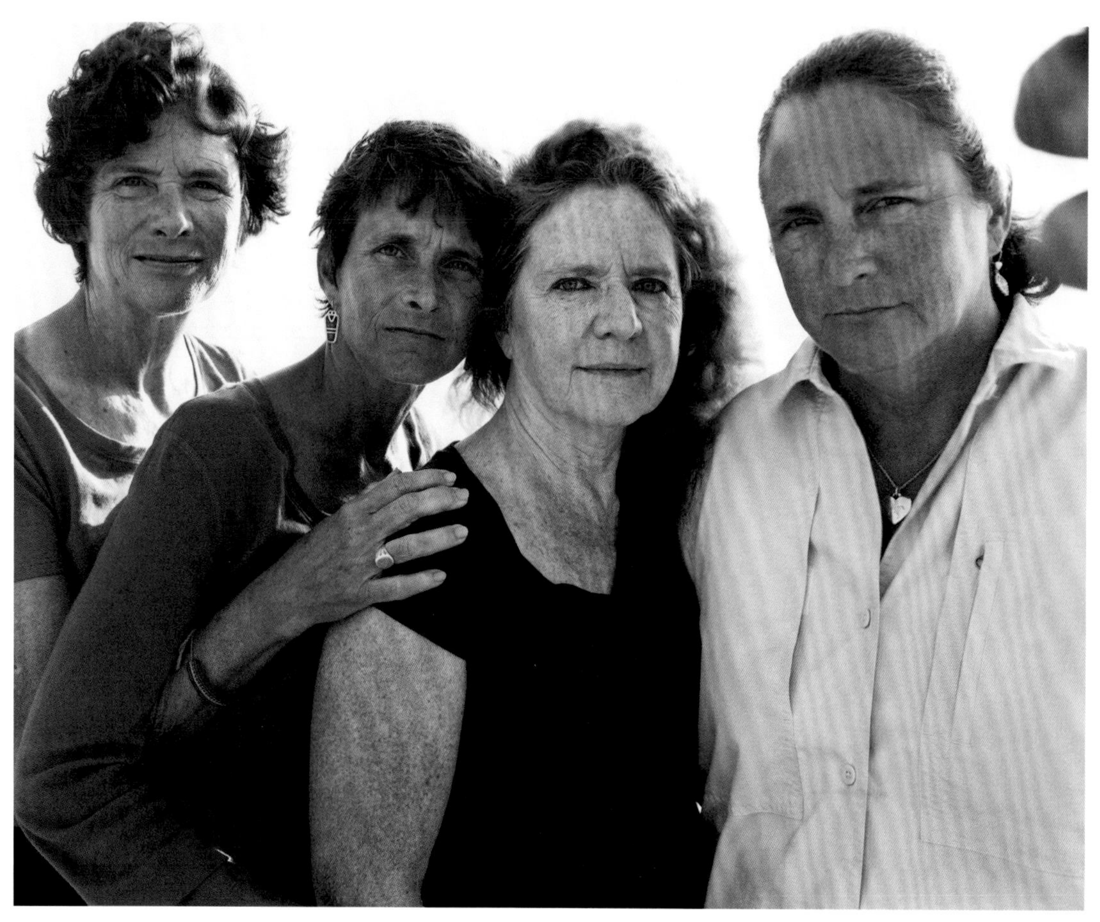

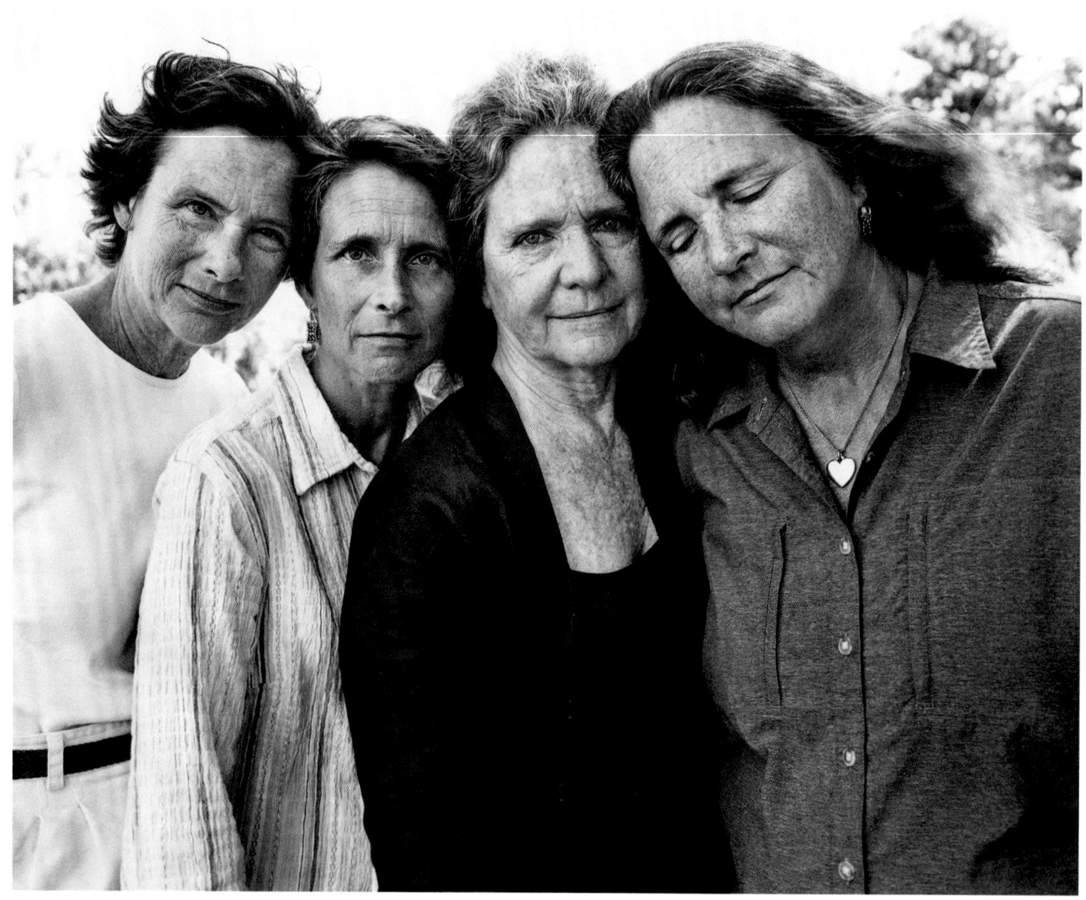

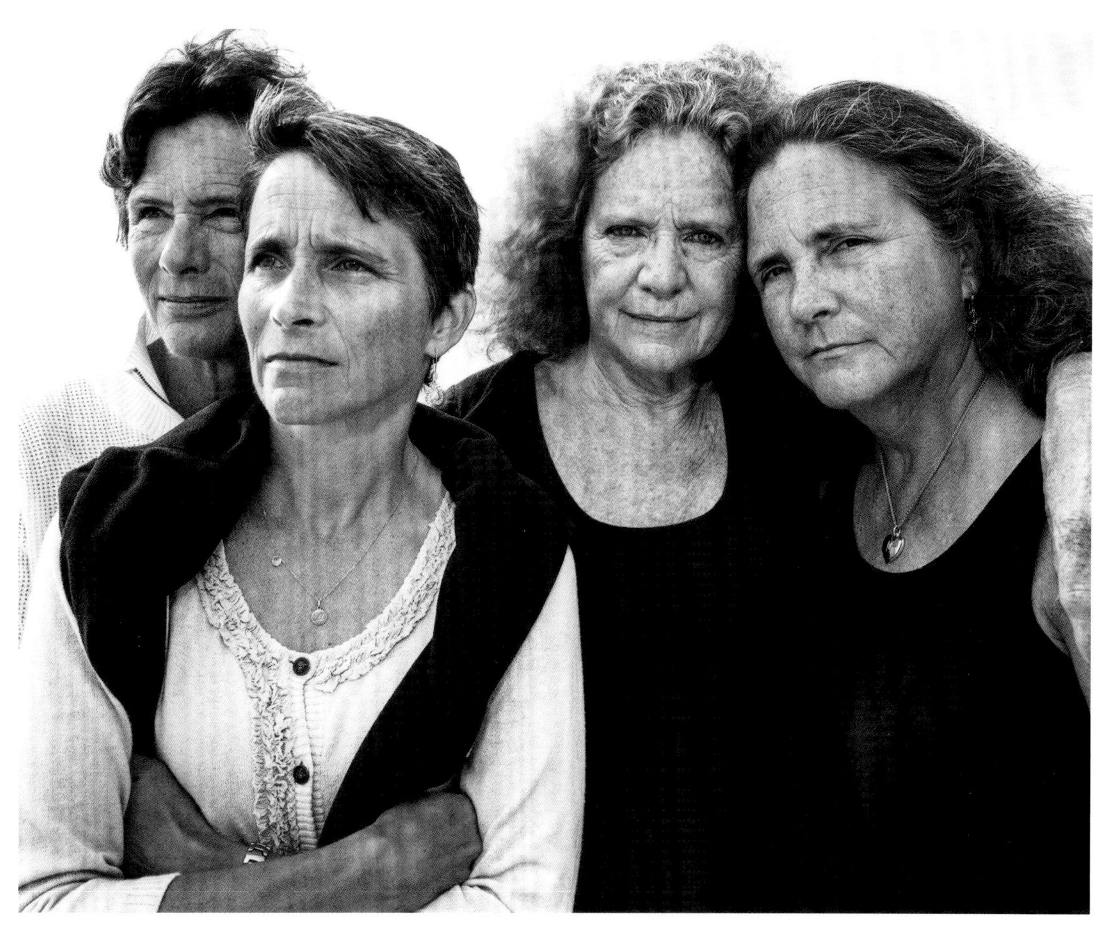

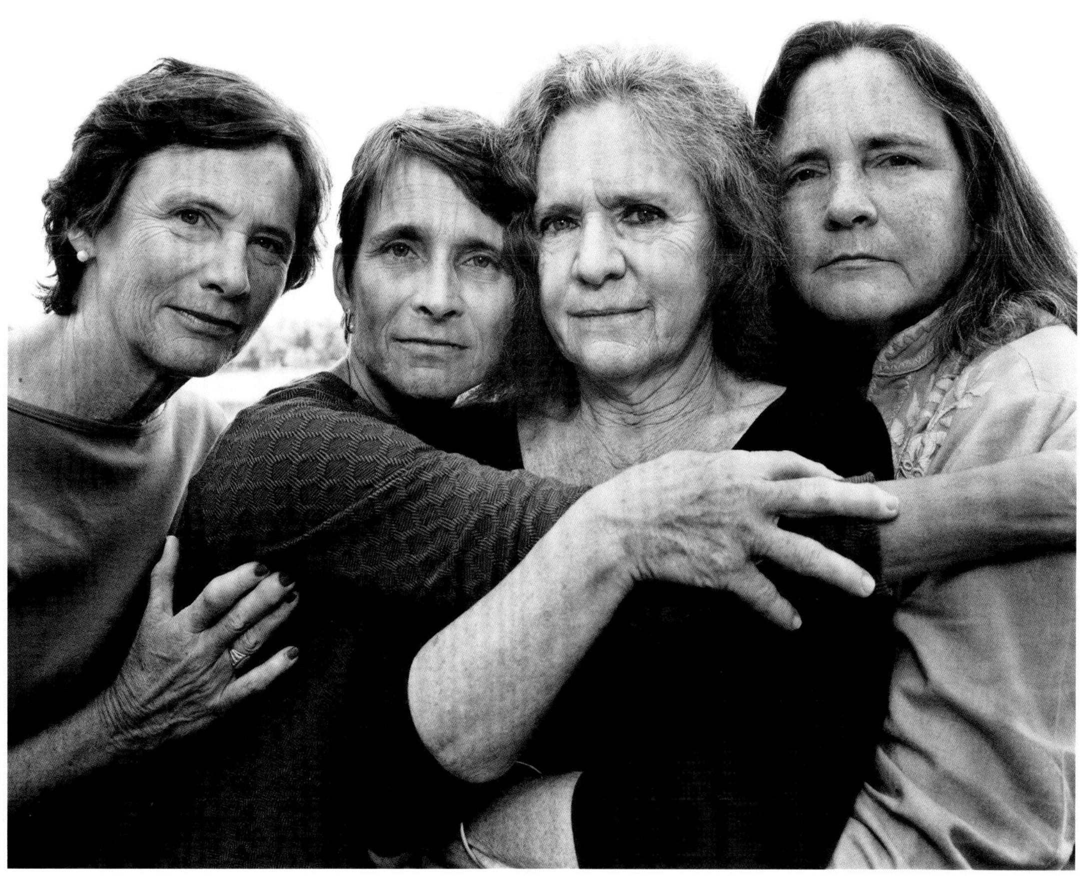

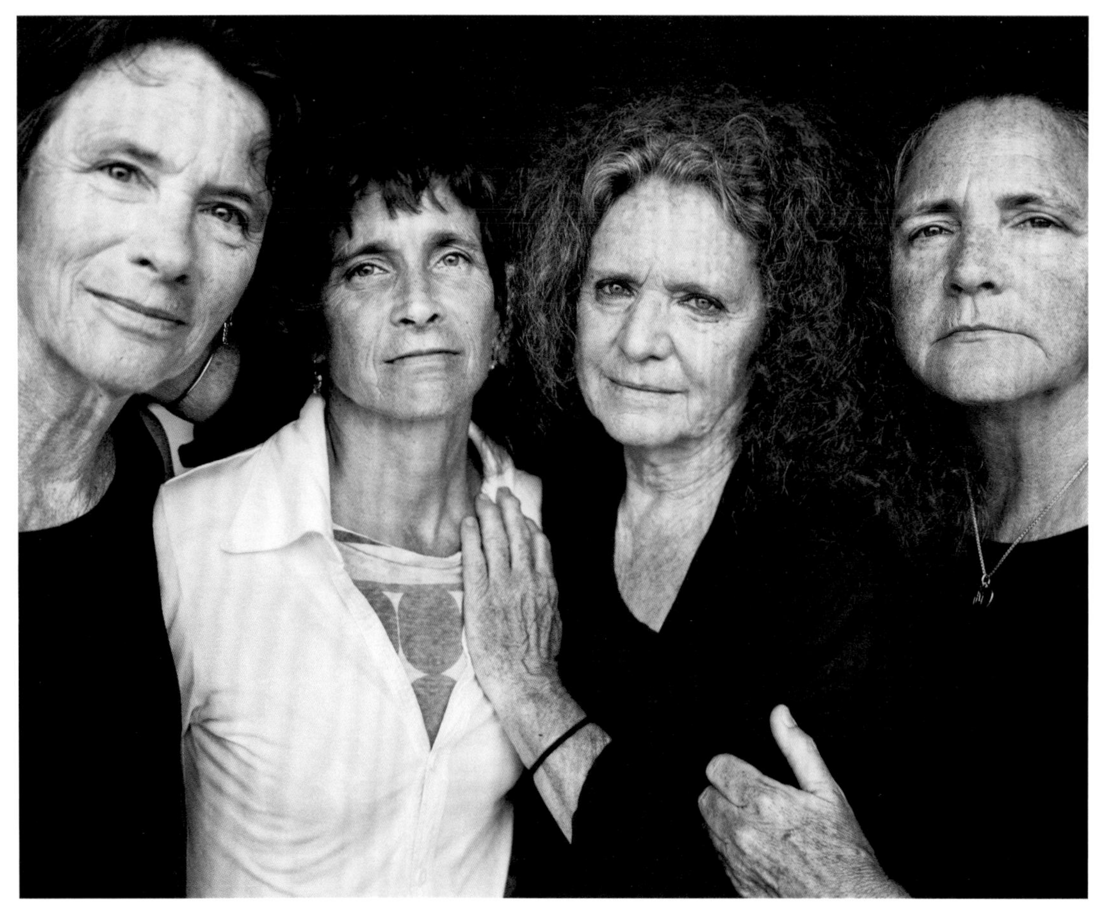

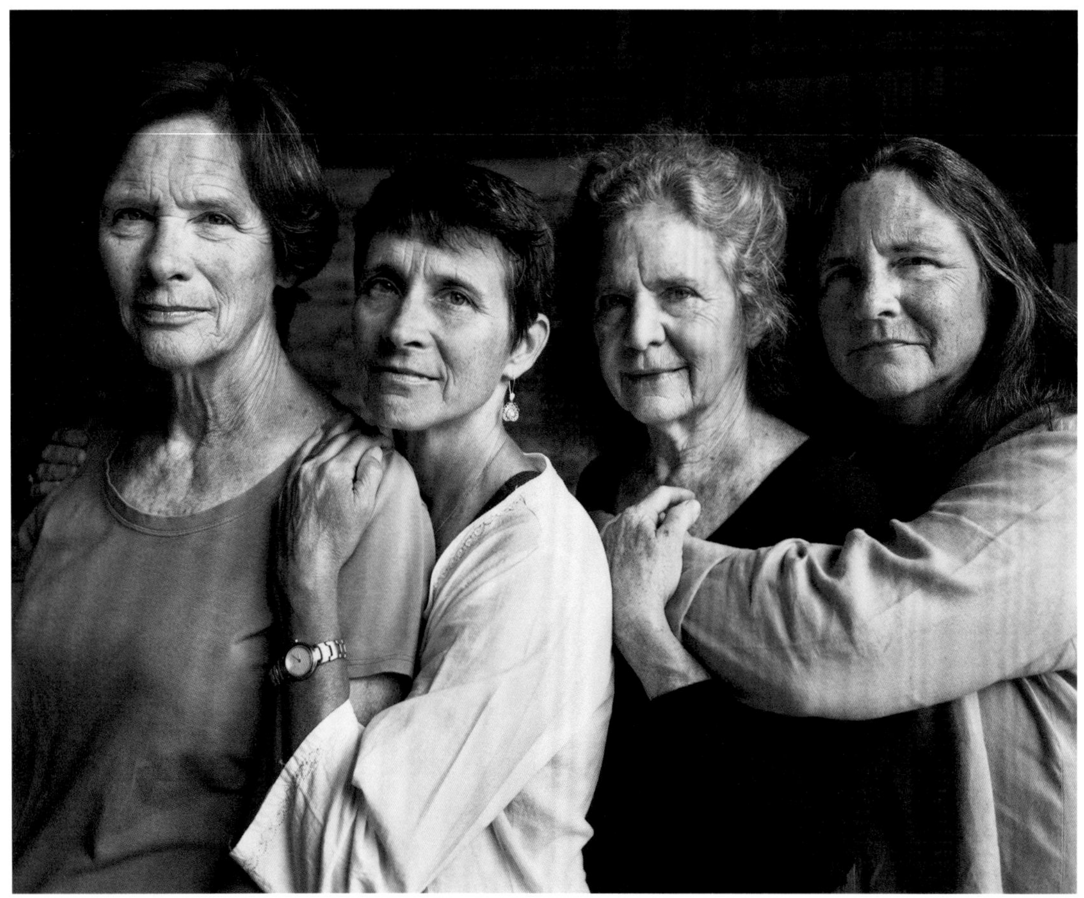

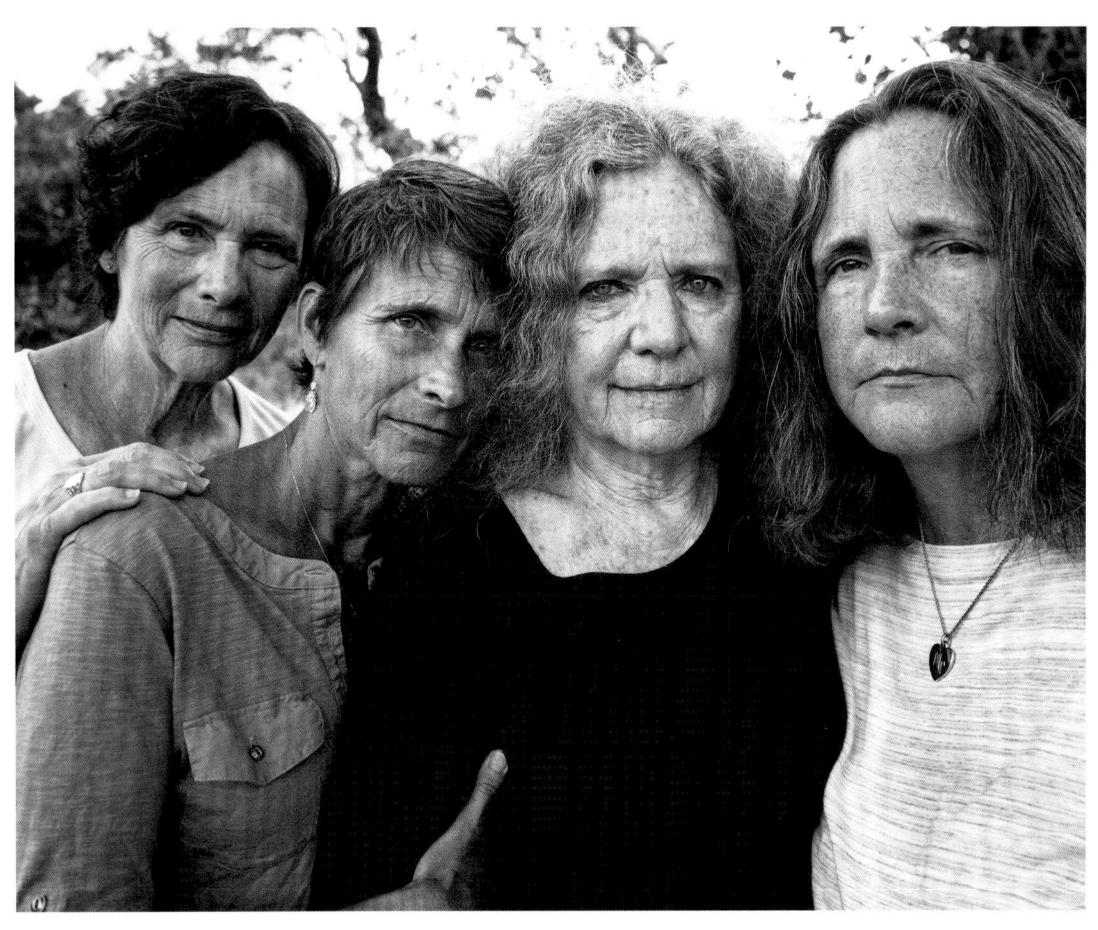

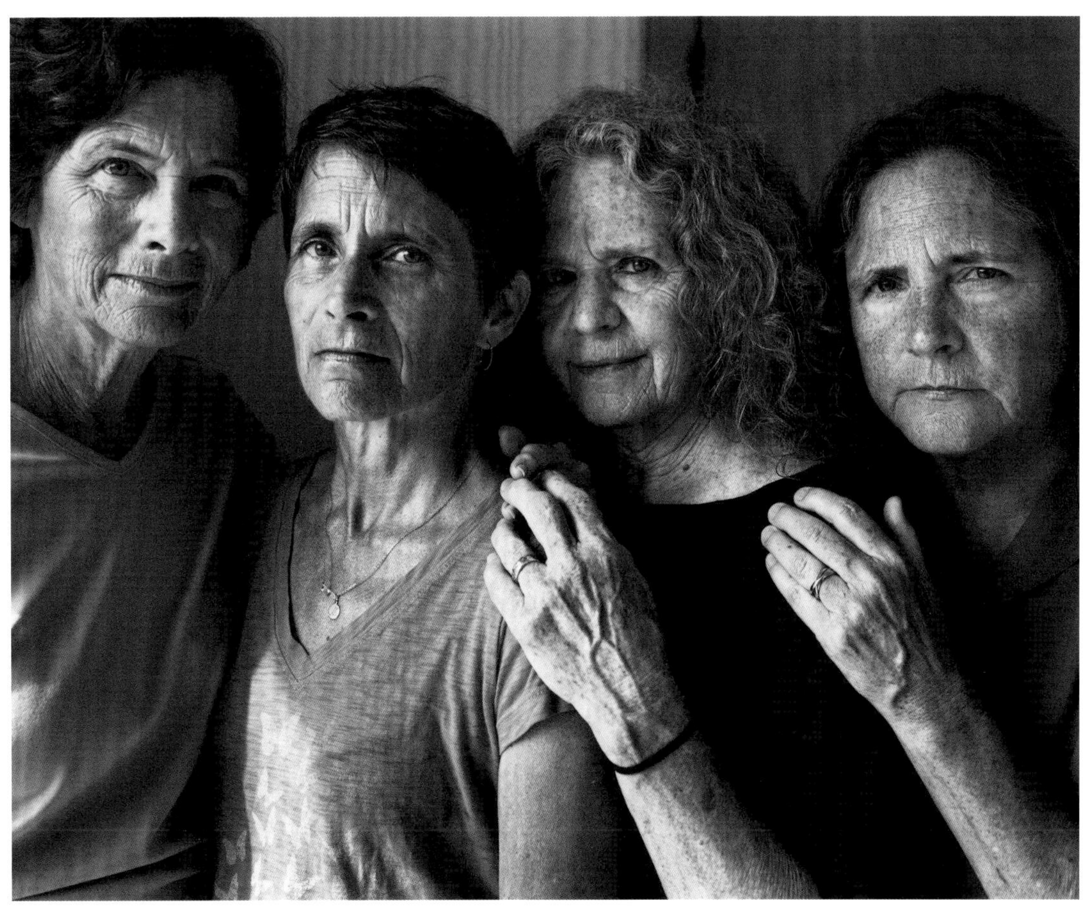

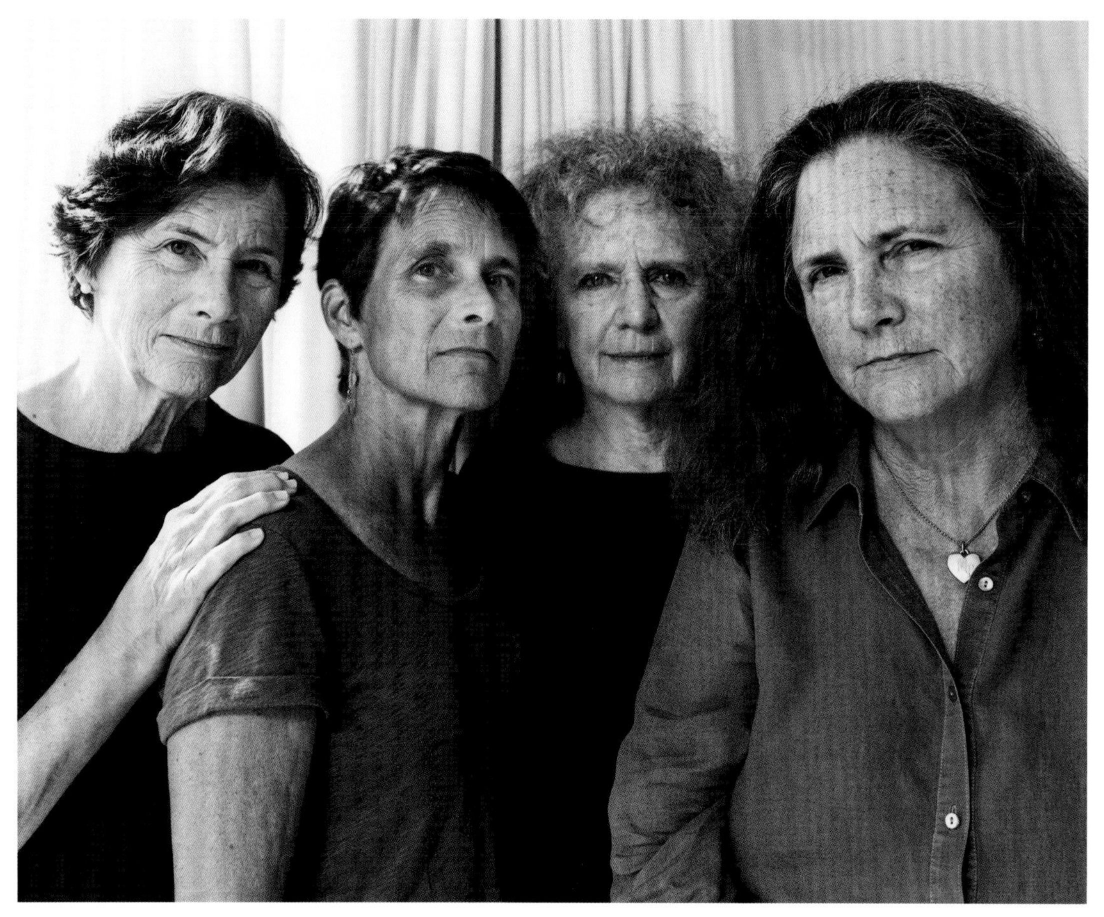

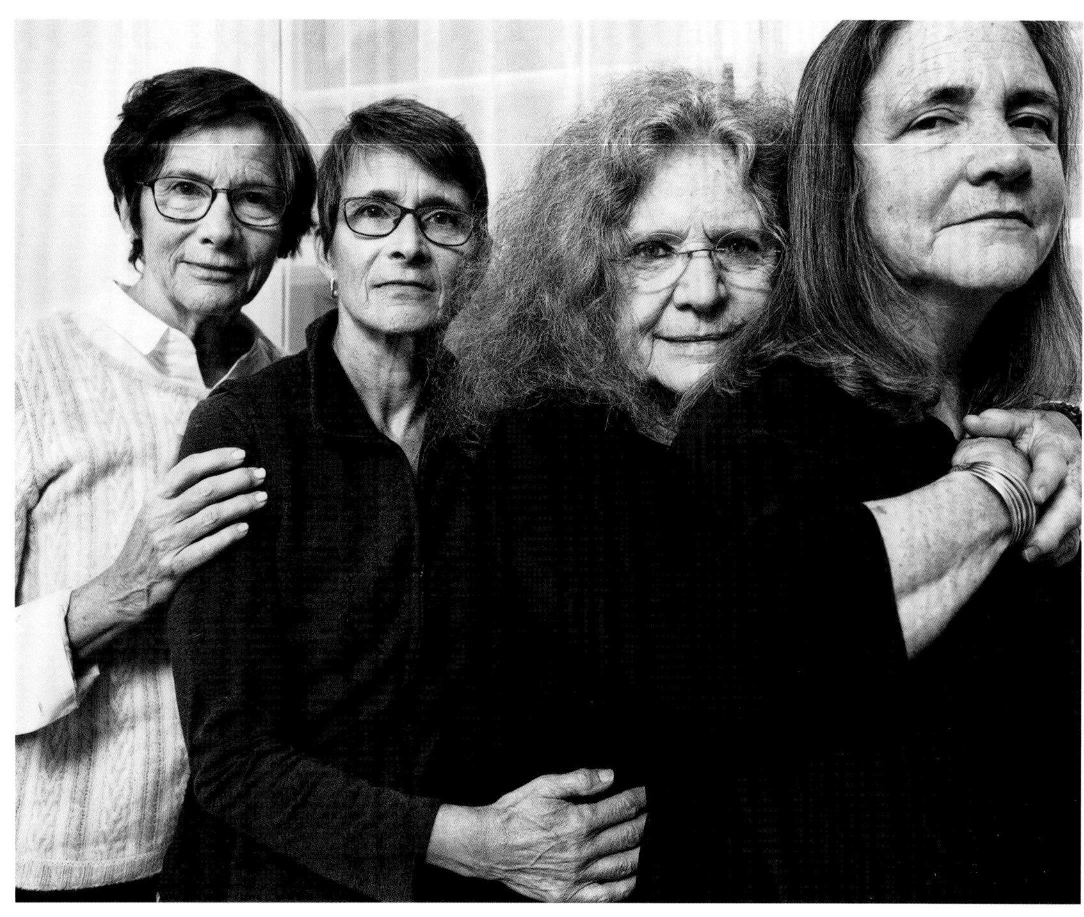

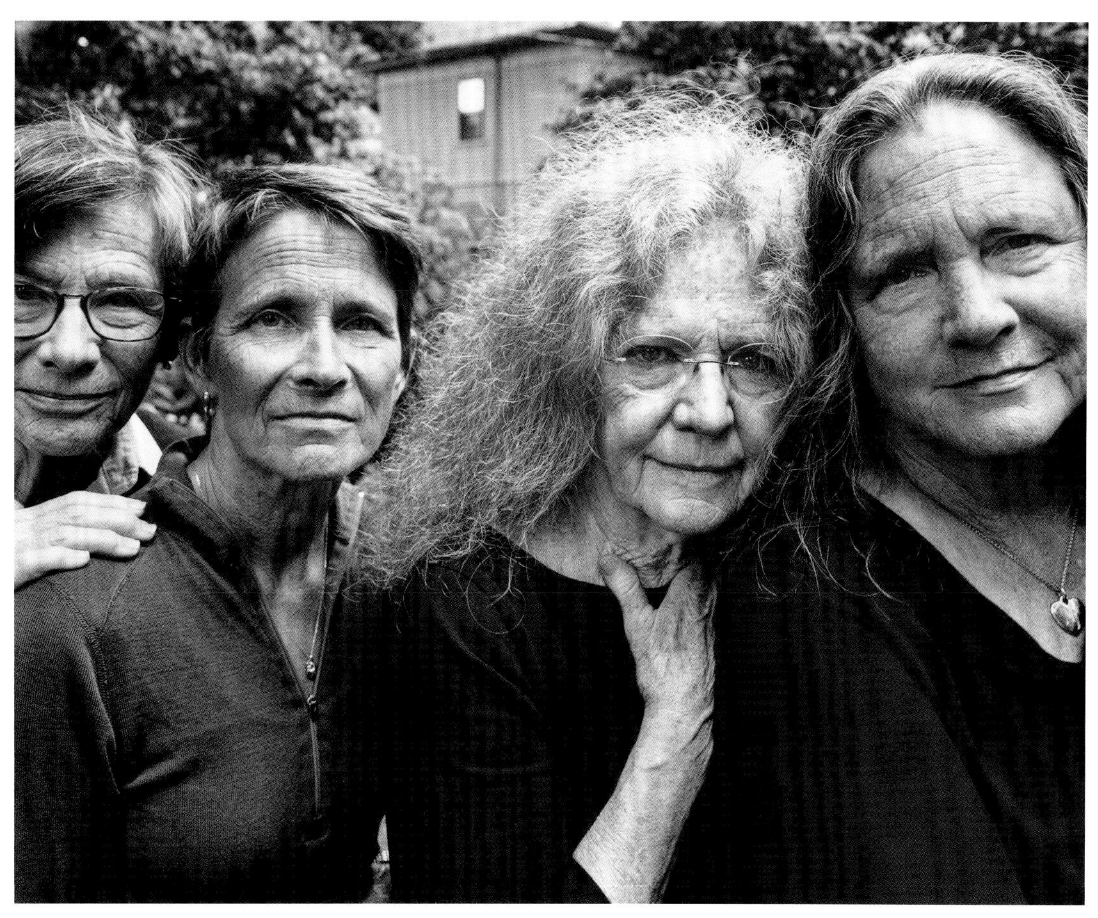

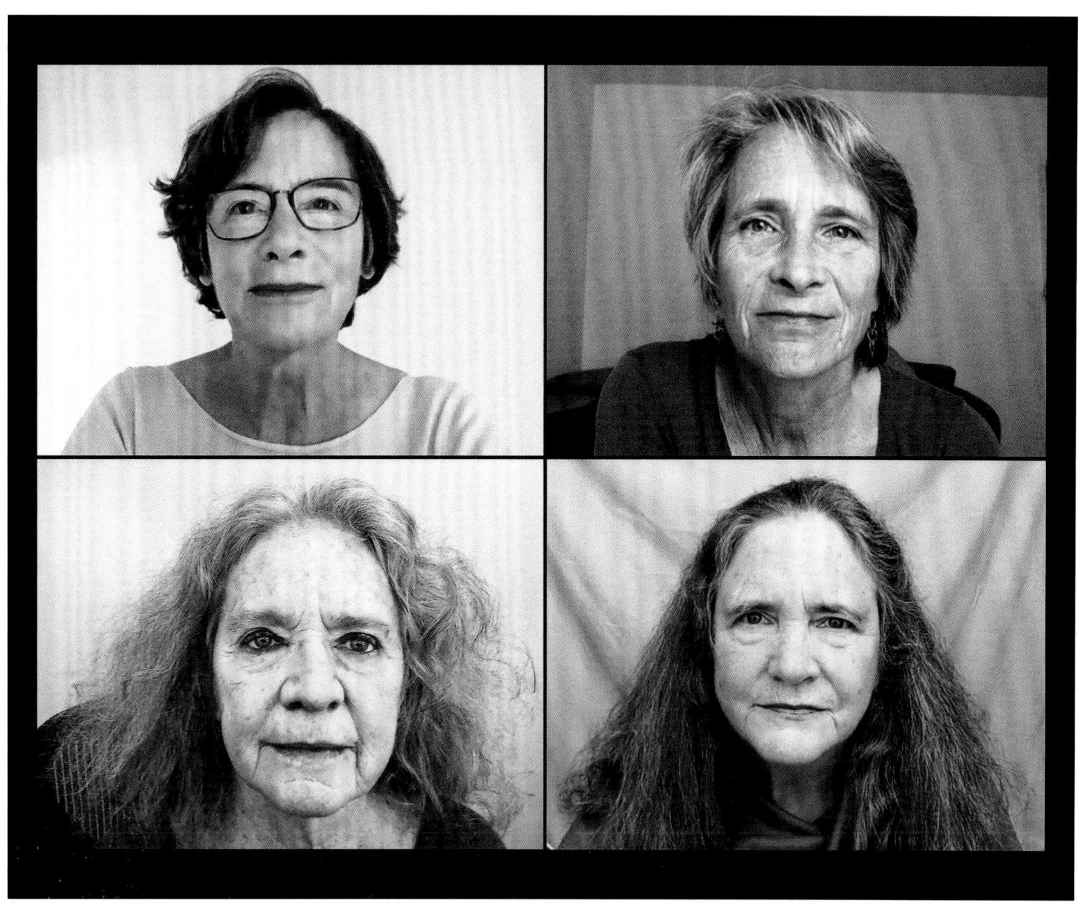

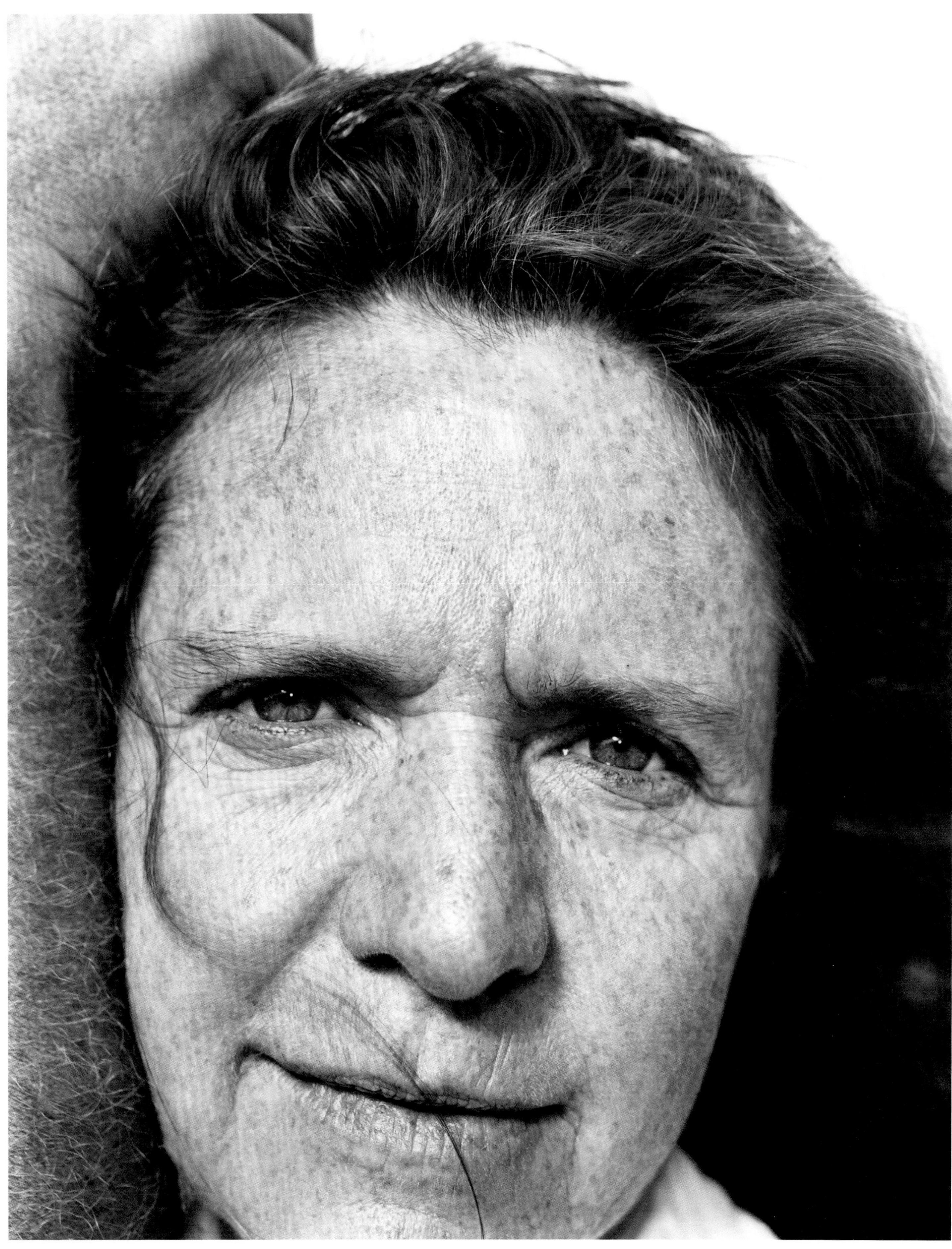

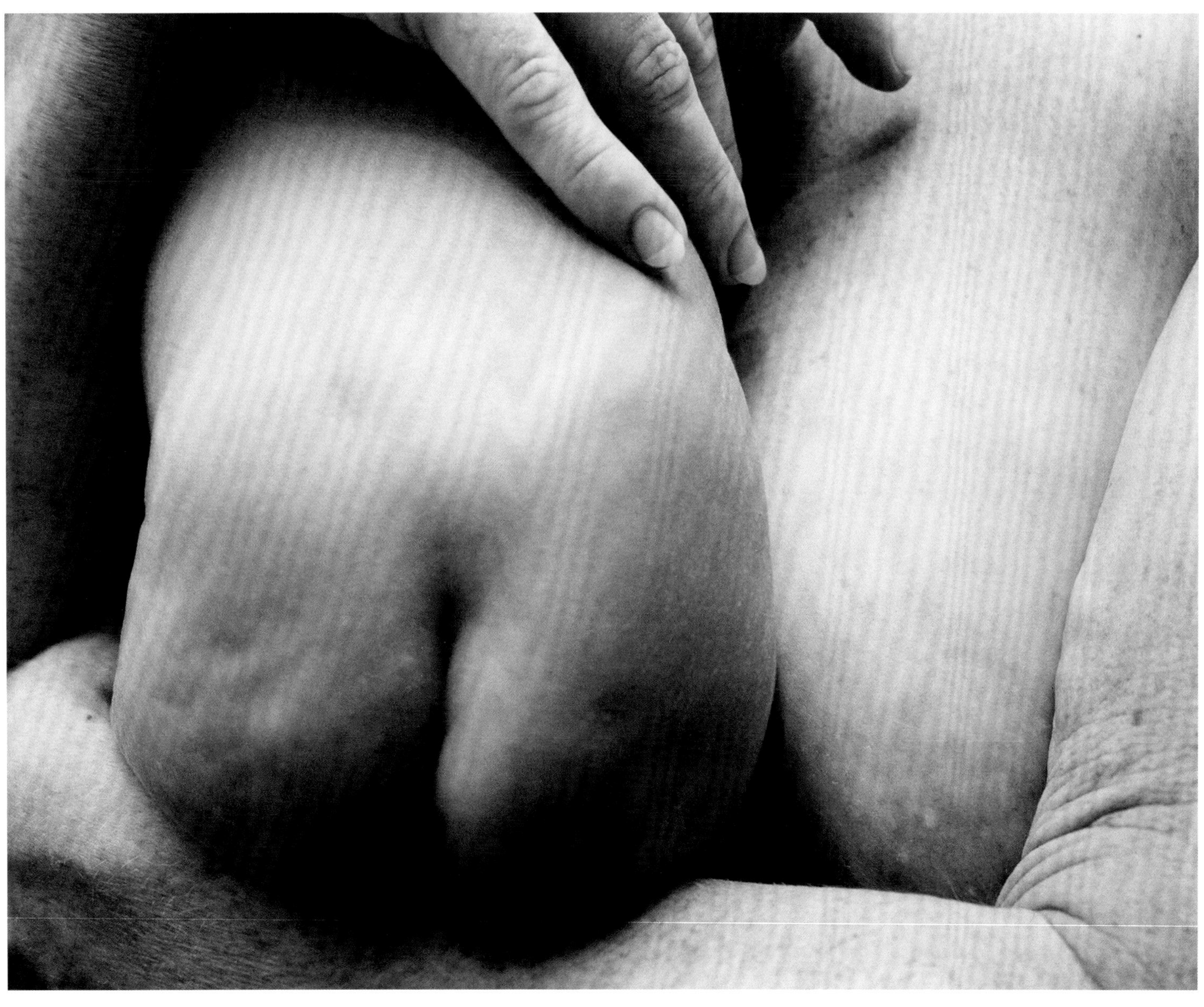

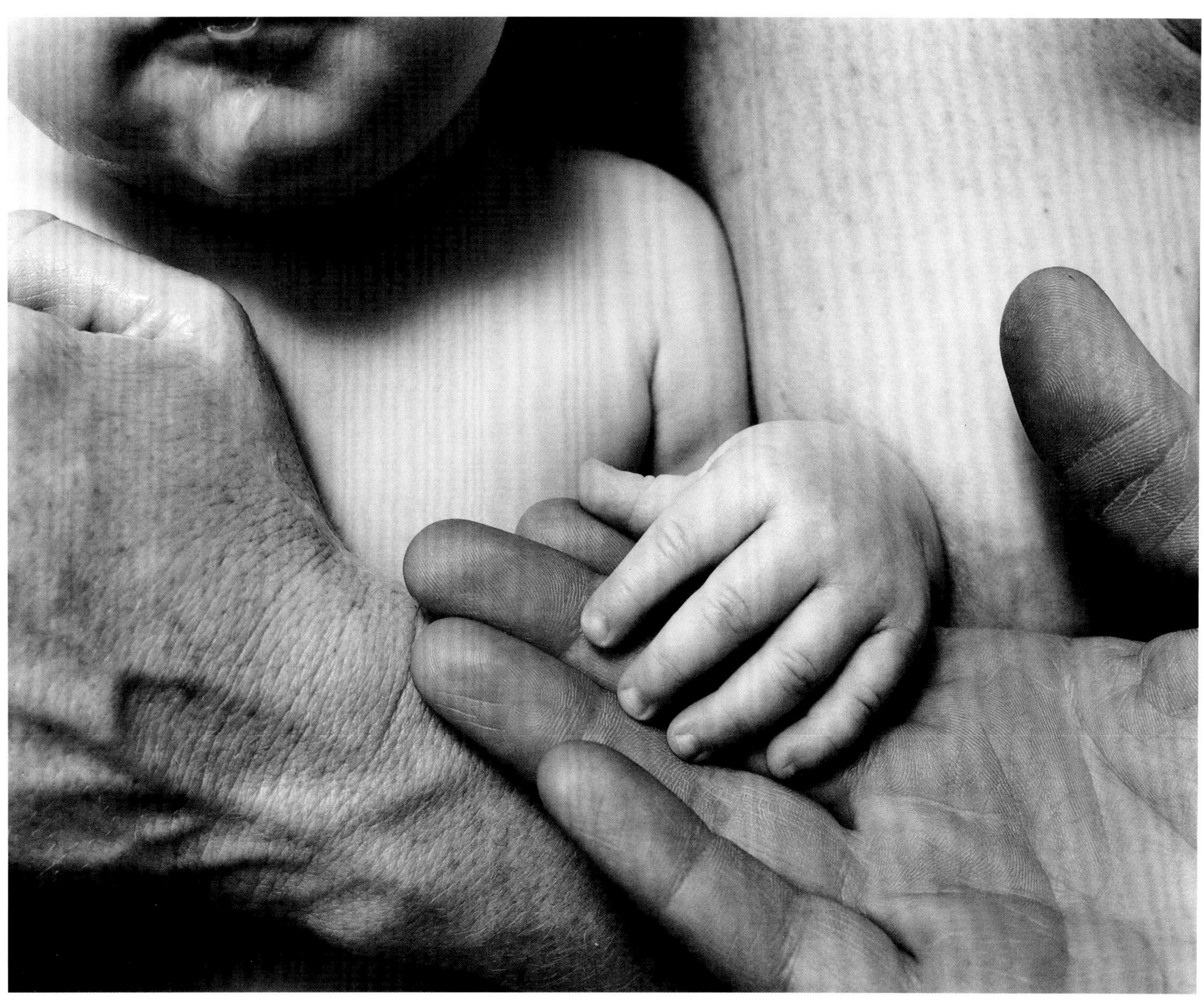

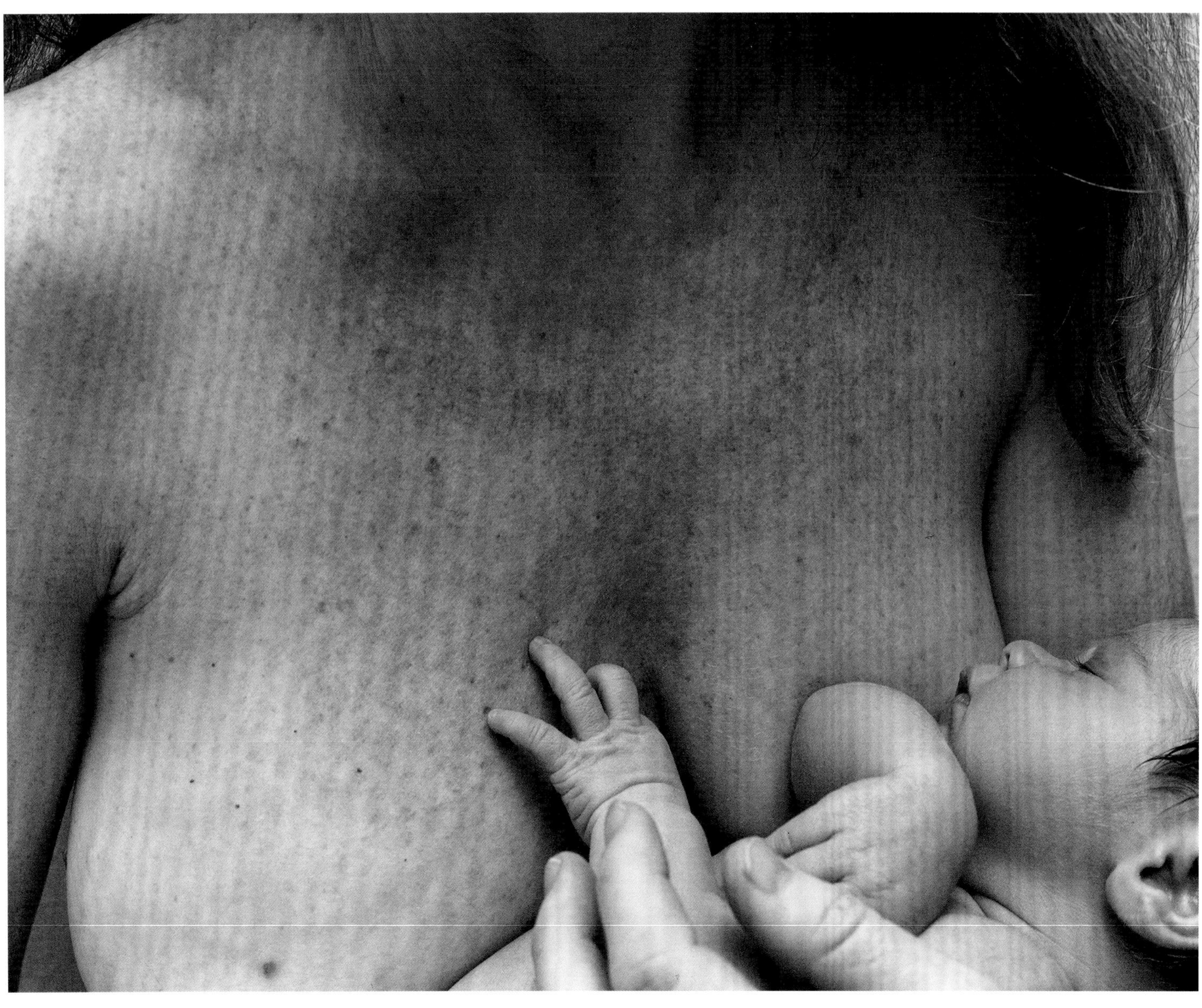

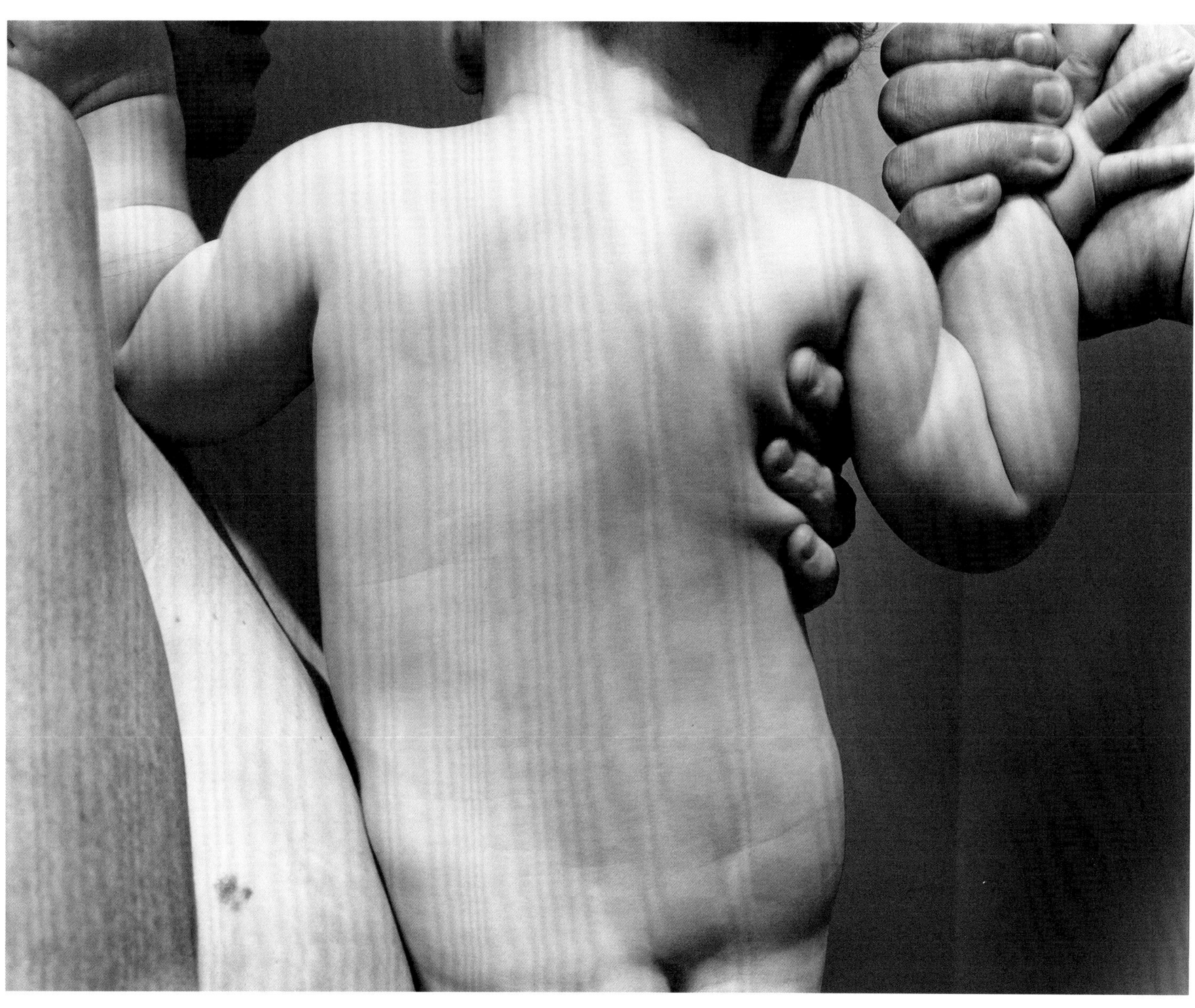

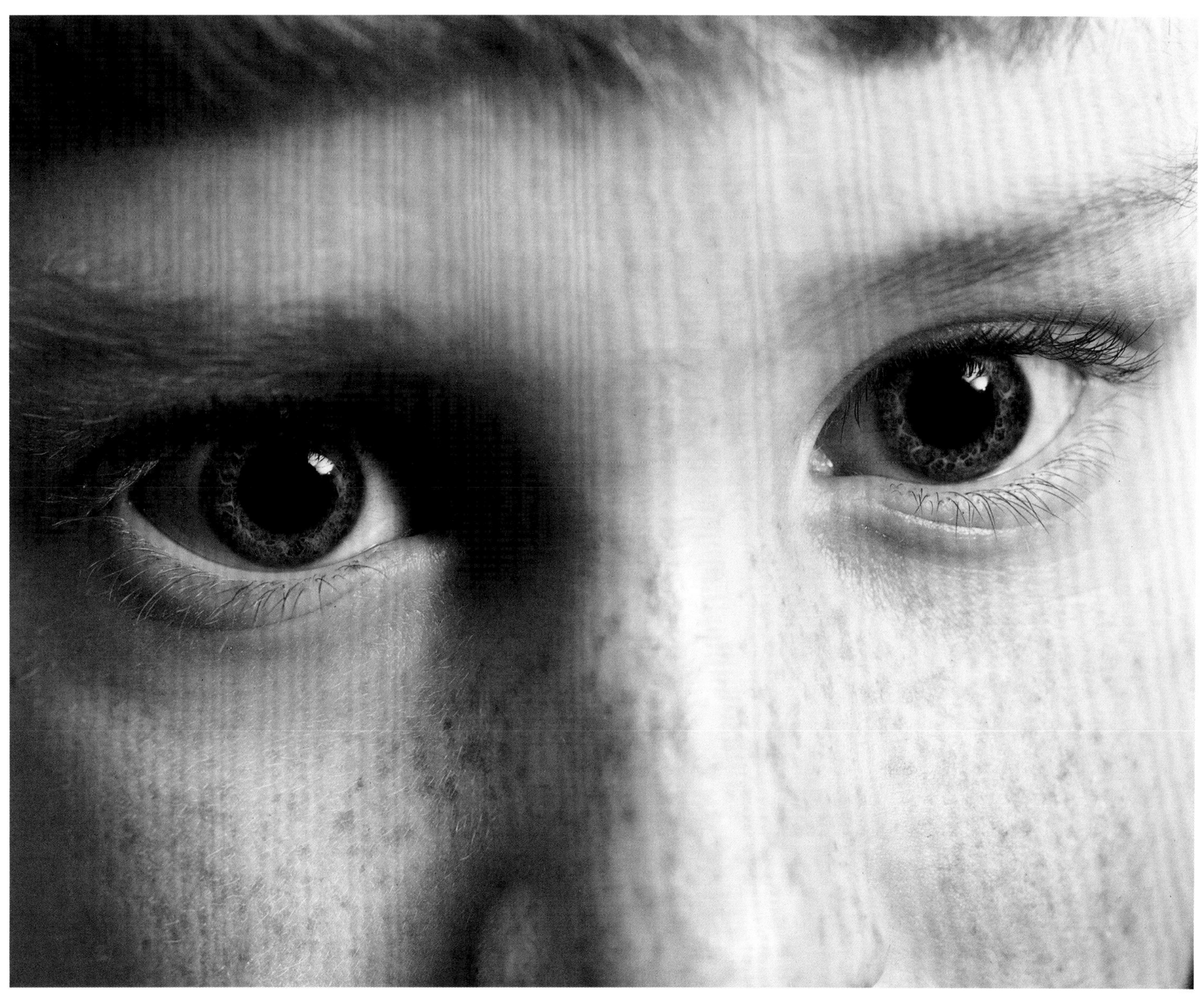

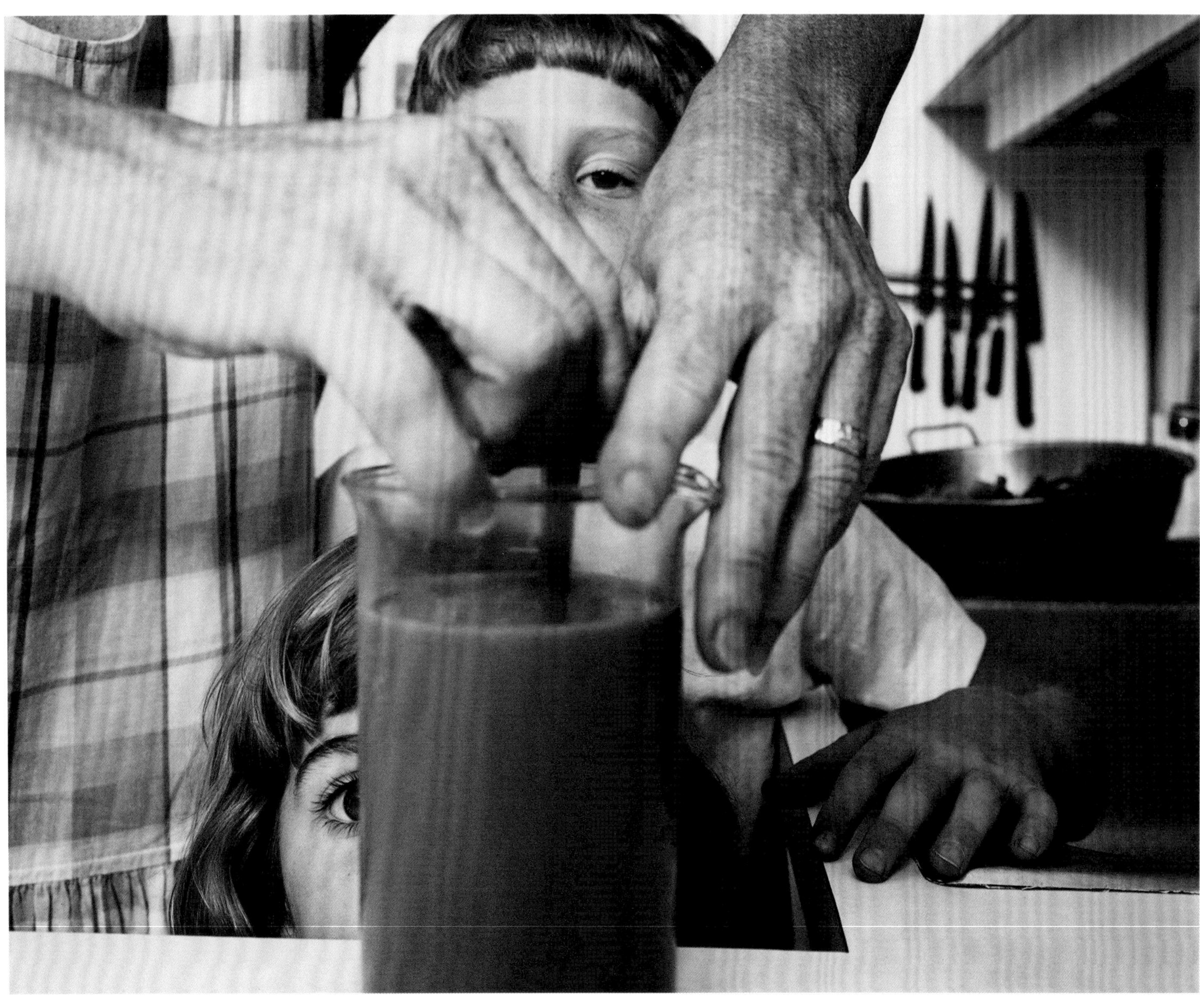

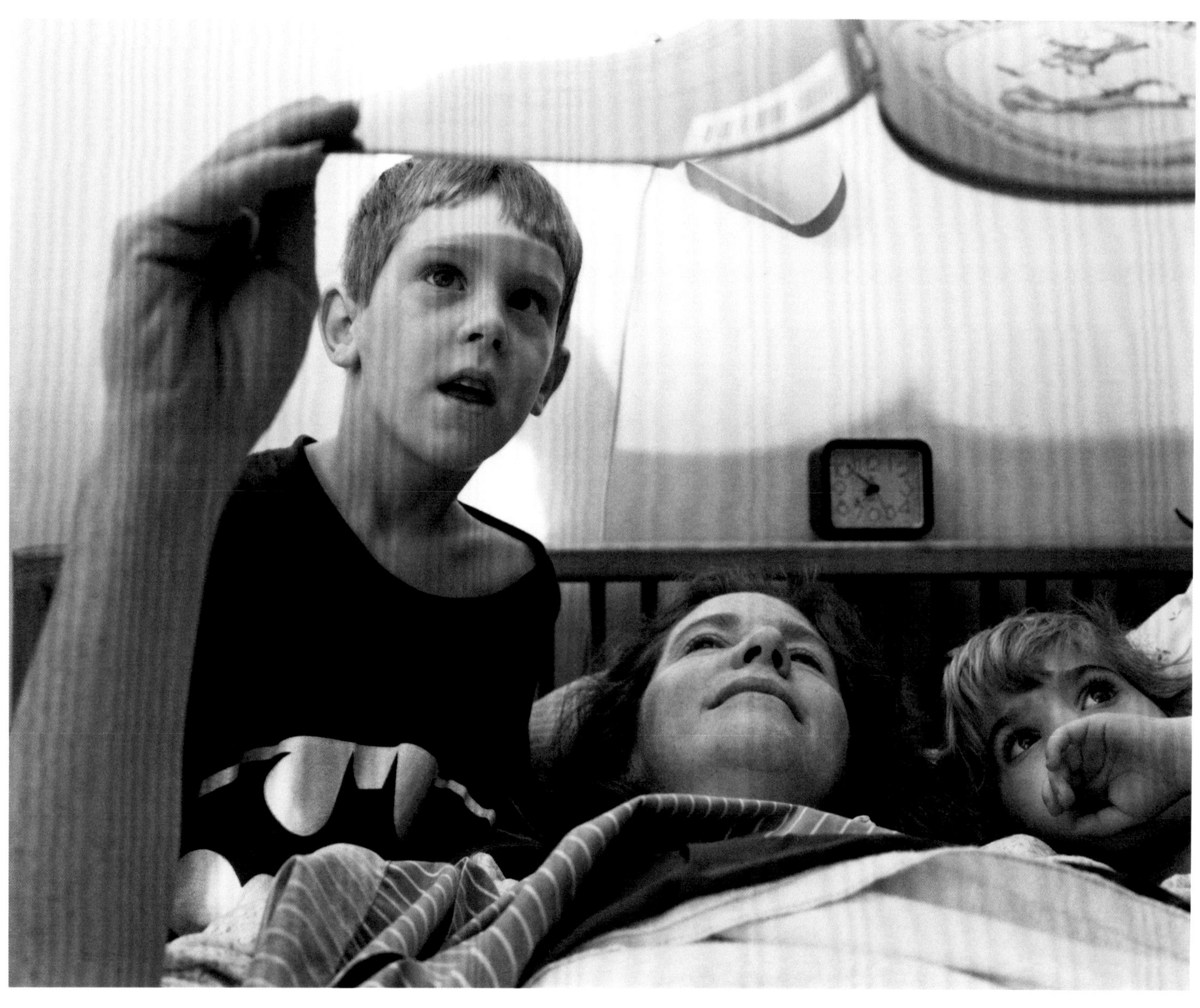

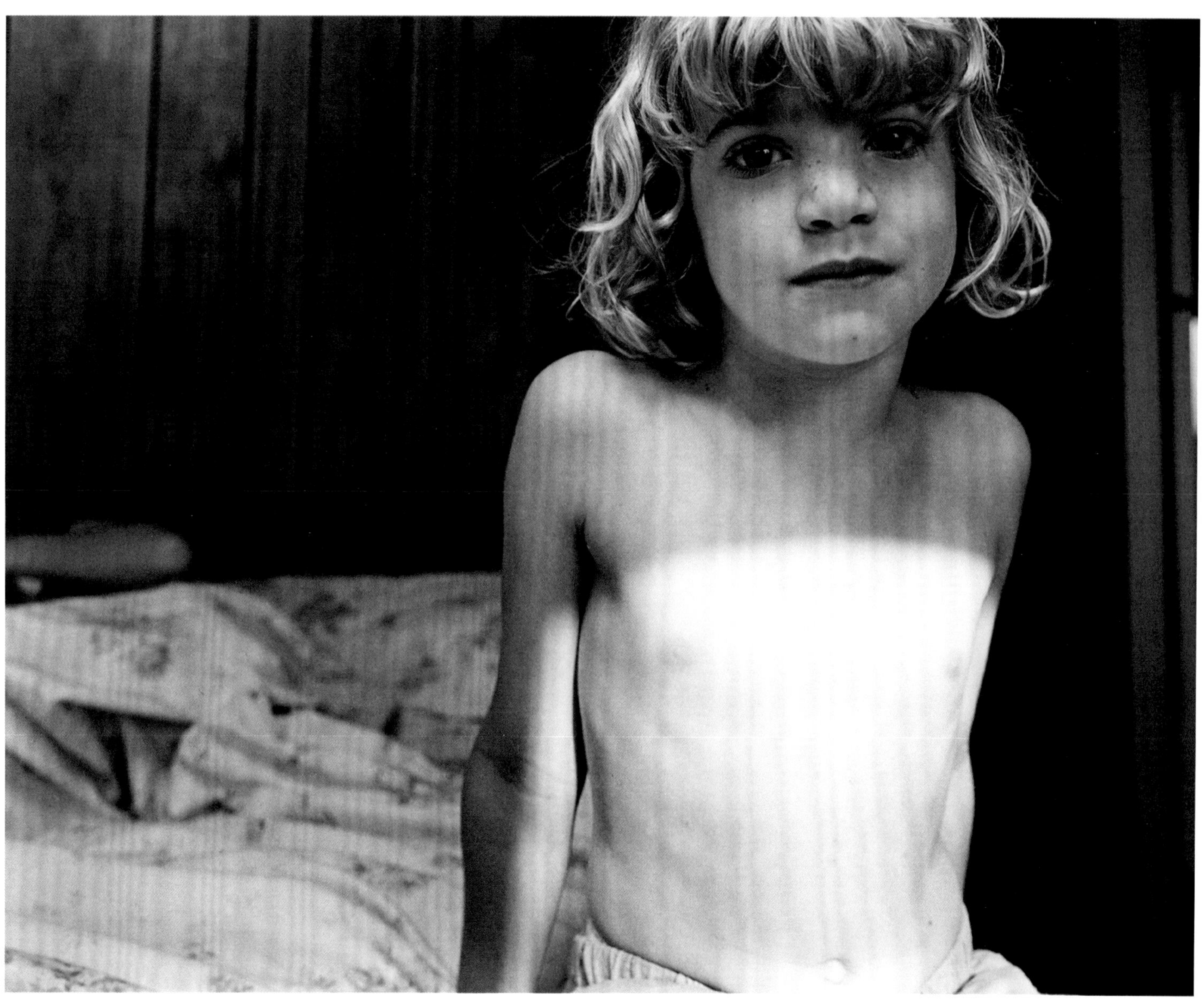

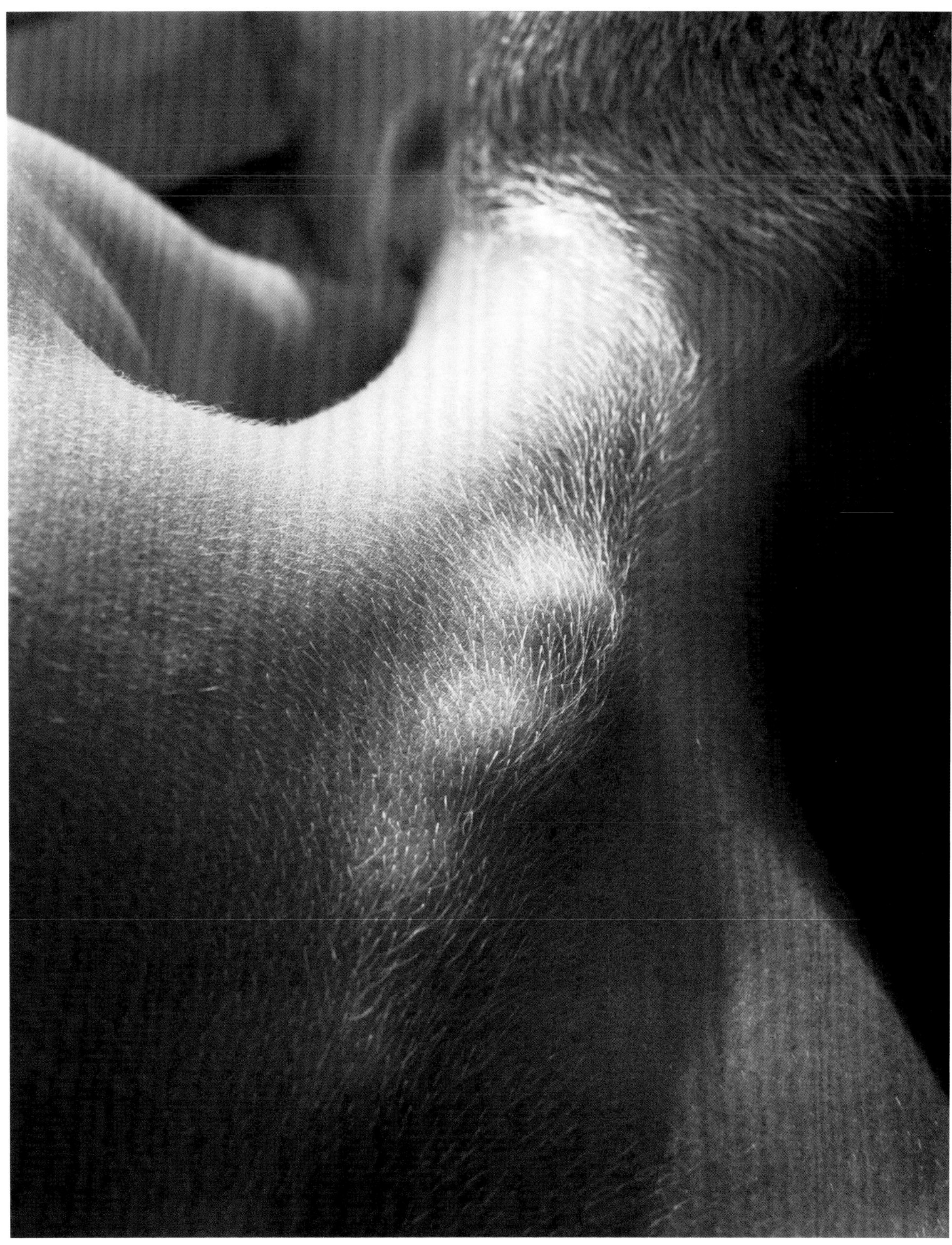

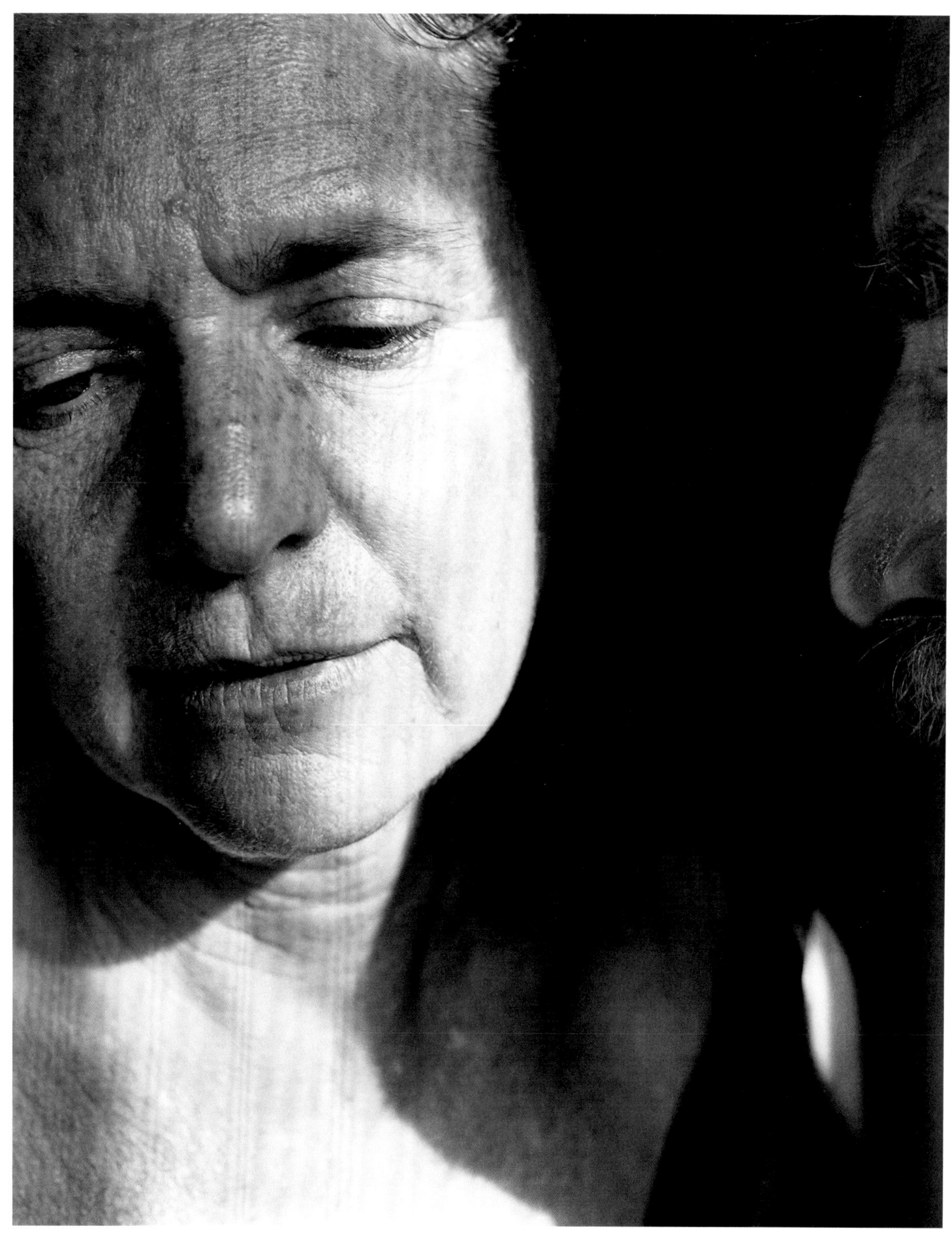

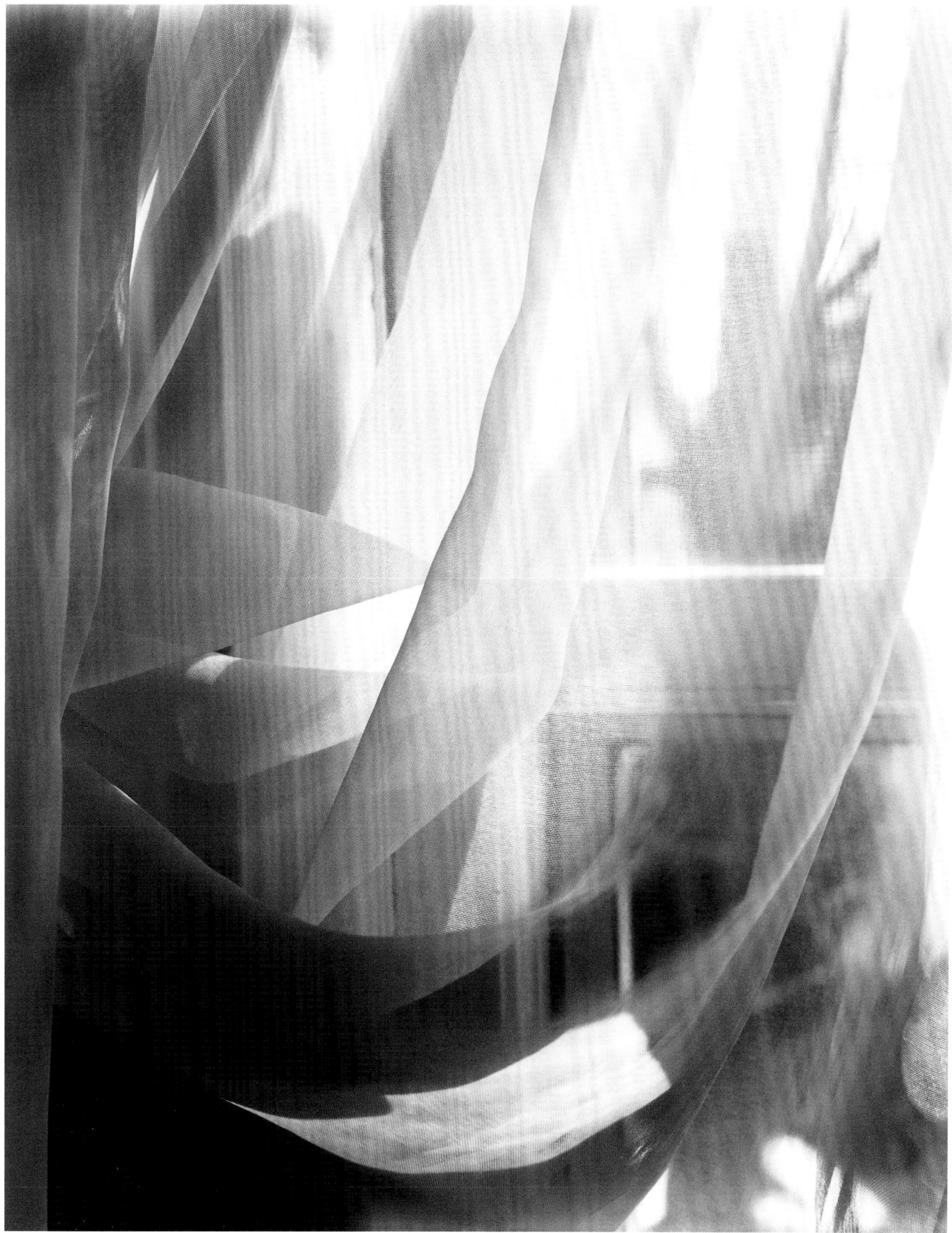

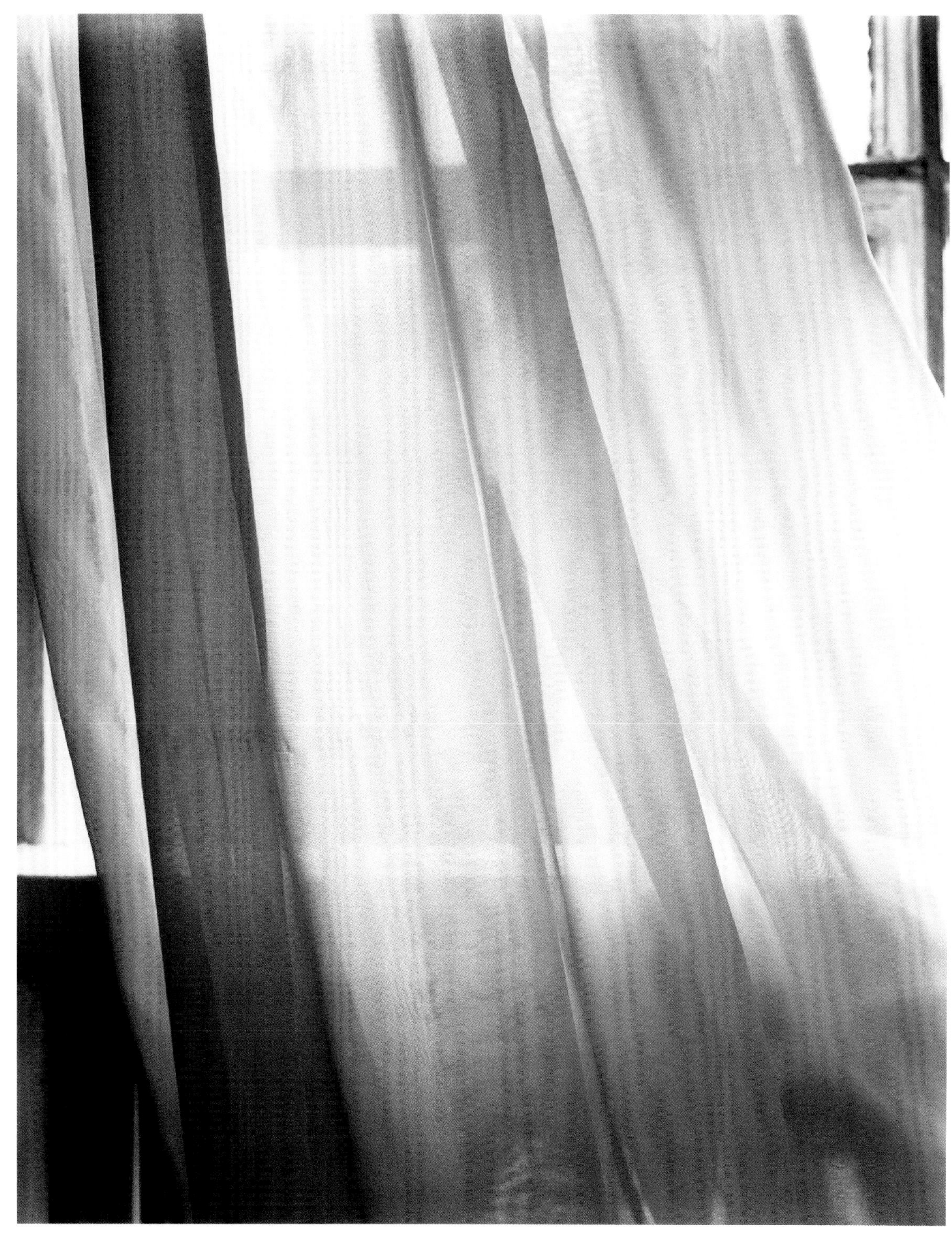

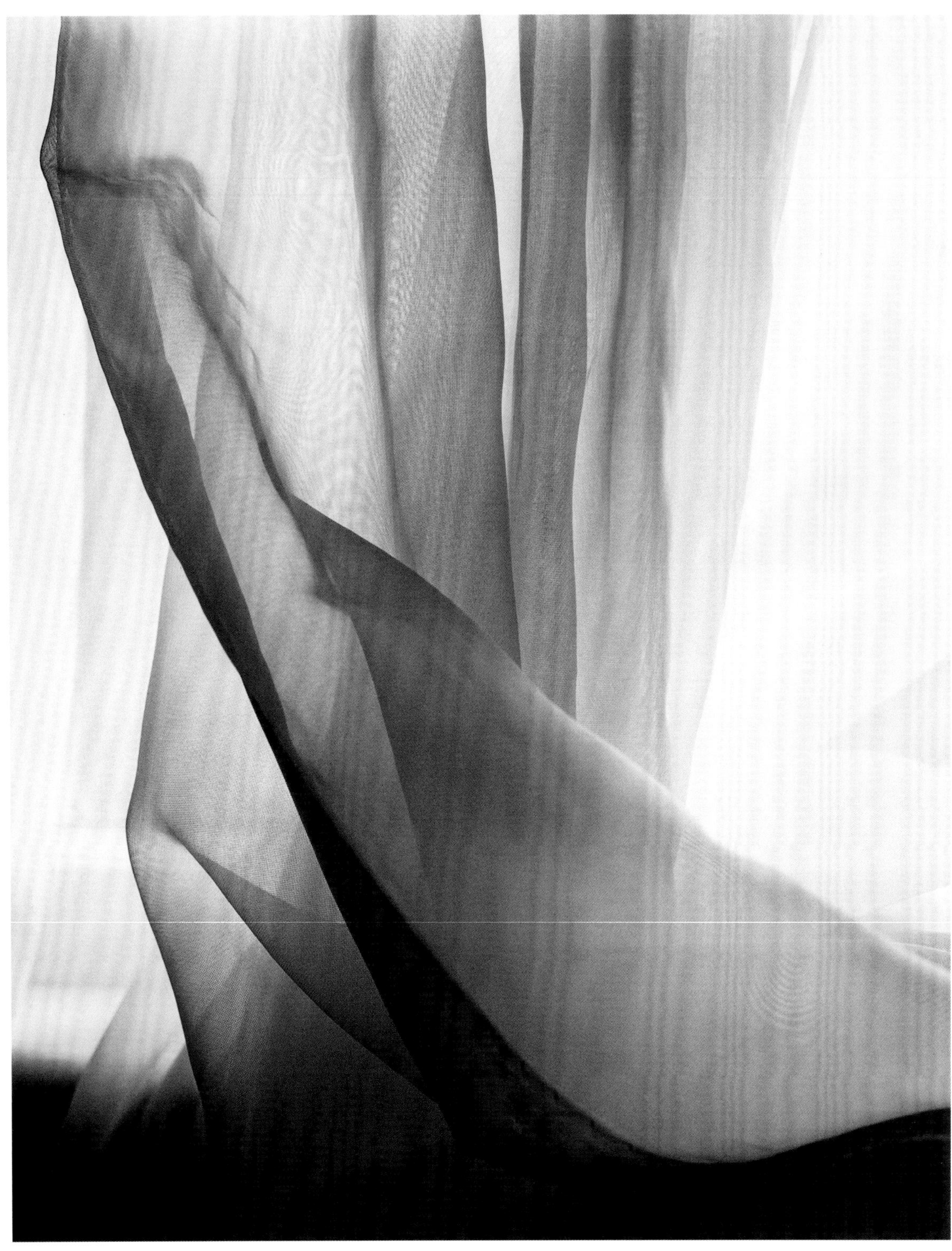

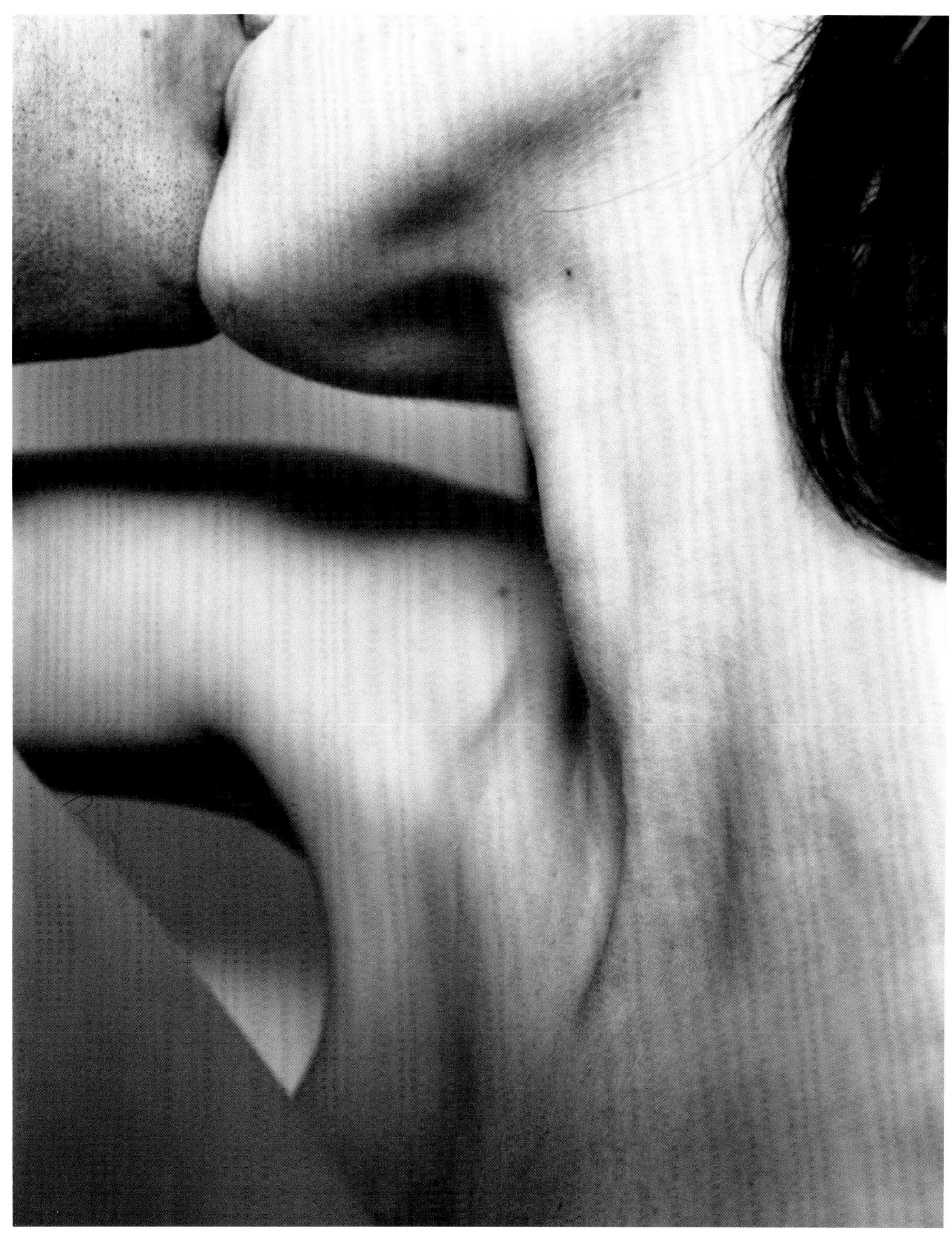

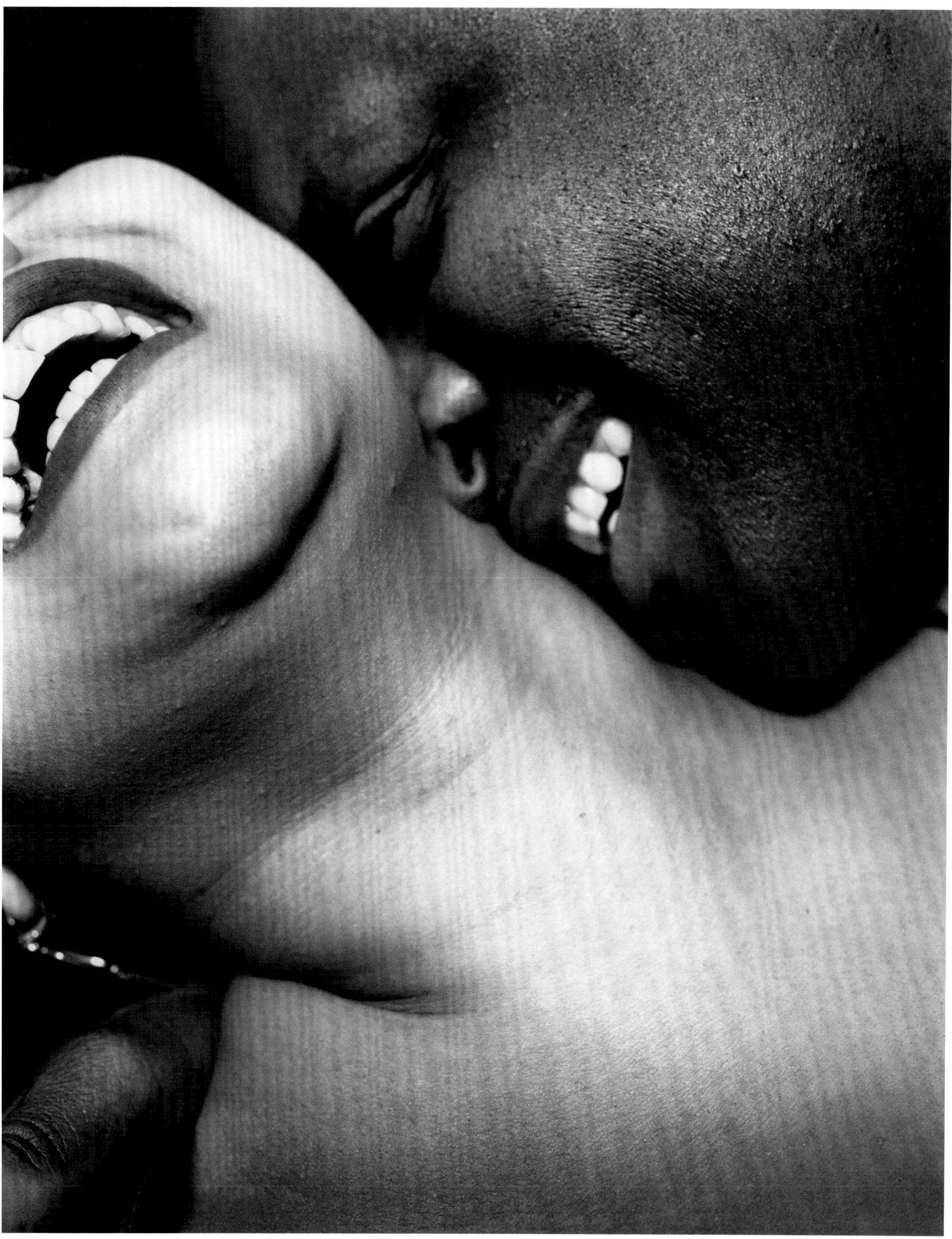

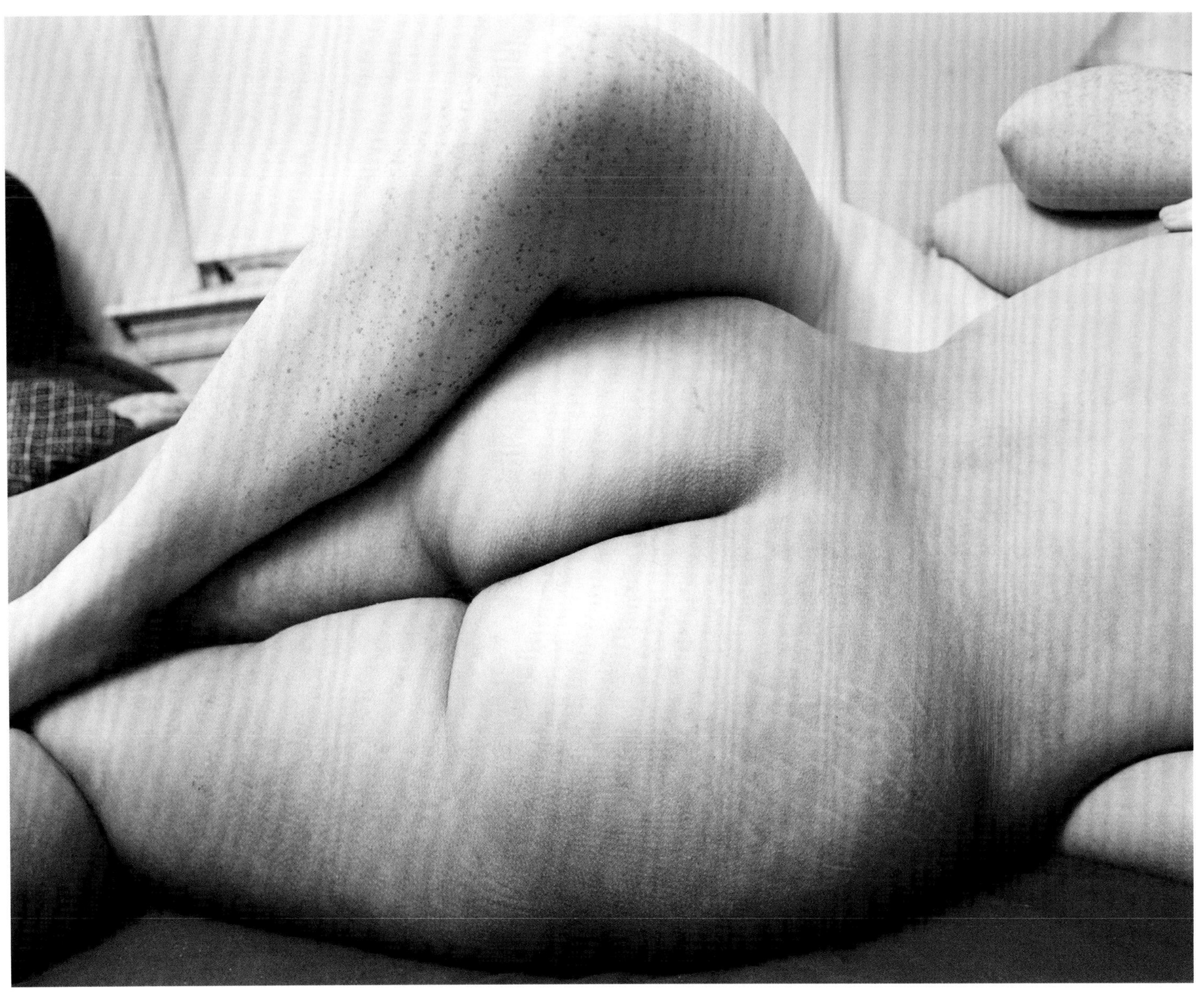

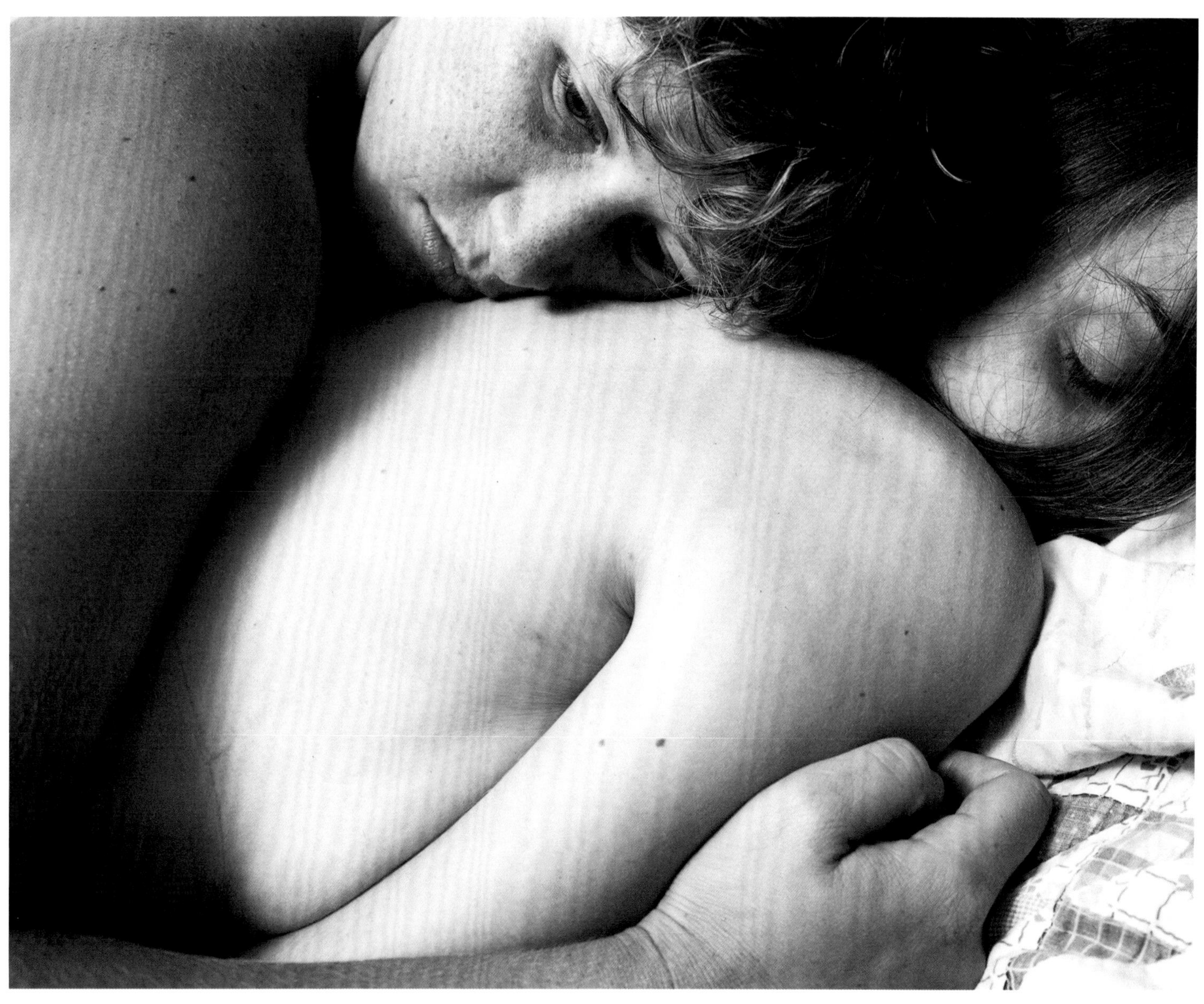

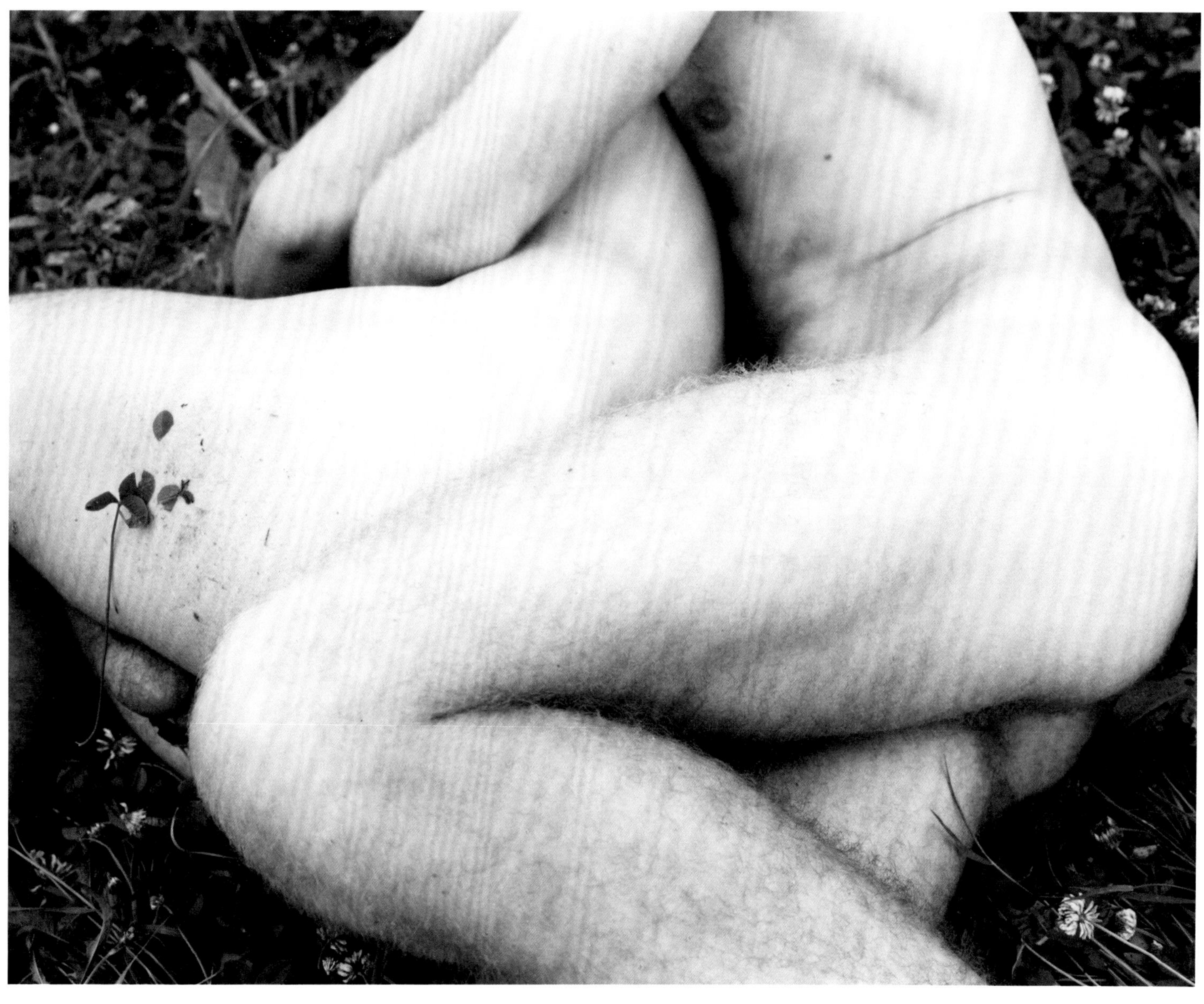

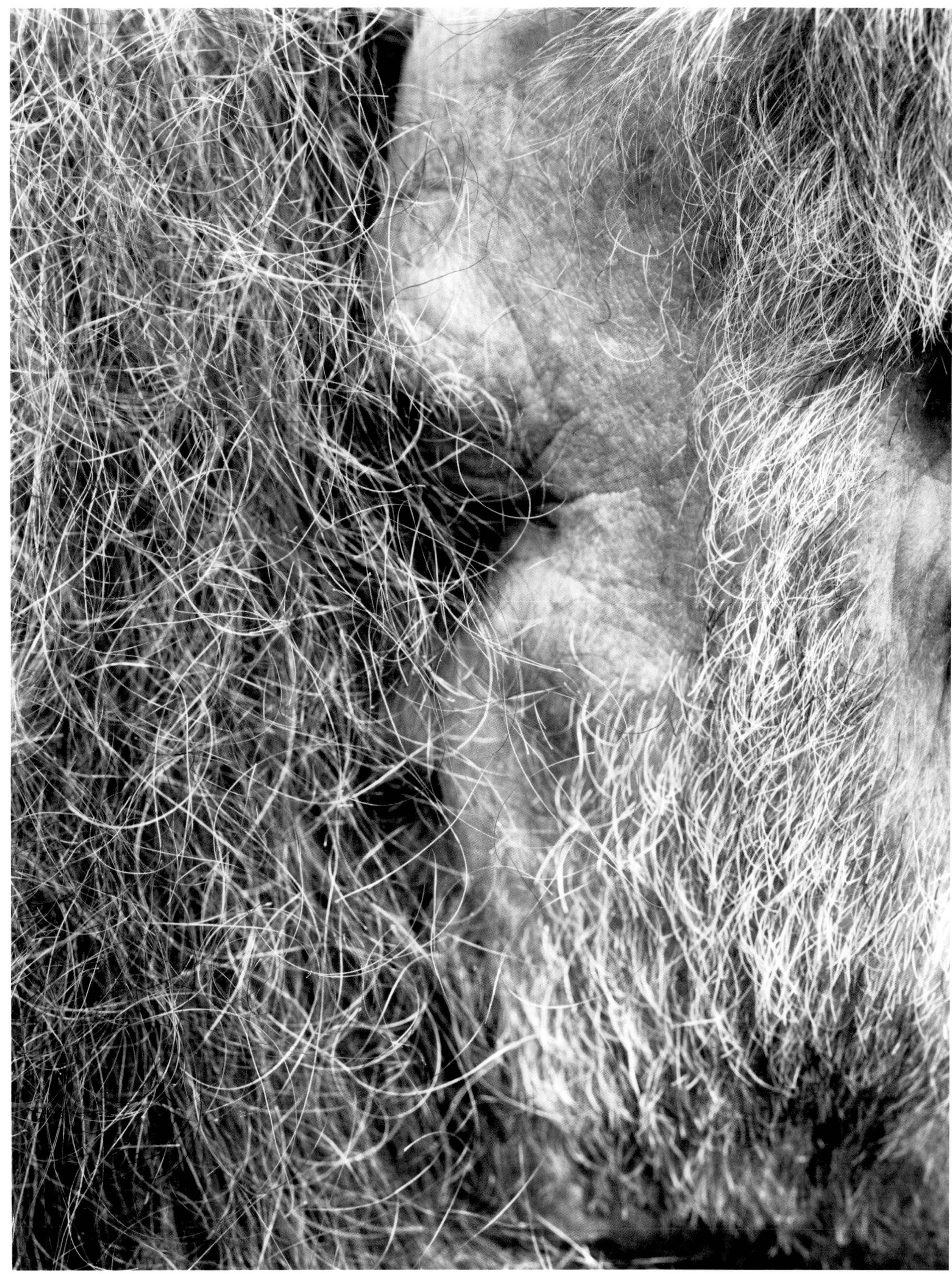

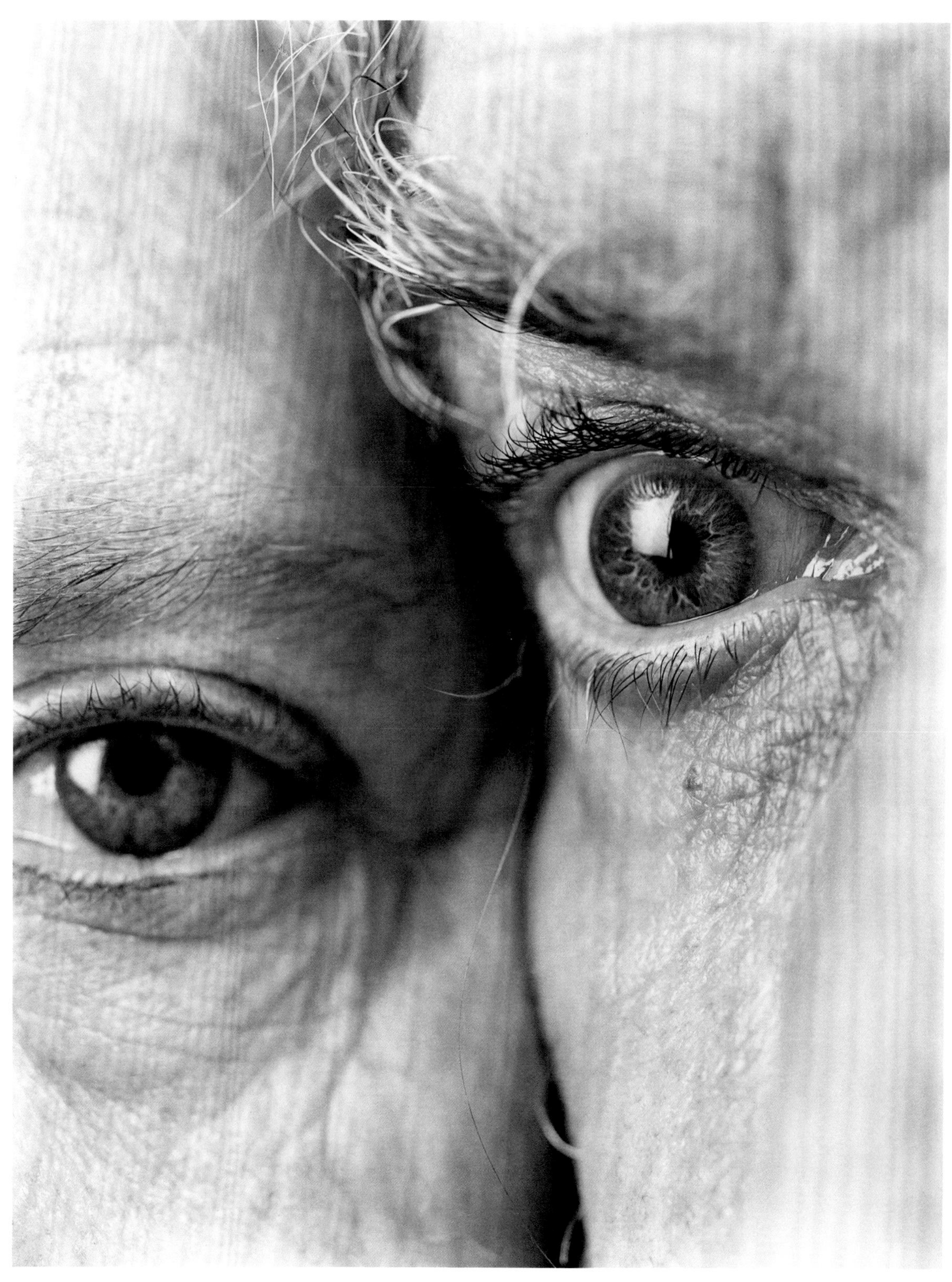

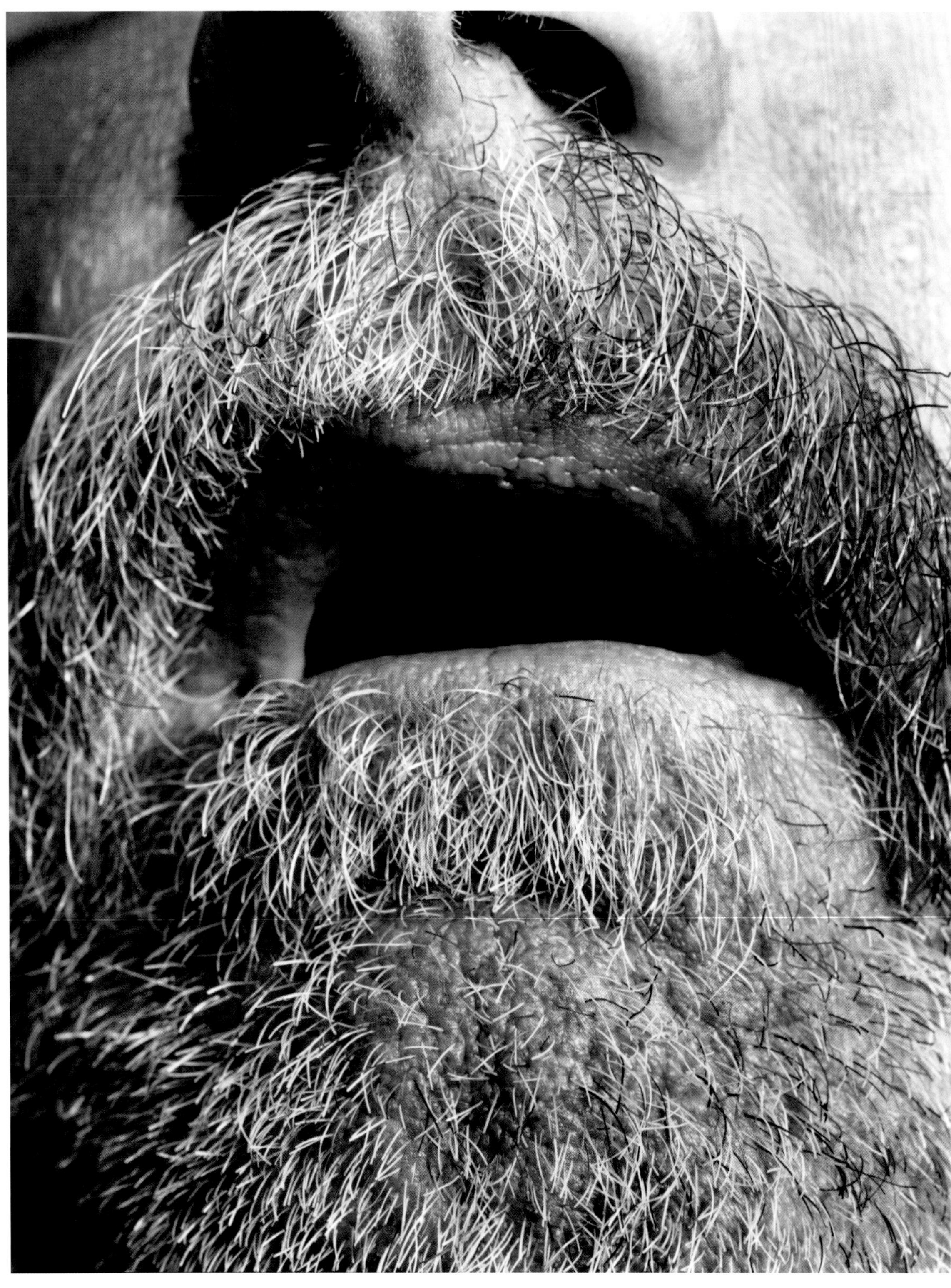

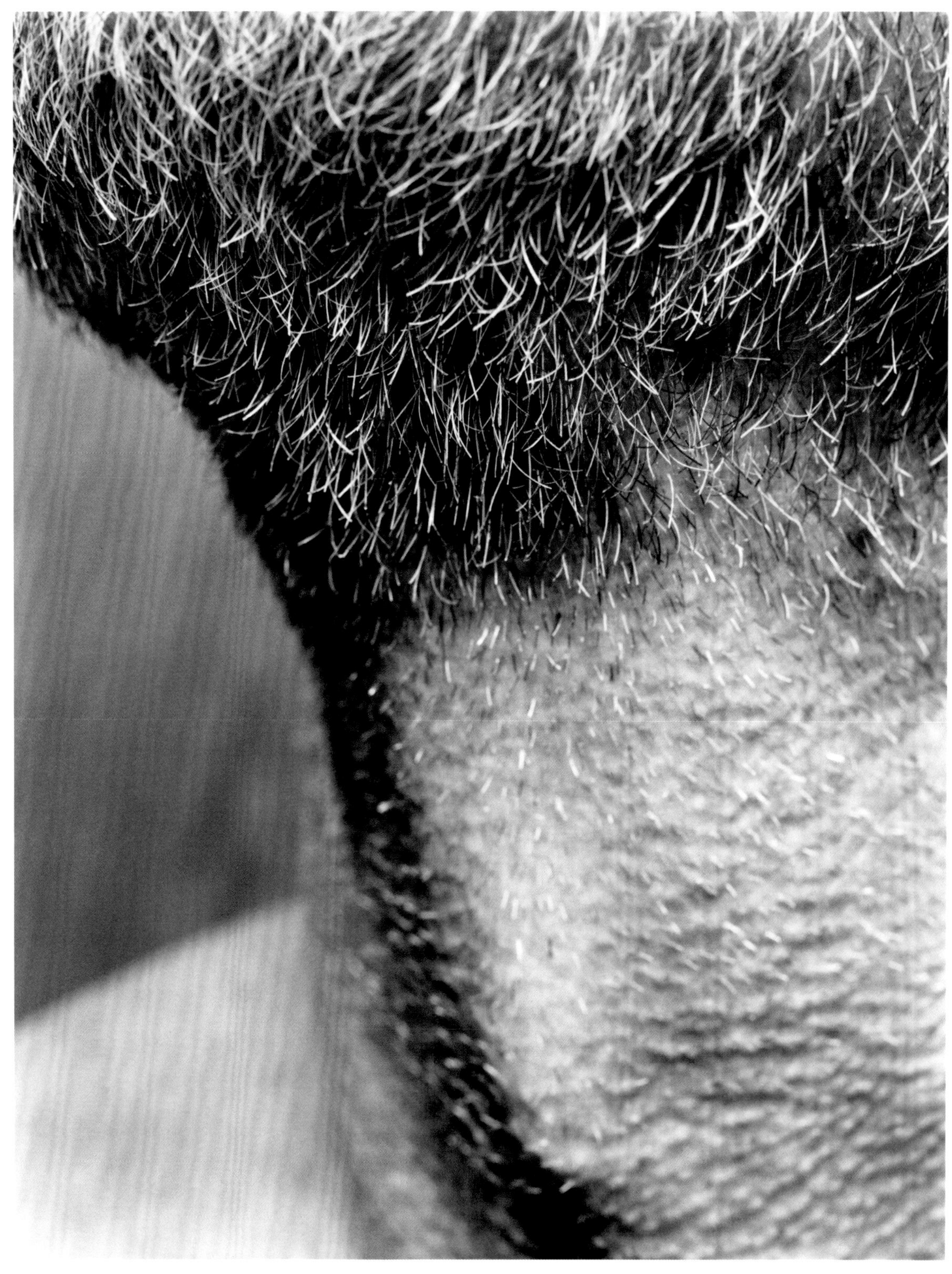

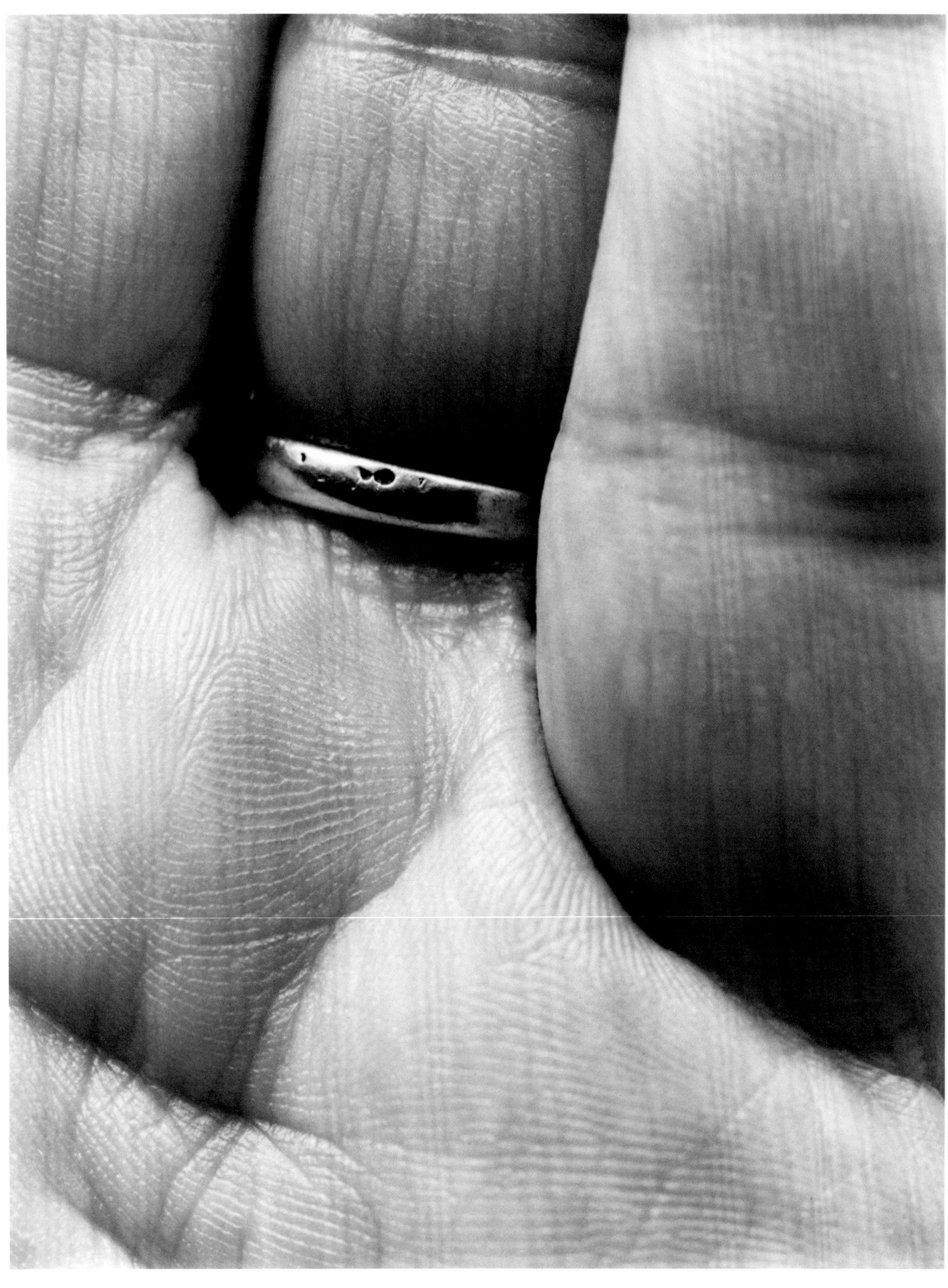

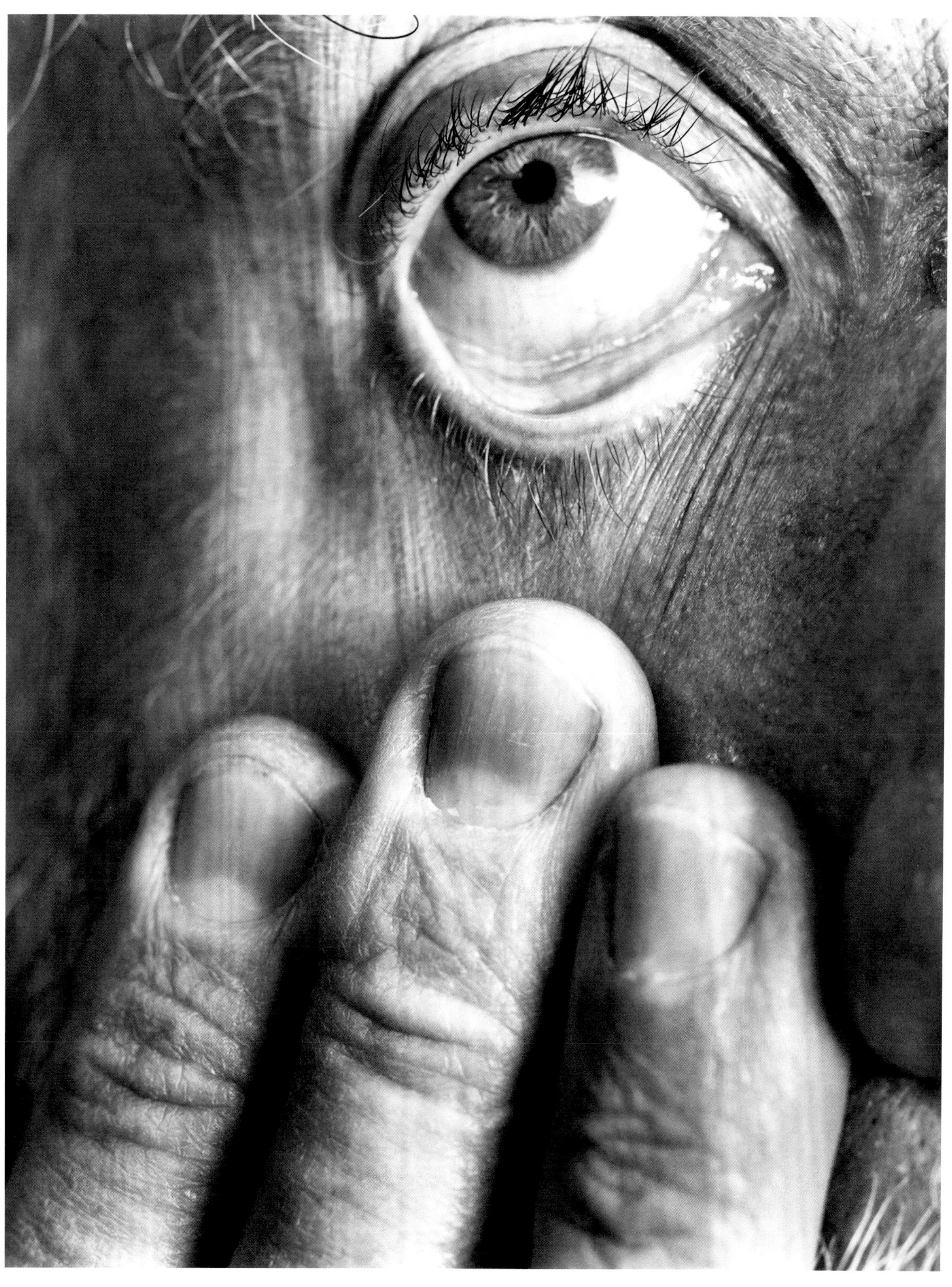

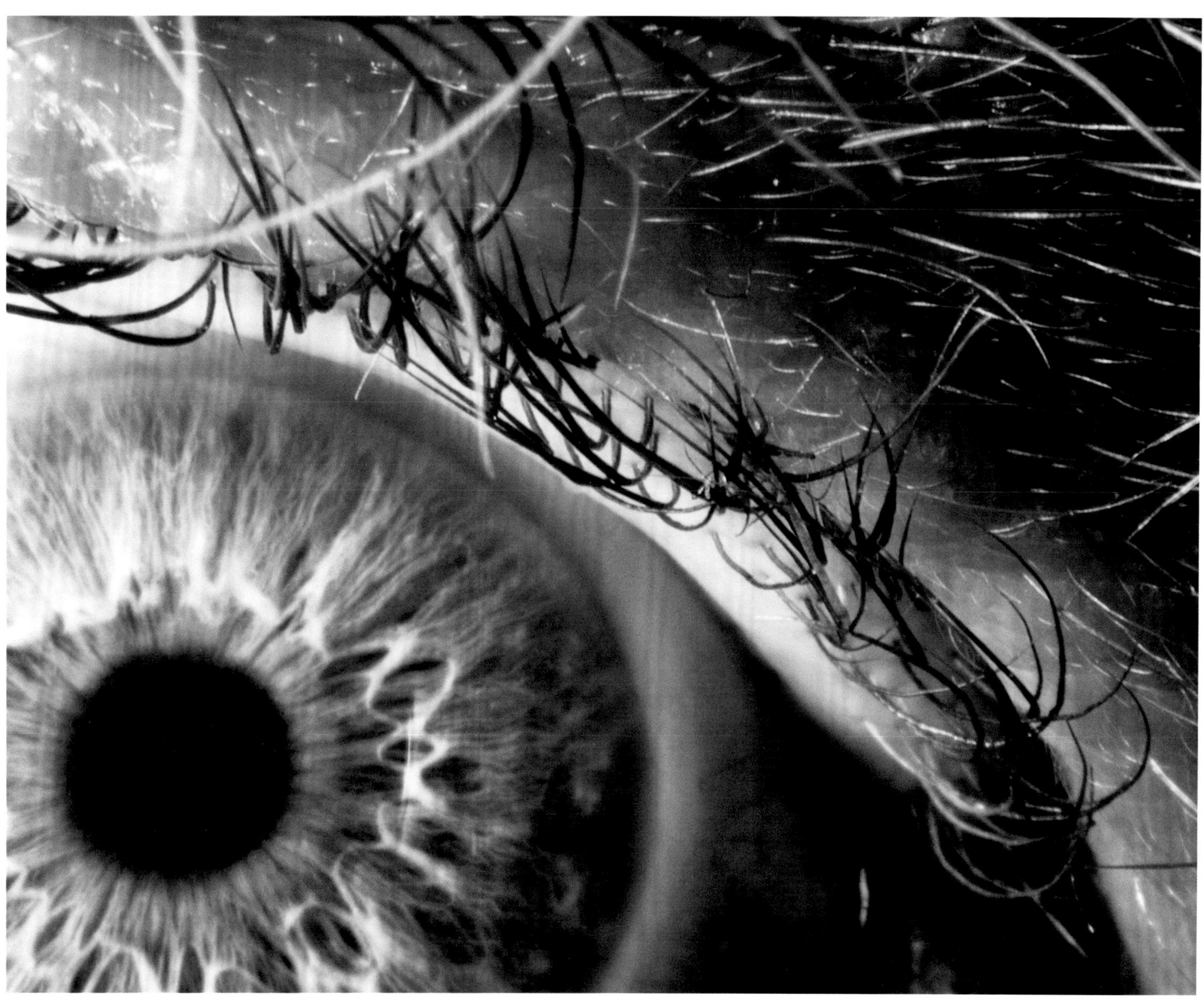

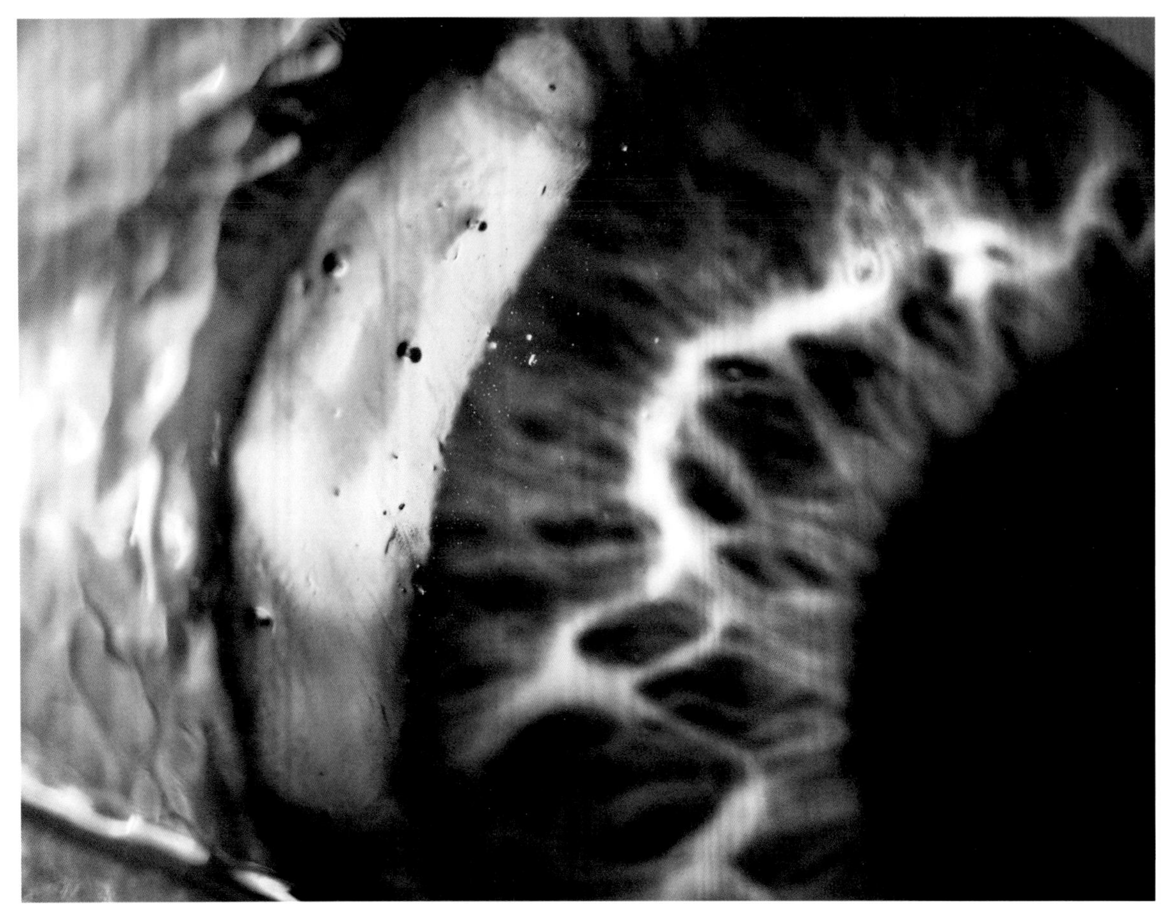

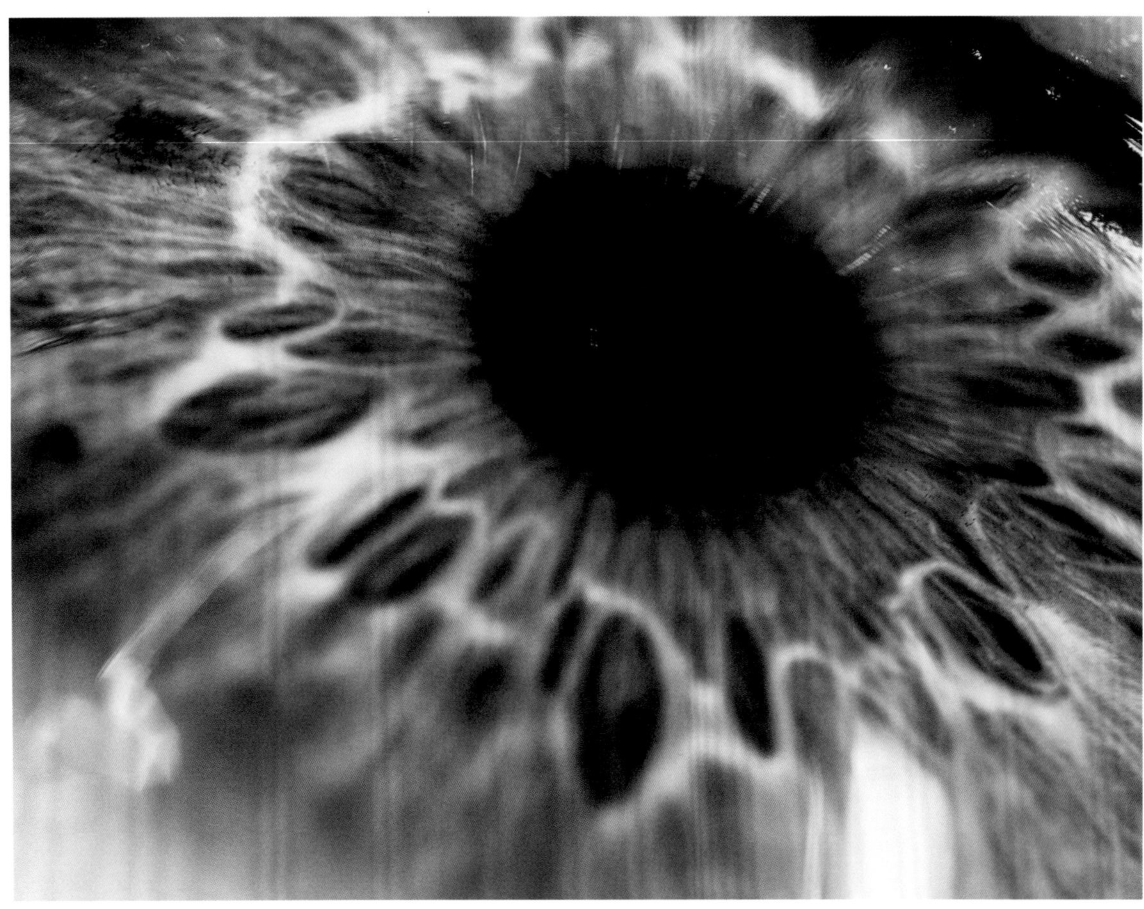

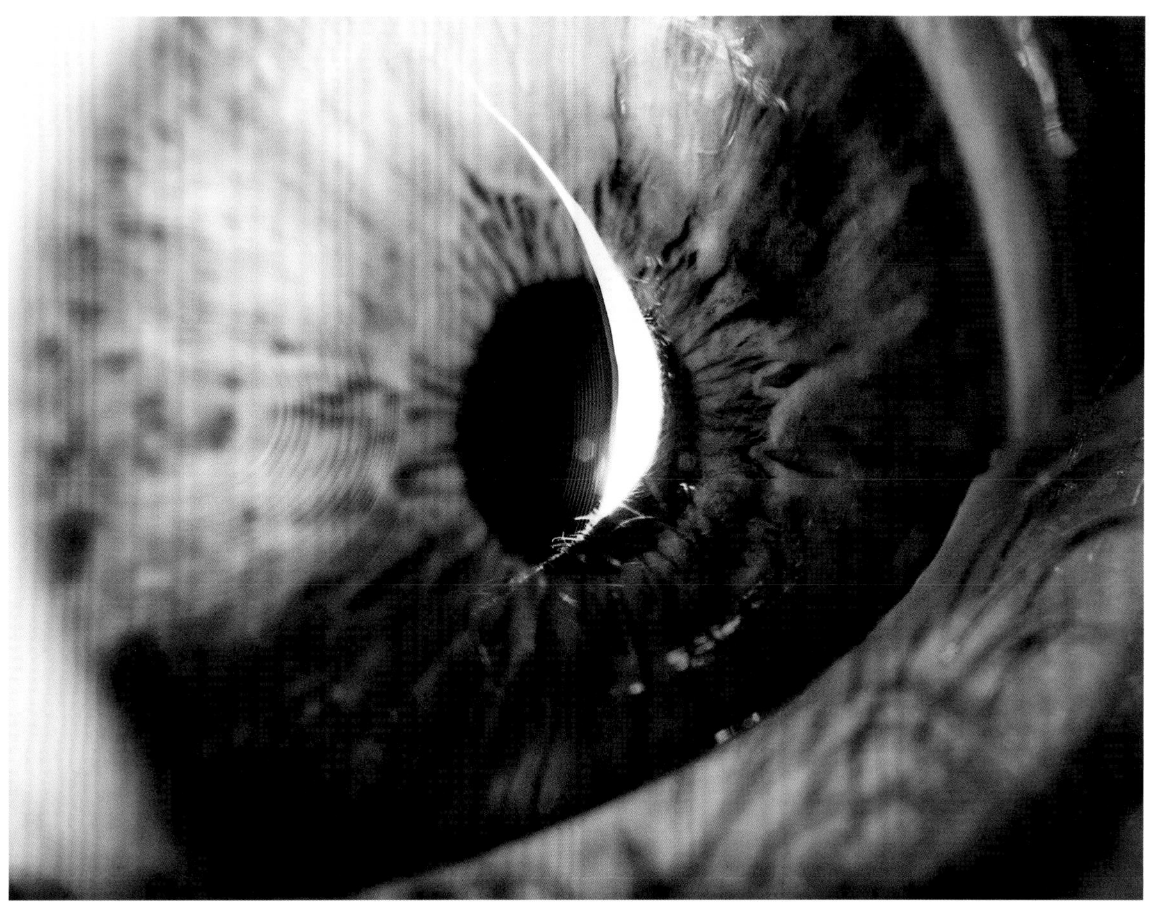

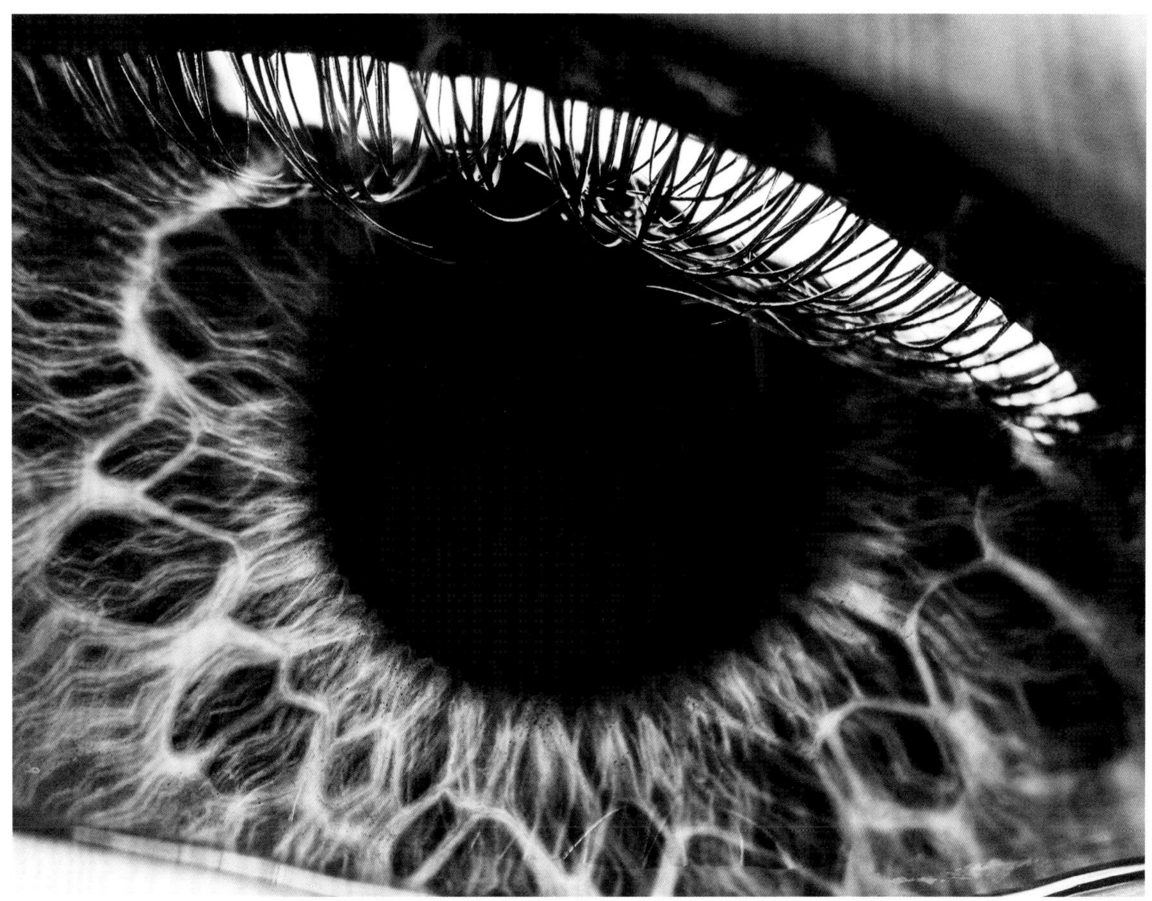

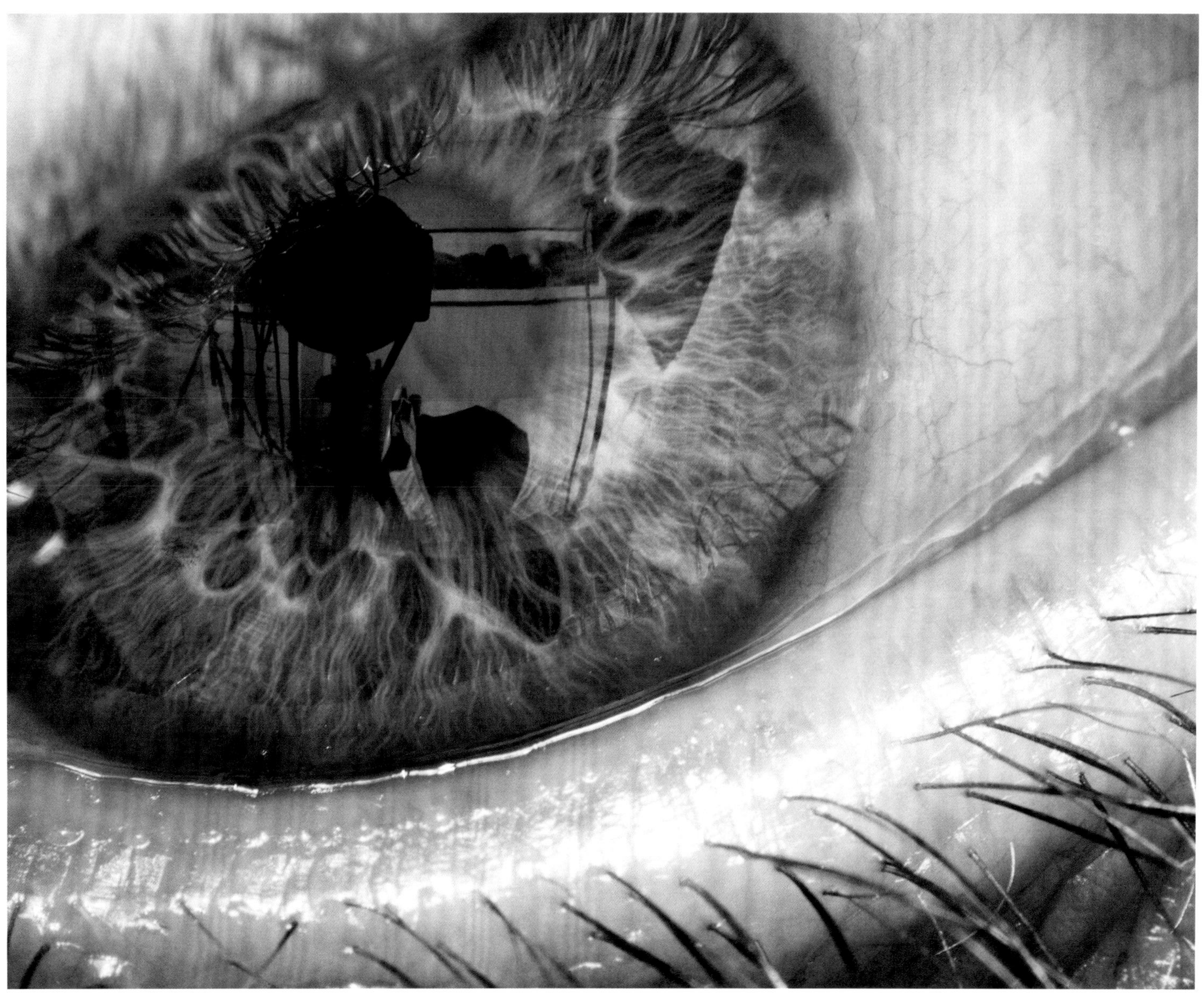

...one becomes a discoverer, seeing a new world through the lens. And finally the complete idea is there, and completely revealed.

Edward Weston

We met Nicholas Nixon nearly 20 years ago. He first entered our lives alone. A mutual friend had told him about us, about the ocean that runs the length of our city, and the beauty of the Basque Country. He was in search of new faces, couples, people who love each other. He was also eager to travel and practice his French. We wanted to talk about photography and know more about his work. One day, he arrived. He had hired a bicycle to discover the surrounding cities and villages with his large-format camera, a magnificent, timeless and mysterious object. When evening came, he told stories, evoked his family, friends, students, and all his models. And he photographed us, us and our son who was still little, who he had tamed.

The following year, he returned with his wife Bebe, who we felt as though we'd known since she was teenager, like her three sisters. Then it was the turn of Clementine, his daughter, who put down her luggage at our place on her tour of Europe, her mind brimming with projects. From one voyage to the next, through email messages, letters, and images, we had together seen our families, friends, the world and its inhabitants change. For 20 years, we spoke of waves here, trees there, the snow in their garden, hydrangeas on our hills, French books or films we had liked or disliked (both Nicholas and Bebe are real Francophiles), about our friends, children, shockwaves in the news, our fears and joys. Nothing more, nothing less, as in his photographs.

Today, our son is a young adult and there are obviously many more photos of the Brown Sisters in the series than when I discovered it. It is also thanks to these portraits—his, theirs, ours—that I see the passage of time. That is what it's all about. Time made visible. About time, which of course unravels us, but also binds us. Nicholas's gaze is a perspective on time. Over the years, it is as though it has become more acute and rigorous, almost vertiginously.

When he photographed AIDS patients in the late 1980s, emaciated and nearing death, hiding nothing of the ravages of the disease, he forced us to look deep into their eyes and in so doing, even though their days were numbered, their end announced, he built bridges. Moreover, he transmuted our gazes, all gazes, into bonds.

Nicholas photographs life—and therefore also sometimes death—in the eyes of all those who agree totally to abandon themselves before his lens, as though placing their trust in a caregiver. Nothing is foreign to him when it comes to what crops up along our path on earth and all of it is found in his images: newborns, children, caresses, couples, kisses, the softness of the skin and wrinkles that furrow it, the hair whitening, the questions, joys, illness, extreme weakness, tenderness, great age, the end of the struggle, peace.

And everywhere, love. Love for his wife of course, Bebe, who has been present throughout his work and life, ever since they met, and who is also—was it an accident?—engaged in the care and support of the sick. Love for his children Clementine and Sam. For those or that which he photographs: a family on a porch, a tree with 100-year-old bark, or a city by night. But also, the love of photography, for the black and white that he has always carefully crafted, for his forays into color, and for the work of others, for this man who is both an art-book collector and infinitely curious about other artists, friends, students or strangers.

Certain photographs have a surprising ability to closely capture their subjects, fearlessly, unobtrusively, discreetly. When humans are the subject matter, and this is the case for Nicholas Nixon, the images explode the rules of proxemics, penetrating unobtrusively within our personal space so that an intimate distance between beings becomes the norm and not the exception. I have seen Nicholas approach his subjects, position his large-format camera more than a metre from them at first, respecting the ordinary rules of social distancing. Then he will disappear under the black canvas, and gently draw closer, to the point of reading the shiver of a grain of skin, the light on a cheek, a shock of stray hair, implicating himself and physically implicating his models, making them our loved ones, new members of our family.

I have seen him, over the years, dig deep into the poetry of intimacy, probing the gaze into its farthest reaches, composing his images like increasingly streamlined haikus. As though he had taken Robert Capa at his word, he went ever closer, allowing body fragments to become subjects in their own right and invade the image.

Nearly 60 years ago, John Szarkowski listed the five choices that in his view were incumbent upon the photographer: the thing itself; the detail; the frame; time; and vantage point. Each of Nicholas's photos seems to respond to these criteria. The subject, detail, frame, time, and vantage point here all give rise to an ever-stronger bond between the various participants in the image: photographer, subjects and viewers. This is how, over time, despite the thousands of kilometres that separate us, I still feel Nicholas's friendly, attentive, precise, and curious worldview, and I know that in his quest for closeness and connection between beings, as well as between beings and nature, he progresses a little further each day, to the point where his eye, in both the literal and figurative senses, becomes what in the 13th century Peter of Spain called "precious succor on a dark path".

Isabelle Darrigrand

LIST OF WORKS

p.66 Tom Moran, East Braintree, Massachusetts, September 1987

p.67 Tom Moran, Boston, Massachusetts, January 1988

p.69 Savignac de Miremont, 2011

p.70-71 Savignac de Miremont, 2012

p.72-78 Arnold Arboretum, Boston, Massachusetts, 2021

p.79 Longwood Mall, Brookline, Massachusetts, 2019

p.81 Arnold Arboretum, Boston, Massachusetts, 2021

p.83 Longwood Mall, Brookline, Massachusetts, 2019

p.84 Marion, Massachusetts, 2012

p.85 Cadenet, 2012

p.86 Our Front Porch, Brookline, Massachusetts, 2014

p.87 Bebe's Dogwood, Brookline, Massachusetts, 2012

p.88 Moby Dick on Porch, Brookline, Massachusetts, 2014

p.89 Brookline, Massachusetts, 2014

p.90 Front Steps, Brookline, Massachusetts, 2014

p.91 White Place, Brookline, Massachusetts, 2008

p.92 My Shawl, Brookline, Massachusetts, 2016

p.93 Bebe's Desk, Brookline, Massachusetts, 2013

p.95 The Brown Sisters, New Canaan, Connecticut, 1975

The Brown Sisters, Hartford, Connecticut, 1976

p.96 The Brown Sisters, Cambridge, Massachusetts, 1977

The Brown Sisters, Harwichport, Massachusetts, 1978

p.97 The Brown Sisters, Marblehead, Massachusetts, 1979

The Brown Sisters, East Greenwich, Rhode Island, 1980

p.98 The Brown Sisters, Cincinnati, 1981

The Brown Sisters, Ipswich, Massachusetts, 1982

p.99 The Brown Sisters, Allston, Massachusetts, 1983

The Brown Sisters, Truro, Massachusetts, 1984

p.100 The Brown Sisters, Allston, Massachusetts, 1985

The Brown Sisters, Cambridge, Massachusetts, 1986

p.101 The Brown Sisters, Chatham, Massachusetts, 1987

The Brown Sisters, Wellesley, Massachusetts, 1988

p.102 The Brown Sisters, Cambridge, Massachusetts, 1989

The Brown Sisters, Woodstock, Vermont, 1990

p.103 The Brown Sisters, Watertown, Massachusetts, 1991

The Brown Sisters, Concord, Massachusetts, 1992

p.104 The Brown Sisters, Boston, Massachusetts, 1993

The Brown Sisters, Grantham, New Hampshire, 1994

p.105 The Brown Sisters, Marblehead, Massachusetts, 1995

The Brown Sisters, Lexington, Massachusetts, 1996

p.106 The Brown Sisters, Wellesley Hills, Massachusetts, 1997

The Brown Sisters, Falmouth, Massachusetts, 1998

p.107 The Brown Sisters, Brookline, Massachusetts, 1999

The Brown Sisters, Eastham, Massachusetts, 2000

This book is published on the occasion
of Nicholas Nixon's exhibition
at the Galerie le Château d'eau, in Toulouse,
France.

Editor: Jordan Alves
Consulting editor: Nadine Barth
Project management: Adam Jackman,
Hatje Cantz
Copyediting: Tom Ridgway
Translations: Anna Knight
Graphic design: Jérôme Saint-Loubert Bié
Typefaces: Tungsten Bold,
Spectral Regular, Spectral Italic
Production: Charlotte Debiolles

Reproductions: Les Artisans du regard, Paris
Printing: Offsetdruckerei Karl Grammlich,
Pliezhausen
Paper: Condat Matt 170g.

Published by arrangement
with Atelier EXB, Paris

Published by
Hatje Cantz Verlag GmbH
Mommsenstraße 27
10629 Berlin
www.hatjecantz.com
A Ganske Publishing Group Company

ISBN 978-3-7757-5189-6

Printed in Germany